JAN   2012

DAVID STUART & GEORGE STUART

Palenque

ETERNAL CITY OF THE MAYA

*with 167 illustrations,
27 in color*

NEW ASPECTS OF ANTIQUITY
General Editor COLIN RENFREW
Consulting Editor for the Americas JEREMY A. SABLOFF

To Alberto Ruz Lhuillier (1906–79) and Heinrich Berlin-Neubart (1915–88), pioneers in the discovery of Palenque's secrets

FRONTISPIECE *The temples of the Cross Group at Palenque in 1942, prior to their excavation and restoration.*

© 2008 Thames & Hudson Ltd, London

First published in 2008 in hardcover in the United States of America by Thames & Hudson Inc., 500 Fifth Avenue, New York, New York 10110

thamesandhudsonusa.com

Library of Congress Catalog Card Number 2008901127

ISBN 978-0-500-05156-6

Printed and bound in China by SNP Leefung Printers Ltd

Contents

Preface

Each of the authors of this work has had a long and close relationship with Palenque and also with many colleagues, some now deceased, who were intimately associated with the ancient city.

Gᴇᴏʀɢᴇ ꜱᴛᴜᴀʀᴛ: Memories of Palenque and its people stand high among the most wonderful and rewarding parts of my life. I first glimpsed the place some 40 years ago through the dingy Plexiglas window of a plane – a small patch of white all but lost in a seemingly endless ocean of deep green forest. At that moment it was difficult to reconcile this minute speck of land with the immensity of the ruins, much less the story behind them. I have been fortunate to have known a few of the parade of investigators who were there at various times, each of whom made his or her unique contribution to our knowledge of Palenque and those who built it.

I first met Alberto Ruz Lhuillier in 1959, when he came to Mérida, Yucatán, following the last of his ten seasons of archaeological research at Palenque. I was 24 at the time, brand new to the Maya area, where I had arrived as E. Wyllys Andrews IV's field assistant to begin mapping the sprawling ruins of Dzibilchaltun, north of the city.

One evening, at a party at the home of his friends Dick and Anita Hedlund, Bill Andrews introduced me to a tall, distinguished-looking man who, Bill told me, was the famous discoverer of the great royal tomb at Palenque. I knew almost nothing about Palenque at the time, or, for that matter, about the Maya, but I remembered well the name and the tomb. The date of its discovery, 15 June 1952 – the Sunday that Ruz, along with archaeologist César Sáenz and master mason Juan Chablé, and a few others, entered the tomb chamber for the first time – coincided almost exactly with the start of my own first job in archaeology. That fell on the following morning, Monday 16 June, when I reported for work at the Mulberry mound site near my hometown in South Carolina.

That evening in Mérida, Dr. Ruz spent ten astonishing minutes telling me of his incredible day of discovery, and I have never forgotten it. Soon afterward, I became friends with Juan Chablé, the master stonemason from Oxcutzcab, Yucatán, who was then supervising the consolidation of the Temple of the Seven Dolls at Dzibilchaltun. Juan told me how he had been the first to notice the unusual triangular pattern on the side wall of the final landing of the interior stairway of the Temple of the Inscriptions that famous day in June, and how he began to chip away at its edges, finally revealing the entry to the crypt. On another occasion, Juan revealed to me the story of *his* "discovery" of the sarcophagus. "All the archaeologists," he recalled, "thought the big stone was an altar. I asked Don Alberto if he would grant me permission to drill a small hole into the side, just to confirm that it was indeed solid. To me, the stone on top seemed more like a lid than a table top." Juan was right, of course. The block was hollow, and soon Juan, Ruz, and the crew were poised around the great block, each manning an automobile jack, raising, ever so carefully, centimeter by centimeter and perfectly level, the five-ton slab to reveal the royal burial.

Years later, on a trip to Uxmal with my family, I met archaeologist César Sáenz. That evening as we sat in the shade by the Instituto Nacional de Antropología e Historia (INAH) *campamento*, César shared his vivid memory of those first moments inside the crypt. While Alberto, Juan, and other members of the small group stood awestruck, César impulsively knelt on the floor and pointed his flashlight into the open space under the massive stone block – and saw the two magnificent stucco heads that had been carefully placed there.

Although I had seen Palenque from the air, my first actual visit to the site took place late in 1968, when my wife Gene and I, with our children George, 12, Gregg, nine, Ann, seven, and David, three, took the overnight train from Mérida to Palenque station. Early that morning we found ourselves standing at the western base of the Palace, where a throng of workers and a large INAH dump truck were undertaking the task of restoring the great staircase. There we met Jorge Acosta, archaeologist in charge, and he outlined for us INAH's plans to complete the consolidation of central Palenque over the next few seasons. At that moment my profound appreciation of the extraordinary achievement of the Mexican government in saving Palenque for future generations was born.

Given my relatively short experience with Palenque prior to 1973, I have never fully understood why my wife Gene and I received an invitation to attend the First Mesa Redonda at Palenque that coming December. This, as it turned out, was only the first of many gatherings of Maya and Palenque experts at the site, and I shall be ever grateful to Merle and Bob Robertson for their thoughtfulness in including us neophytes. My entry to the gathering was quite undistinguished to say the least. Unknowingly, I drove to the ruins instead of to the real meeting place at La Cañada, on the north edge of town, directed by well-meaning townspeople to another "mesa redonda," the huge circular stone resting at the base of the stairway of the Temple of the Inscriptions! I parked beside it – one could drive into the site center in those days – and wondered where everyone else was.

The Palenque meeting introduced me to David Kelley, Peter Mathews, Linda Schele, and Floyd Lounsbury, whose lasting friendships strengthened my ever-growing bond to Palenque. At later Mesas Redondas, I was privileged to run the sessions as moderator, where I continued to learn from Peter Mathews, Beatrice de la Fuente, Marta Foncerrada de Molina, Paul Gendrop, and the many others who attended over those years.

I also learned more than he ever suspected from Heinrich ("Henry") Berlin, hero of hieroglyphic research, whose incisive and rigorous work with the inscriptions of Palenque set the stage, and the standards, for all such work since. I only met Henry once, for a long lunch at a Mexico City restaurant, where we mainly discussed his deep interest in railroad history! He hadn't gone to the Mesa Redonda, he told me, because it seemed a good time for the next generation to take over. Not long after my return home, I received a large packet and a long letter from him. It contained reprints of all he had ever written on Palenque, and soon I came to realize the enormity of his contribution.

It is regrettable that, like Berlin, Alberto Ruz didn't come for that first meeting. Alberto later told me that he had his own good reasons for being wary and, besides, he was somewhat resentful of this group of enthusiasts suddenly descending on a place to which he had devoted his career. Alberto's feeling soon abated, however, as I learned from my last conversation with him: in 1977 I was engaged in writing a book on the Maya and trying desperately to reconcile his initial reading of the name of the individual buried in the Temple of the Inscriptions, "Eight Ahau," a logical calendar name based solidly on known ancient Mesoamerican custom, with the name "Pakal" ("Shield"), a then newly proposed phonetic reading by David Kelley and Floyd Lounsbury. Alberto quickly solved my problem. "No matter what we disagree on," he told me on the telephone as we were nearing press time, "we are all after the same thing: we want to know all we can about that man in the tomb." I have often thought of this as an effective statement of the ultimate goal of archaeology in its pursuit of the understanding, not only of Palenque, but also of the whole of the human past.

DAVID STUART: Some of my earliest memories are of Palenque, where I first visited in 1968 as a toddler, and so it isn't hard to explain how the name and the place have always conjured in me a sense of wonder and excitement. To tell the truth, what impressed me most as a three-year-old was the large INAH dump truck used to haul the backdirt away from the front stairs of the Palace. The backdirt itself was also wonderful. The ruins themselves left a more ghostly impression on me, but I still recollect the sight of the Temple of the Inscriptions looming over our family and the hustle of activity around the excavations. It was the first of many visits, and a place that ultimately drew me into a life with the ancient Maya.

Palenque was thereafter an exotic destination where exciting things often seemed to happen. Some years later, in 1973, I recall my parents leaving us Stuart kids with a babysitter as they went off to something called a Mesa Redonda at Palenque, and on their return I could sense my father's excitement – something important had happened down there. As an eight-year-old, I could clearly see that Palenque was "the place" for exciting archaeology, and I always looked forward to a chance to return. Brief stopovers there came in the mid-1970s during our long drives from North Carolina to Cobá, Quintana Roo (where my father was working), but I knew I wanted to spend more time at Palenque and explore. The labyrinth of the Palace's galleries and *subterraneos* was enough to excite any kid bitten by the romance of archaeology.

In 1977 I met Linda Schele and Merle Greene Robertson, the two people who, besides my parents, fostered my interest and enthusiasm for the Maya world. I met Linda with my parents in the offices of the National Geographic Society in Washington, D.C., when she arrived to consult on their soon-to-be-published book on the ancient Maya. Linda's name was much the buzz in Maya studies in those days, she was the charismatic, up-and-coming star of glyph decipherment. I knew this, of course, and was thrilled to meet her. What she thought of me at that point – I was a 12-year-old with scraggly hair – I can't say, but our conversations about glyphs must have left something of a mark, because she was impressed enough to invite me to Palenque later that summer to help her correct her drawings of the Cross Group tablets. Once there, my mother and I spent a wonderful time at Merle's house, with Linda and I devoting our mornings to the ruins, scanning the tablets with flashlights and clipboards in hand, adding and omitting lines from her preliminary drawings. The experience taught me so much about the intricacies of the glyphs, and it made me know I was going to be a Mayanist. It was the seed of a friendship and collaboration that would last two more decades, until Linda's death in 1998.

Later in life, as a student, my fieldwork took me far away from Chiapas, to ruins in Honduras and Guatemala, but Palenque always stayed with me, defining my early experience and education. I was suddenly reminded of this in 1998, when Alfonso Morales e-mailed me with photographs of the stunningly beautiful tablets he and his team had just uncovered in Palenque's Temple XIX. Drawing and studying them over the following months, it was easy to be taken back to my formative experiences at Palenque, and I soon knew I could never spend any extended time away from the ruins. Palenque's story is always being re-written because of new discoveries such as Temple XIX, and finds in the coming years will no doubt lead to even more exciting revisions of what you will read in these pages. I grew up in and with Palenque, and in many ways I am still there.

CHAPTER ONE
Palenque and its World

*Here were the remains of a cultivated, polished, and peculiar people who had
passed through all the stages incident to the rise and fall of nations; reached
their golden age, and perished, entirely unknown …. We lived in the ruined
palace of their kings; we went up to their desolate temples and fallen altars;
and wherever we moved we saw the evidences of their taste, their skill in arts,
their wealth and power.*

JOHN L. STEPHENS, PALENQUE, JULY 1840[1]

The famous 19th-century traveler John L. Stephens got it right, as he
usually did. More than a century after he wrote of the brilliant human
achievement he saw reflected in the Maya ruins of Palenque, a small group
of privileged individuals literally stood on the threshold of what many consider the greatest archaeological discovery ever made in the Americas. It was
Sunday 15 June 1952 when Alberto Ruz Lhuillier squeezed through a narrow
opening into a large vaulted chamber deep inside the pyramid under the
Temple of the Inscriptions, one of the largest structures in Palenque.

Ruz let his flashlight play over walls half hidden by sparkling stalactites
of limestone. In the center, dominating the room like a gigantic table, a huge
rectangular stone could be seen, resting upon a massive stone block (fig. 1).
Both bore carvings as fresh as the day they were made. The portrait of a
reclining man, poised amid symbols of earth and sky, dominated the surface
of the great slab; a long hieroglyphic text ran along its thick edge. Other portraits and glyphs marked the sides of the block beneath it (see figs 45 and 58).

Ruz had discovered, as it came to be known in the years of research that
followed that fateful summer, the tomb of K'inich Janab Pakal, or simply

Pakal, the greatest king of ancient Palenque. The amazing find also revolutionized Maya archaeology; before that, the stepped "pyramids" of the Americas were thought to function simply and solely as platforms for the buildings on their summits. This is not all. Pakal's sarcophagus and its lid, along with the extraordinary bas-relief panels and hieroglyphic texts from other buildings in Palenque, were among the earliest clues that Maya inscriptions held not only dates, but also names and histories of real people. By virtue of its spectacular mountain setting, the profound esthetic appeal of its art and architecture, and the knowledge it has provided about those who lived and died there, Palenque ranks high among the enduring achievements of the human past. Fittingly, in 1987 the ancient city was proclaimed a UNESCO World Heritage Site.

Between about 500 BC and AD 900, the Maya people, builders of Palenque, created one of the most distinctive and accomplished of the many civilizations that flourished in the Americas before the arrival of European invaders. The story of the ancient Maya played out over a territory of some 390,000 sq. km (150,000 sq. miles) – an area roughly the size of the state of Montana, extending from the northernmost coast of the Yucatán Peninsula southward some 800 km (500 miles) to the dark volcanic sand of Guatemala's Pacific shore, and from the Isthmus of Tehuantepec to the Caribbean Coast. The landscape is remarkably diverse. The northern lowlands, mostly a riverless limestone plain punctuated by cenotes, or natural wells, make up about a third of the Yucatán Peninsula before grading into the slight undulations and extensive depressions, or *bajos,* that characterize the southern lowlands. Even farther south, and forming about a third of Maya country, lies the broad highland base of the Yucatán Peninsula – a closely packed mass of mountain ridges that extends southeastward from the Isthmus of Tehuantepec through most of Chiapas, much of Guatemala, and practically all of El Salvador. A chain of active volcanoes marks these mountains of the Maya, which end along the narrow band of land bordering the Pacific Ocean. In terms of modern political borders, then, the Maya area consists of the nations of Guatemala and Belize, the western portions of Honduras and El Salvador, and the Mexican states of Yucatán, Quintana Roo, and Campeche, along with parts of Tabasco and Chiapas.

1 *Alberto Ruz Lhuillier inside the burial chamber of the Temple of the Inscriptions in 1977, the 25th anniversary of his momentous discovery of the tomb of K'inich Janab Pakal. Beside him stretches the enormous carved sarcophagus lid that nearly fills the room.*

The Maya area forms the eastern third of "Mesoamerica," the term anthropologists use to refer to an area whose people shared a distinctive set of beliefs and practices between about 1500 BC and the coming of the Spanish at the end of the 15th century – customs that continue today to varying degrees among their living descendants.[2] These range from subsistence agriculture, mainly involving maize, beans, and squash, to a belief system reflected in a large pantheon of supernatural beings intimately related to land, water, and sky. In this schema of sacred geography are recurring themes of ancestry, death, and destiny. Related ceremonies include the ritual ball game and the sacrifices of animals and humans.

Mesoamerica extends roughly from north-central Mexico to the Pacific coasts of Nicaragua and Costa Rica (fig. 2). Its landscapes range from near desert on the northern frontier through rugged snow-topped volcanic highlands of south-central Mexico to coastal lowland zones of dense forest, savannah, and swamp. All of Mesoamerica lies within the tropics, where the patterns of climate, though fluctuating now and then over the millennia, are distinguished by alternating seasons of dry and rainy weather that set the annual pattern of life for its inhabitants.

Those who study Mesoamerica customarily divide its culture history into named "periods." This is done more for convenience than as a reflection of the character of the period or what really happened during the time in question. These terms, as well as the time spans they refer to, vary greatly in the literature of the last half century or so, depending upon who employs them, and when.[3] In this book, we conform generally to current conventions of nomenclature in Mesoamerican archaeology, flawed as they may be. Thus, we treat the 3,000-year span that preceded the European invasions in terms of three main periods: Preclassic (c. 2000 BC to AD 250), Classic (c. AD 250 to 900), and Postclassic (c. AD 900 to 1500). In speaking of these date spans, we may separate them even further, into early, middle, or late subdivisions.

As early as about 2000 BC, the beginning of the Preclassic period, Mesoamerica had become a farmer's world. In the ensuing centuries peoples of different language groups living in both the highlands and lowlands formed, in effect, a cultural "melting pot." From it came the Mesoamerican way of life.

Around 1500 BC, the Olmec culture emerged in the general area of the tropical Gulf Coast lowland of what are now the Mexican states of Veracruz and Tabasco. Olmec centers such as San Lorenzo and La Venta reflect the development of Mesoamerica's first powerful and recognizable art style, evident in the famed sculptures of colossal heads as well as miniature masterpieces of jade carving. These artifacts, in turn, reflect the development of complex society and elite power by the Olmec and their neighbors from Mexico's central highlands across the Isthmus of Tehuantepec to Pacific Guatemala. This "Isthmian" region saw the crystallization of most of the fundamental cultural characteristics that would define Mesoamerica from about 500 BC on.

Cities begin to appear in the Mesoamerican record in the centuries before the beginning of the Christian era. One in particular, Teotihuacan, rose to greatness on the plateau of Mexico's Central Highlands, not far northeast of present-day Mexico City, and prospered until about AD 650. As a hub of trade and perhaps of militarism, the metropolis of Teotihuacan – its population has been estimated at between 125,000 and 200,000 – exerted a powerful influence on other Mesoamerican civilizations whose heyday generally defines the Classic period, particularly the Zapotec of Monte Alban in the Valley of Oaxaca; the Huastec of Veracruz; and the highland and lowland Maya.

The Classic Maya area consisted of a patchwork of small kingdoms stretching from Comalcalco in the west to Tulum in the east and from Ek Balam in the north to Copán in the south (fig. 2). Populations of the largest – Calakmul, Tikal, Cobá, and Caracol among them – may have exceeded 75,000, and served as the regional centers for powerful kings and queens and their royal courts. These large cities, and even much smaller places such as Palenque and Toniná, traded, raided, warred, and intermarried, depending upon the time and circumstances.[4]

The Postclassic period, based on the fall of Teotihuacan and the apparent abandonment of Tikal, Palenque, and other Maya capitals of the southern lowlands, saw the rise and fall of the legendary Toltec in central Mexico and, later, the arrival of the Mexica, or Aztec, who came from a legendary "Place of the Reeds" somewhere on the northwestern Mesoamerican frontier to settle in the Basin of Mexico. There they built their island capital, Tenochtitlán, and made it the powerful center of a tribute empire that covered much of the highlands and lowlands stretching east to the frontier of Maya country – until the autumn of 1519, that is, when Hernán Cortés entered the city to confront the emperor Motecuzoma II in the first momentus act of the Spanish Conquest.

The Postclassic Maya, meanwhile, continued their lives in a succession of regional centers – Uxmal, Chichén Itzá, Mayapan, and others, mostly in the northern lowlands, until the coming of the Spaniards. The Maya highlands fell to Pedro de Alvarado in 1524; Yucatán and the north yielded to

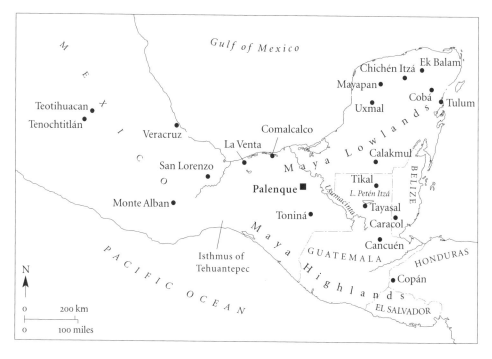

2 *Map of Mesoamerica showing places mentioned in this chapter.*

Francisco Montejo the Younger in 1542. Finally, the last Maya capital, Tayasal (now Flores), on Lake Petén Itzá in the southern lowlands, yielded to the Spanish in 1697, when the priests and soldiers entered the city unchallenged – the Itzá Maya saw their conquest as a prophecy fulfilled on schedule.

By the time Spaniards set foot in Tayasal, a much earlier Maya city lay abandoned and deserted in the dark forest to the west. It was only 225 km (143 miles) from Tayasal, but more than 700 years away in time – and no one would even hear about it for another century. We now know that city as Palenque, and it is the subject of this book.

Ask a professional Mayanist or anyone else who knows about Palenque what the place means to him or her, and you will likely get a different answer from each. Almost certainly the responses will come with some degree of passion, for whatever Palenque does to the mind, it does not evoke indifference. For Alfred Maudslay, one of its early visitors – and he had seen them all – it was "the queen of Maya cities." For Gillett Griffin, a later visitor and a scholar of profound artistic perception, Palenque stands as "the most enigmatically moving of all Maya sites." And to anyone interested in the history of research in American archaeology, Palenque marks the spot where it began just over two centuries ago.

For the epigrapher, the scholar of ancient Maya writing, the hiero-glyphic inscriptions of Palenque are both special and memorable not only for their abundance and remarkable preservation, but also for what they have told us over the past three decades about Palenque history, cosmology, and myth. For the historian of art and architecture, the elegant buildings and the miraculous bas-reliefs of stone and stucco that adorn them repre-sent one of the great esthetic achievements of the ancient world. To the disciples of New Age thought, Palenque ranks as one of the most powerfully spiritual destinations for the modern pilgrim. Thus, in these and many, many other ways, Palenque has transcended time itself to re-live its old glory among the discriminating minds of our present age. Indeed, it is probable that today more people recognize the name "Palenque" than knew, or knew of, the city at the pinnacle of its greatness some 1,300 years ago.

City among Mountain Streams

The Maya who lived in and around the city knew it as Lakamha', or "Big Water." The name surely came from the cluster of small rivers – the Murciélagos, the Otolum, the Picota, and others – that come out of the upper slopes, cascade through ravines and over great natural stair-steps of water-worn limestone, and pause occasionally in quiet pools in the semi-darkness of the rainforest that now cloaks most of the site. The modern name of the ruins comes from the colonial town of Santo Domingo de Palenque, about 8 km (5 miles) to the east (fig. 3). In Spanish, the word *palenque* refers to a stockade, or wall of poles made to set off an area for pur-poses ranging from defense to public events.[5]

The ruins of Palenque cluster on a narrow, irregular shelf of land a quarter of the way up the face of the 400-m (1,300-ft) high escarpment that marks the northern edge of the Chiapas highlands (plate 16). Rain falls on the area in abundance – an average of 300 cm (120 in) a year, with July and

October normally being the wettest months; April and May and, to some extent August, the driest. From this well-watered and lofty setting the city faced north, its orderly buildings silhouetted against a backdrop of natural hills, slopes, and valleys recalled in miniature by Palenque's inner cityscape of pyramid-platforms and plazas. A prominent peak, El Mirador, immediately southeast of the main city center, holds a small ruined structure on its artificially flattened summit, suggesting that it may have been venerated, in the Mesoamerican way, as a sacred mountain, and in this instance also as the location of the source spring of the Otolum River. Appropriately, the temples clustered near the base of El Mirador hold ancient hieroglyphic texts that celebrate the birth of Palenque's patron triad of gods at Matwiil, their mythical place of destiny – or Palenque.

At the base of the slope far below the ruins, Palenque's streams join the Michol River, which flows westward to join the Tulija at Salto de Agua, some 35 km (22 miles) away. To the south, just beyond the ridge of the Sierra Palenque, the Chacamax River wends its way east, then north to join the Usumacinta River at Emiliano Zapata, about the same distance away. After crossing most of the Tabasco plain both the Tulija and the Usumacinta Rivers join the Grijalva just before entering the Gulf of Mexico some 140 km (87 miles) northwest of Palenque.

In his study of some 3,400 sq. km (c. 1,300 sq. miles) centered on Palenque, Moises Morales observed that about a third of the region – mainly interior mountain valleys rich in humus – held land excellent for planting. The remainder was divided almost equally between steep slopes and seasonally flooded lowlands and swamps, both with indifferent soils for farming. Where there is forest, it is true rainforest of almost stupefying abundance – indeed, fruiting trees may have been a major source of food for the city – a dense and fast-growing realm of mahogany, cedar, and the sacred ceiba, and other forest giants draped with lianas or holding the dark starbursts of hundreds of species of orchids amid their foliage. These forests house an abundance of animals ranging from monkeys, both spider and howler, to jaguars, peccary, and deer, as well as wild turkeys, scarlet macaws, parrots, eagles, and owls. Here, too, are snakes, including the deadly coral and fer-de-lance, scorpions, and an inventory of insect varieties so vast that it virtually

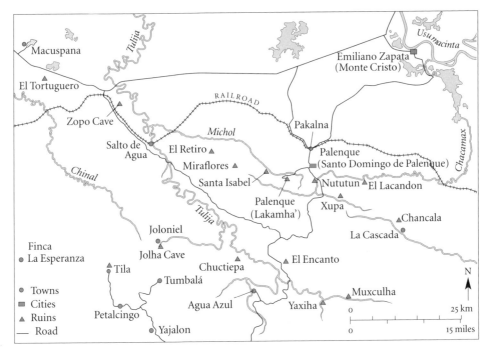

3 *Map of the Palenque region showing the pattern of the Tulija, Michol, and other rivers as they flow northward from the highlands through the coastal plain to empty into the Gulf of Mexico. Cities, towns, and other modern features are shown for clarity.*

defies description. This richness of life in the forest around Palenque stands in direct contrast to the silent stone world of the ruins themselves.[6]

What remains of the urban core of old Palenque occupies an area measuring 2.2 sq. km (0.8 sq. miles), only slightly larger than the Principality of Monaco, and consists of the remnants of some 1,500 structures, mostly visible only as mounds, that cluster in at least 35 major building complexes (fig. 4).[7] The heaviest concentrations of structures end on the east, where level ground gives way to a series of uninhabitable slopes and ravines. On the western edge of the site an area almost three-quarters the size of the mapped ruins is known to contain mounds, but remains to be surveyed.[8]

Within the densely packed archaeological zone, carefully constructed stone aqueducts and walled stream banks reflect an intensive and efficient management of the water supply – a matter never to be taken for granted in the capricious alternations of dry and wet seasons that characterize this area

4 *The archaeological zone of Palenque as mapped so far by Ed Barnhart and his team contains the remnants of some 1,500 buildings in an area of 2.2 sq. km, or nearly one square mile. These remains, now mostly overgrown mounds of fallen stone, cluster in some three dozen groups, each located amid the streams that probably drew the first inhabitants of Palenque to this site. The modern road from Palenque town, upper right, generally follows the old trail that brought visitors to the "stone houses," beginning in the 18th century.*

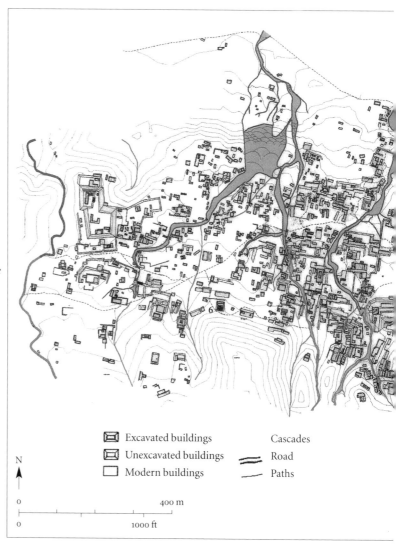

▥ Excavated buildings	Cascades
▥ Unexcavated buildings	══ Road
☐ Modern buildings	— Paths

N ↑

0   400 m

0   1000 ft

(see fig. 60). Other measures to conserve water and to prevent erosion and flooding are evident in the 16 or so kilometers (*c.* 10 miles) of ancient terraces that mark the slopes of ravines.

Not the least of ancient Palenque's resources lay in the quality of its building stone. While virtually all lowland Maya sites had an abundance of stone readily at hand near the surface, the limestone at Palenque was special, seemingly as dense and flawless as fine lithographic stone. And, just as

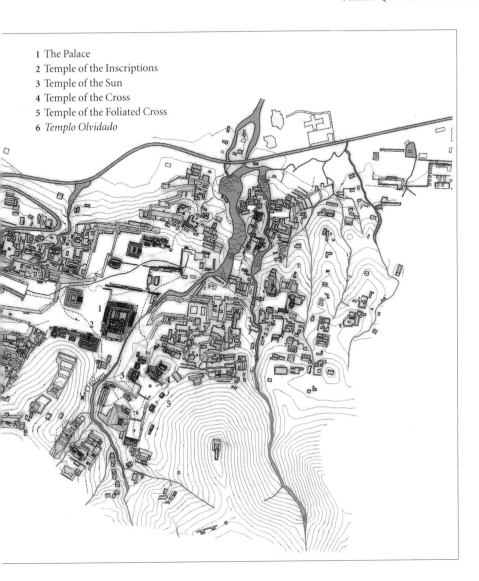

1 The Palace
2 Temple of the Inscriptions
3 Temple of the Sun
4 Temple of the Cross
5 Temple of the Foliated Cross
6 *Templo Olvidado*

important for the masons, the deposits in and around Palenque possess natural cleavage planes that not only caused it to break easily into great slabs, but also made its quarrying and working relatively easy. Local stone workers employed this perfect construction material to produce buildings of astonishing beauty as well as the great panels of scenes and hieroglyphic texts that, set into the interior walls of the most important buildings, form one of the distinctive architectural hallmarks of Palenque.

"Downtown" Palenque

The modern visitor to Palenque rarely sees more than about ten per cent of the whole archaeological zone – the cleared central precinct carefully maintained by Mexico's INAH (figs 5, 6, plate 15). This relatively small area, however, holds some of the greatest known examples of ancient Maya architecture. Ever since 1784, when the first modern visitor of record described "a Palace that by its construction and magnitude could be nothing less," Palenque's buildings have borne various names.[9] Understandably, the "Palace" described by José Antonio Calderón retains that designation to this day. Other structures, however, have had different names, depending upon who labeled the building and when. What we now call the Temple of the Inscriptions, for example, has also been known as "Casa No. 1," "the study," and the "Temple of the Laws." In our treatment, we generally follow the policy of INAH and the Palenque Mapping Project (1998–2000) in the labeling of buildings and groups, a system based on Frans Blom's pioneering effort of 1923 and Merle Greene Robertson's 1983 map.[10] Thus, we label some buildings by letters (e.g., "House E" of the Palace); others by roman numerals ("Temple XVIII"); and still others by traditional names ("Temple of the Count"). One must realize, however, that the designations implying specific functions such as the ubiquitous "temple" or even the "palace" itself are but terms of convenience, and do not necessarily reflect their ancient function, which often remains unknown.

All the largest and clearly most important buildings of Palenque adhere to the general principles of Maya architecture, and also reflect the remarkable design and engineering skills of the city's architects, stonemasons, sculptors, and painters. The Palace, likely the ceremonial and administrative center for the ruler and other members of Palenque's court – the royal family, members of other noble and favored families, the scribes, priests, and others of privilege and power – dominates the cleared area of downtown Palenque. A massive, irregular quadrangle, more a parallelogram than a rectangle in overall plan – sometimes Maya architects were strikingly casual when it came to horizontal corner angles – it consists of a complicated system of vaulted buildings, some forming lengthy halls, or galleries, arranged to enclose three courtyards of varying size (plate 16). All these lie

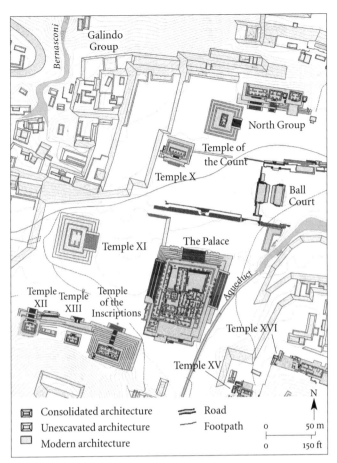

5 *Central Palenque as mapped by Ed Barnhart and the Palenque Mapping Project between 1998 and 2000. The Palace, lower center, beside the aqueduct of the Otolum River, dominates this part of the site, along with the nearby Temple of the Inscriptions and the row of buildings adjacent to it.*

Galindo Group

Bernasconi

North Group

Temple of the Count

Temple X

Ball Court

Temple XI

The Palace

Aqueduct

Temple XII Temple XIII Temple of the Inscriptions

Temple XVI

Temple XV

N

▢ Consolidated architecture   ═ Road

▢ Unexcavated architecture   — Footpath

▢ Modern architecture

0   50 m
0   150 ft

on a gigantic platform with monumental staircases on the west and north sides. The numerous blocked doorways or partitions added to existing structures show clearly that this bewildering array of structures, patios, and rooms was continually expanded and modified over a long period of time. To help bring order to this architectural confusion, the 12 discernible "houses" have been assigned alphabetical labels from A through L. Beneath all this, buried within the supporting platform, lies an earlier series of passageways and chambers, appropriately named the *subterraneos*. Many of these remained open and accessible via stairways from the buildings above.

Miraculously, and fortunately for us, much of Palenque's exterior stucco art has survived the continual assault of more than a millennium of intense rains and humidity for which the area is famous (plate 4). The conservation of the "piers," or exterior wall surfaces separating the entry doorways, was greatly helped by the wide overhanging eaves provided by the architects' foresight. Despite accumulated limestone deposits and the mold – as well as the continual cleanings that have taken place over the last two centuries – portions of the red, yellow, blue, and other brightly colored paints have endured in the deeper, protected parts.[11] Therefore it is not difficult for today's visitors to Palenque to imagine these stucco sculptures as their makers left them. Such a privilege is denied the visitor to most Maya sites – and indeed much of Palenque as well, where partially collapsed building exteriors have been worn down by the elements to bare masonry.

Scenes of people or mythical figures, often accompanied by hiero-glyphic inscriptions, decorated the piers and other exterior wall spaces as well as the panels flanking the interior sanctuaries. Of the stucco glyphs themselves, each was a masterpiece in its own right, a detailed block of writing about the size of a large, thick book. These were apparently pro-duced in accordance with directions and drawings from the scribes, then formed and literally glued in place with wet stucco by the construction workers. In one instance, on the west wall of the Palace, a worker, in haste or ignorance, stuck one glyph on sideways!

Within the Palace, the square Tower, a four-storey construction unique in all of Maya architecture, stands 18 m (60 ft) high to dominate the Palace and the entire central area of Palenque (see plate 16). The small patio beside it, the Tower Court, bordered by Houses E, I, and K, features a small chamber containing three of the six toilets in this general area of the Palace.

Temple of the Inscriptions

Just southwest of the Palace rises the great bulk of the Temple of the Inscriptions, so called for the three large hieroglyphic panels that grace the interior walls (plate 20). Unlike most Maya buildings at Palenque or else-where, the Temple of the Inscriptions was built relatively quickly, virtually in a single stage of construction, as a noble endeavor for the single purpose of memorializing Palenque's greatest ruler Pakal, whose remains Alberto Ruz discovered as we have seen in 1952, in the crypt deep in the center of the pyramid. The inscription in the building high above the crypt is Palenque's

6 *Aerial view of Central Palenque, showing the Palace, center, with the Temple of the Inscriptions behind.* 25

longest. It not only recounts Pakal's achievements, but also places the revered ruler in the context of eternity and the rich panorama of myth and history as the ancient Palencanos saw it. One can easily imagine the almost overwhelming awe experienced by elite, literate visitors who had climbed the steep staircase to pay homage to their king.

Extraordinary as it was in its time – and ours – the Temple of the Inscriptions provides an instructive example of the general canons of ancient Maya architecture – rectangular in plan with mirror-image symmetry based on the centerline. And, like the typical Maya building, it rises vertically from basal molding, or plinth, to a horizontal medial molding that passes above the doorway lintels and extends outward to form wide overhanging eaves. Inside, this lowest range of medial molding masonry also serves as the lower, or "spring," course for the face of the sloping vault face above. The Temple of the Inscriptions, like most other Palenque structures, holds a wall that divides the building into two long parallel rooms, and also supports the spring courses of both interior vaults, the faces of which converge toward the capstone. The corbelled arch thus formed, often with wooden crossbeams added for reinforcement, is perhaps the best-known hallmark of Maya architecture.

To this basic Maya formula the architects of the Temple of the Inscriptions and other buildings in downtown Palenque added their distinctive mark. On the upper building exteriors, between the medial molding and the superior molding, the designers made a sloping, rather than vertical, upper façade, in effect a "mansard roof," with its exterior slope parallel to the vault face inside. This method of building substantially reduced the mass and weight of the masonry pressing downward on the walls below, allowing the building relatively thin walls, remarkably wide rooms, and large entryways, giving the whole structure an esthetically pleasing illusion of lightness.[12]

The Temple of the Inscriptions features another characteristic trait of Palenque architectural art – the presence of a *cresteria*, or "roof crest," a vertical masonry slab-like construction that rises above the long centerline of the roof.[13] Such structures were made as light as possible by constructing their opposing faces with a hollow space between, and openings in the faces themselves. These masonry roof crests served as foundations for painted stucco sculptures that stood much like modern billboards over Palenque's most important buildings. The whole weight of these massive yet graceful constructions rested directly on the central wall directly below it.

The Cross Group

To early European visitors, two wall panels in the group of temple-pyramids immediately east of the Temple of the Inscriptions appeared to depict crosses as their central motif. Although we now interpret these cruciform elements as Maya representations of plants, the names "Temple of the Cross" and "Temple of the Foliated Cross" have endured, as has the

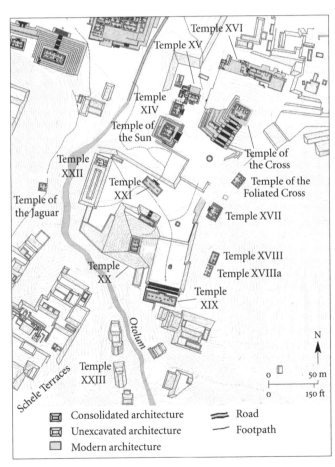

7 The Cross Group lies partially embraced by the Otolum River, which falls from a spring on El Mirador hill, immediately to the southeast. The buildings here, dominated by the Temple of the Cross, which gives its name to the group, are among the last major buildings constructed at the site.

designation for the whole – the "Cross Group." Other buildings related to the same set of plazas include the Temple of the Sun, Temples XIV and XV, and Temples XII through XVII (fig. 7).

The Temples of the Cross, the Foliated Cross, the Sun, as well as other buildings in Palenque, feature an extra interior chamber often called a "shrine" or "sanctuary." Each of these consists of a partially enclosed, low, roofed "room" set against the inside rear wall of a structure with its own wide entryway built to provide access. The extraordinarily special nature of these "inner sanctums" is manifest in their associated sculpture and texts. The usual pattern features tall bas-relief jambs flanking the doorway opening, where curtain holders indicate that the space could easily be closed off after one passed through. Inside, and set flush into the rear wall of the chamber, a monumental tablet bearing a scene flanked by long hieroglyphic texts would have greeted anyone who entered.

Sculpture and Painting at Palenque

The presence of the imposing carved tablets set into the rear walls of buildings or the shrines inside the Temple of the Inscriptions, the Palace, the Cross Group, and other buildings reminds us that in Palenque these and other magnificent bas-reliefs served the very same function as the familiar stelae employed at other Maya sites – to immortalize rulers and to record rituals and the key dates of myth and history. Doubtless the easy availability of fine-grained slabs of soft limestone helped to make such works the premier art form at ancient Palenque. Looking at the limestone panel in Temple XIX, for example, it is almost impossible to believe that, even with the relative workability of the material, the ancient masterpiece was meticulously carved and polished without the metal chisels and manufactured abrasives we would routinely use today (plates 12 and 34). Instead, the Palenque sculptors employed an effective kit of special implements of obsidian, flint, or polished greenstone, fine-grained sandstone, and other abrasives. The seamless manner in which the bas-reliefs appear on two or more limestone slabs indicates that they were carved in place by the sculptors, following guidelines drawn in advance.[14]

Thanks to the painstaking analysis of the "handwriting" of individual carvers by Mark Van Stone, an accomplished calligrapher as well as a devoted Mayanist, we can better understand just how Palenque's imposing stone wall panels were made. Mark's examination of the Palace Tablet indicated that some 20 sculptors were involved in its making, each working on one or more specific areas of the tablet (plate 17). These men ranged from master carvers to others with seemingly less ability, perhaps apprentices just beginning to learn the intricacies and possibilities of hieroglyphic composition and the canons of sculpture. Van Stone estimates the carving of the whole tablet, not counting the time it took beforehand to install the three slabs that formed the whole, nor to paint the finished sculpture, took the artisans between five and eight weeks to do their work.[15]

Equally adept were the specialists in stucco work. Amid the limestone landscape of the Maya lowlands, it is no wonder that the ancient inhabitants became masters of mortar, plaster, and stucco in both construction and carving. And there was never an absence of wood for the essential process of burning of the lime into powder – at least it must have seemed so at the time. Much of Palenque's artistic fame stems from its elegant stucco relief carvings that adorned the piers, roof crests, upper façades, and other significant walls and surfaces of the major buildings (plate 32). The carvings required special stone armatures to serve as structural foundations for the heavier high-relief figures.

As Merle Greene Robertson discovered, the making of a stucco-decorated pier was much like dressing a living human figure. The piers on the Temple of the Inscriptions, for example, involved first the wetting of the flat stucco background and that of the yet "unclothed and unadorned sculptural figures." This dampened the stucco and thus served as a bonding agent for the color, applied next. Then, when clothing, bracelets, sandals, and other accoutrements were added to the "naked" figure, a thin watery coat of lime was applied as a kind of glue, followed by wetting and painting the additions in their selected colors. These colors apparently served as a kind of visual language that followed certain rules, depending, for instance, on whether the figure depicted was human or supernatural.[16]

The painters of ancient Palenque bore the ultimate responsibility for the basic look of the place. Virtually every painted surface, from the stucco coating on the exteriors of buildings and platforms to the ornate carvings that graced the most private royal spaces, demanded continual maintenance and renewal, a never-ending task, especially during times of torrential rainfall, humidity, and with the ever-present mold and lime incrustation.

The Scribal Arts

The artist-scribes who worked with delicate brushes of fine animal hair and other precision tools of their craft – even quill pens according to Michael D. Coe – were clearly masters of their specialty. Aside from the murals, they also painted the careful line "cartoons" that served as guides for bas-reliefs. The famed Tablet of the 96 Glyphs, carefully carved in stone to replicate the character of brushstrokes, attests to their calligraphic skill (plate 29). And, like all good Maya scribes, they were thoroughly schooled in the complexities and possibilities of the hieroglyphic script. They also employed this talent on smaller, portable works, including accordion-fold hieroglyphic "books," known to have existed during the Classic period, although no example from that period has survived intact; and on special ceramics that they adorned with scenes and hieroglyphic captions.

The writing system used at Palenque and elsewhere was based on the version of Ch'olan Maya spoken during the Classic period. To construct texts, the scribes had at their disposal some 800 different glyphic signs, each of which could appear in simple form or more elaborate versions such as profile heads or even full figures of people or supernatural beings. Each sign served as a word or a syllable – or as an extra graphic element to clarify, if necessary, a subtlety of sound or grammar. With such symbols the scribes could render any word, sound, or phrase they chose – numbers and time periods, names of kings, gods, objects, buildings, cities, states, mythical realms, and even food, and they did so with dazzling virtuosity. For example, Palenque scribes could, and did, render the complete version of the name of their king, K'inich Janab Pakal, in at least ten different ways, and using from one to three separate "glyph blocks," the gently rounded rectangular units that characterize most ancient Maya texts.

With the text blocks laid out in rows and columns – long texts were normally read from left to right in pairs, and downward – as well as L-shapes and other arrangements, the inscriptions of Palenque were created in stone, stucco, and painted line. The subjects of such texts range from mere nametags on possessions to grandiose proclamations of the lives and exploits of rulers set within the chronological framework of history and myth.

Like the rest of the Maya, the calendar specialists of Palenque used the unique system inherited from their Preclassic forebears and employed in various forms at different times throughout Mesoamerica. It utilized two distinct calendar cycles – one of 260 days (itself made up of two smaller intermeshed cycles of the numbers one through 13 and 20 names) and another of 365 days, divided into 18 "months" of 20 days each, with a five-day period at the end. At some point in the process of invention, someone decided to combine the 260- and 365-day cycles into a grand cycle of 18,980 days, or approximately 52 true solar years. Within this "calendar round," each single day bears a twin label – its number plus name in the 260-day cycle, and its number and month name in the 365-day cycle.

Even the 52-year interval between repetitions of one of any given calendar round date must have seemed inadequate to the calendar keepers, for in Late Preclassic times they took the vigesimal, or base-20, system they used for everyday counting of such things as cacao beans, maize plants, bolts of cloth, or rubber balls, and modified it slightly for counting days. The resulting "Long Count" is simply a number of days, usually expressed as an ordered notation of five respective spans – the *baktun* (144,000 days), the *katun* (7,200 days), the *tun* (360 days), the *uinal* (20 days), and the *k'in* (one day). In order to express any number of days, such as those elapsed since the beginning of the count, the Palenque scribes, like their counterparts in other Maya cities, attached a numerical coefficient, or multiplier, to each of these five periods. These numbers could be simple – bars as "fives" and dots as "ones" – or portraits, profile heads or full figures, of the gods of the numbers. To construct a Long Count date, then, one would simply attach the appropriate number glyph to the special hieroglyph for the period, place them in correct order, and end the whole with the Calendar Round designation of the day reached. In this manner, the Long Count became a kind of majestic odometer of time, clicking off each day in turn, in lockstep with the Calendar Round, providing a precise tempo to which the astronomers could match the movements of the visible planets, the constellations, or the visits of gods and ancestors.

Ceramics of Palenque

Palenque's hieroglyphic inscriptions tell us much of both the real and mythical history of the place, and dates as well, from the viewpoint of the Palenque elite of the Late Classic period. But while these texts are eloquent on matters such as the exploits and accomplishments of the ruler and royal ties to mythical gods and heroes, they are mute on such things as the history of settlement, population, and economics involving Palenque and neighboring cities. This is where pottery comes into its own as the universal friend of the archaeologist, not only at Palenque and throughout Mesoamerica, but also in every quarter of the world where people made it. Pottery, whether as whole vessels or, more often, in the form of fragments, is not only durable, but it also indicates by changes in its make-up, shape, and decoration such useful data as sources of clay, methods of firing, and, if one pays proper attention to the sequence of its layered deposits, changes in style and taste over both space and time. Precisely these sorts of data have been meticulously sampled and studied by Robert L. Rands, who has spent much of his 55-year career seeking to understand Palenque better in terms of its ceramic history. Despite the difficulties – even the most durable pottery surfaces, one of the diagnostic features the archaeologist uses for analysis, deteriorate rapidly in Palenque's humid conditions – Rands has meticulously constructed a chronology for Palenque in terms of "phases" named for the streams that pass through the archaeological zone. He has carefully correlated them with other archaeological and epigraphic evidence to construct a framework for looking at the history of the settlement.

The Living City

Palenque's situation on the border between two enormously different environmental zones, the vast plain on the north and highlands immediately south, gave it the advantage of exploiting both lowland and highland resources. The city also lies on the geographical divide between two drainage systems, one flowing west and the other east (fig. 3). Awareness of both these benefits may well have helped Palenque's first settlers select the place. Whatever the reasons, the ceramic record – the appearance of red-brown paste bowls, hallmarks of the Picota phase – shows people living in the western part of the present site as early as 500 BC, near the eponymous stream.

By AD 400, the community had grown considerably. We know only the names of some of Palenque's first rulers, for instance, K'uk Bahlam, Butz'aj Sak Chihk, and Ahkal Mo' Nahb I. The sudden appearance at this time of pottery from the Petén region to the east helps to define the Motiepa phase, a period of some two centuries that witnessed the maturing of the city as a major center – and the beginnings of military conflicts with neighbors to the east.

The 7th century AD corresponds with the renaissance of the kingdom as a major political force under the long rule of K'inich Janab Pakal, Palenque's "king of kings." This Otolum ceramic phase reflects both stability and prosperity in the sheer variety of local wares – and a dramatic increase in the importing of fine polychrome vases by the status-conscious elite. At the same time Palenque witnesses massive building programs in the expansion of the Palace and the construction of the Temple of the Inscriptions. As the period ends, Classic-period Palenque has reached what many consider its high point of art, architecture, and elite society – a city characterized by art historian Mary Miller and epigrapher Simon Martin as "an exemplary Maya court in an ideal setting of physical spaces and social arrangements."[17] At the same time, the other end of the social spectrum – Palenque's laborers, merchants, and farmers – pursued their daily routines based in sturdy dwellings of pole and thatch, some built amid the open low platforms of the city center, others on the outskirts of the city, or nearby.

The 8th century at Palenque, corresponding generally to the ceramic phase named for the Murciélagos River, saw the reigns of Pakal's immediate successors. His son, K'inich Kan Bahlam, began the expansion of the Palace, and ordered construction of the temple-pyramids forming the Cross Group. Half a century of excavation there, most recently by Martha Cuevas García, has uncovered dozens of what surely rank among the most spectacular examples of ceramic art ever produced by the ancient Maya – remarkable incense stands, ornate flanged cylinders, some more than a meter in height – bearing stacked portraits of Palenque's patron gods and revered ancestors. These striking objects were locally produced by the hundreds – Rands has identified at least one studio-workshop about 1 km (0.6 mile) east of the Palace – and were carefully set at regular intervals on the horizontal zones of the main buildings of the Group of the Cross, to support containers of burning incense. From the vantage point of, say, the east end of the Temple of the Inscriptions, these ornate, brightly painted countenances, all in a row and staring from the dense aromatic haze like some supernatural army at attention, must have presented a lasting memory for all who beheld them. During this Murciélagos phase, our best estimates place the population of the urban core of Palenque at no more than 7,500. While this figure is small in relation to other Maya cities, in the sheer density of structures, 673 per sq. km, downtown Palenque ranks second highest in the whole Maya area (after Copán).[18]

The final discernible ceramic phase of Palenque, the Balunté (c. AD 770–850), saw increased interactions with communities on the plains to the north, reflected in fine paste grey wares, as well as a general fading of the expressions of royalty and elite culture in the city. Population in the immediate vicinity had spread into arable lands on the plain below the city. Rodrigo Liendo Stuardo's detailed survey of 37 sq. km (14 sq. miles) extending east of Palenque's urban core to the bank of the Chacamax River and west along the Michol yielded around ten habitation sites for the Otolum phase, and more than 80 habitation sites with Balunté pottery.[19] In around AD 850, and for reasons to be sought later in this book, a holdout population appears to have finally abandoned the faded city to the encroaching forest.

CHAPTER TWO

An Ancient City Discovered

These galleries are so extraordinary, their construction so curious, so strong,
so thick, decorated with embossed devices that I defy any language to do
justice to their description or Painter to depict them.

EDWARD FITZGERALD TO LORD KINGSBOROUGH,
PALENQUE, 17 APRIL 1838[1]

The comfortable trail that leads today's visitors from the parking lot to "downtown" Palenque opens onto a spacious plaza where a remarkable panorama greets the eye. Majestic buildings of grey stone rise in silence and sublime dignity from a smooth carpet of grass punctuated by strategically located shade trees. At appropriate points here and there, signs in Maya, Spanish, and English highlight the story of Palenque during the first millennium AD. They also provide a guide to the modern designations of Palenque's buildings and building groups and the names and dates of those who ruled the ancient city. From the signs, it is clear that we know a good deal about Palenque and those who built it more than 1,300 years ago. This, however, has not always been the case.

Between the 10th and 18th centuries AD, the ancient city of Palenque lay out of sight and out of mind, concealed in the tropical forest that blanketed the frontier between the Viceroyalty of New Spain in Mexico and the Captaincy General of Guatemala – the region west of the Usumacinta River where the mountains and coastal plain meet.[2] In the middle of the 16th century, only a few decades after the first Spanish conquerors had arrived, a group of Ch'ol Maya came out of the high country and settled near the base of the mountains between the Zoque people of Tabasco and the Usumacinta

Valley (see fig. 3). Santo Domingo de Palenque, a settlement in what was then part of Guatemala, soon became an important stop on the trail between Ciudad Real de Chiapa (now San Cristóbal de las Casas) and the Mexican provinces of Tabasco, Campeche, and Yucatán to the north. By 1567, the year of its official founding, Santo Domingo boasted two rows of pole-and-thatch houses flanking a single street that ended at the church.

Given that "lost cities" are most often labeled as such by outsiders, it is probable that Ch'ol Maya from Santo Domingo knew of the nearby ruins when they first settled in the region. It was not until 1808, however, that a notice of its discovery came into print: historian Domingo Juarros gave an account of the discovery of the "vestiges of a very opulent city…concealed for ages in the midst of a vast desert, [that] remained unknown until the middle of the eighteenth century, when some Spaniards…penetrated the dreary solitude."[3]

Juarros was likely referring to the family of Antonio de Solís, a cleric from Tumbalá. Around 1746 – and sources variously put the date between 1730 and 1770 – Solís was assigned to Santo Domingo, where he arrived with his married brothers and nephews. Not long afterward, while searching for suitable land to farm, the relatives came upon *casas de piedra*, "stone houses," in the forested heights not far from the village.[4] The news eventually reached Ramón Ordóñez de Aguiar, priest of the cathedral of Ciudad Real and a passionate antiquarian.[5] In 1773, Ordóñez sent a group, including his brother, to visit the ruins. Soon afterward, Ordóñez got word of the discovery to Brigadier Josef Estacharía, recently appointed as president and captain general of the Royal Audencia of Guatemala. Well aware of the deep and active interest of his king, Charles III, in the geography and history of Spain's overseas colonies, and being particularly anxious to please the court in Madrid, Estacharía reacted swiftly to the news of the city in the forest.[6] On 28 November 1784 he signed an order directing José Antonio Calderón, deputy mayor of Santo Domingo, to investigate.[7]

8 OPPOSITE *José Antonio Calderón's 1784 drawing of the central scene of the Tablet of the Sun.*

Early Expeditions to the Lost City

The early trail between Santo Domingo and the stone houses appears to have followed the general course of road that connects the two places today, except in its final approach to the ruins. Today the 8-km (5-mile) road provides a pleasant drive or walk through the undulating terrain at the base of the mountains. In Calderón's day it was quite different – a cruelly narrow and treacherous trail leading through frequent patches of swampy ground, thick with forest growth and teeming with insects. At the site of the present museum, the trail turned quickly left to follow the steep slope upward along the Otolum River. This brought visitors to the base of the Palace at its north side, near the northeast corner.[8]

Calderón spent three days at the ruins on his first official visit in late November 1784. His report to Estacharía in mid-December includes a short description of the Palace and an astonishing tabulation of more than 200 other ruined structures. He also submitted four pen sketches – two of relief carvings depicting standing figures, another depicting the Tower in the Palace, and a fourth showing the central scene on the Tablet of the Temple of the Sun (fig. 8). Today, it is easy to judge Calderón's renderings as both crude and useless, for they are largely so. At the same time, we cannot help but appreciate the difficulty the assignment must have posed for a provincial official with extraordinarily indifferent drawing ability to even approximate a totally alien work of art for impatient and demanding superiors.

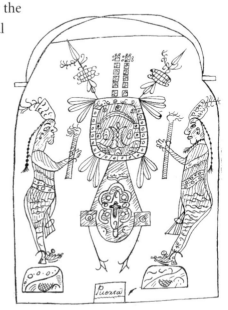

Calderón's report apparently both exasperated and intrigued Estacharía, for after examining it the president immediately ordered a second expedition to investigate the ruins. This time, the task fell to Antonio Bernasconi, royal architect of Guatemala, and he soon justified the choice. The neat shaded depictions Bernasconi made in early 1785 include

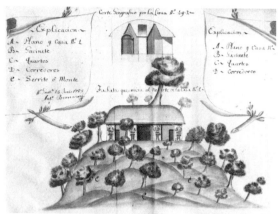

9 *Antonio Bernasconi's 1785 drawings:* A *The "Oval" Tablet and throne in Palace House E, left;* B *A temple in the Cross Group, probably the Temple of the Sun, right;* C *An inscribed tablet from the* subterraneos *stairway, below.*

architectural plans, elevations, and cross-sections; renditions of carved figures; and other features of the site. His renderings, however, were misleading because they adhered to strict standards of geometry, showing the parallelogram of the Palace plan, for example, as a true rectangle, and the Oval Tablet as a perfect circle (fig. 9A). In his elevations, Bernasconi failed to show any of the roof crests on the buildings; perhaps they were overgrown by vegetation. Nonetheless, his elevation view of "Casa No. 2" (probably the Temple of the Sun) atop its mounded platform stands as the first fairly realistic long view of a Palenque temple (fig. 9B). Through his habits as a trained architect, Bernasconi searched for a proper architectural style, or "order" among the ruins, but recognized none. Accustomed to regularity, he rendered his Casa No. 1 on a mound cloaked in a forest of neat, evenly

spaced little trees. And with his depiction of a stone carving containing six hieroglyphs (which he unknowingly showed sideways), Bernasconi also provided us with the earliest known decent, recognizable, and therefore useful, record of a Maya hieroglyphic inscription (fig. 9C).[9]

Bernasconi's report dated 13 June 1785 also included descriptions of many buildings, and also his opinion that the ancient city had not succumbed to destruction by warfare or earthquake as some had perhaps suggested, but rather had collapsed due to abandonment and the ravages of time.[10] With this judgment, Bernasconi became the first person in modern times to reach a correct conclusion about ancient Palenque based on first-hand observation.

Bernasconi's drawings impressed not only Estacharía, but also the influential Spanish court historian Juan Bautista Muñoz, who immediately recognized the potential importance of the ruins.[11] On 7 March 1786, he approached José de Gálvez, marquis of Sonora and secretary to the crown, and requested a more detailed exploration of Palenque, including the recommendation "to bring away pieces of plaster, mortar, stucco, bricks both fired and unfired; potsherds and any other utensils or tools to be found; making excavation where it seems best."[12] Eight days later, Charles III himself made the order to "make it so." This time, the assignment fell to Captain of Artillery Antonio del Río, then serving in the Guatemalan capital.

On 5 May 1787, del Río arrived at the ruined city with an artist, Ignacio Armendáriz, and guides from the village. There they were dismayed to find themselves helpless in "a fog so extremely dense, that it was impossible to see one another at a distance of five paces; and whereby the principal building [the Palace], surrounded by copse wood trees of large dimensions, in full foliage and closely interwoven, was completely concealed from our view."[13] Despite this discouraging start, del Río secured labor assistance with the help of Calderón, and on 17 May, with 79 Ch'ol Maya from nearby Tumbalá and 48 axes, began his work at Palenque. By 2 June, much of the forest choking the Palace had been cleared and was set afire. In the "general conflagration" that followed, the central part of Palenque was opened to the light of day for the first time in a thousand years.[14]

The real work began with only "seven iron crowbars and three pick-axes…and by dint of perseverance," boasted del Río, "there remained neither a window nor a doorway blocked up, a partition that was not thrown down, nor a room, corridor, court, tower, sanctuary, nor subterranean passage in which excavations two or more yards in depth were not effected – all this in accordance with orders."[15]

Following the request from Muñoz for artifacts, del Río removed selected objects from Palenque for shipment to Spain. These included stucco hieroglyphs and figure parts pried from piers, two small hieroglyphic panels of stone from the subterranean halls of the Palace, the right leg of the throne in House E, and various ceramic vessels taken from sub-floor caches (plate 1).[16]

In his report of 24 June 1787, del Río provides some interesting remarks on the hieroglyphs – these would later constitute the very first mention of ancient Maya writing, and certainly that of Palenque, to reach print. His description and rather precocious analysis is based on several stucco glyphs he removed from the exterior of the Temple of the Inscriptions: "Some whimsical designs, serving as ornaments to the corners of the house, I brought away…but all knowledge respecting them is concealed from us, owing to no traditional information or written documents being preserved, explanatory of their real meaning, and the manner in which the inhabitants used such devices for the conveyance of their thoughts."[17]

Del Río's narrative also provides our earliest reasonably complete descriptions of some of Palenque's buildings. His account of the Temple of the Inscriptions and the stucco piers is admirable for its time: "It has square pillars, an exterior gallery, and a salon twenty yards long by three and a half broad, embellished with a façade with life-size figures of women, in stucco relief, with children in their arms. As shown…these representations are without heads."[18]

Del Río's interpretations of what he saw at Palenque coincided with the common view of the time that the "civilized" styles inherent in the sculpture and architecture of some ancient American ruins were certainly the work of Old World migrants, and probably ancient Romans. His "fieldwork," however, appears to have been quite competent, perhaps even a little ahead of its time in terms of architectural description. One may well question del Río's methods as he described them (and all who read the famous description of his "excavations," quoted above, rejoice at his relatively brief stay of three weeks!). Whatever physical damage he did in the course of his explorations, however, soon blended into the rest of the ruins. To the credit of del Río and the Spanish government, the objects removed from Palenque in 1787 may still be seen in Madrid's Museo de América.

While del Río dug and collected, Armendáriz attacked his task with a vengeance. He recorded, among other things, the elaborate stucco *adornos*

10 *Ignacio Armendáriz's 1787 drawings.* A *Palace House A pier, left;* B *West sanctuary jamb, Temple of the Cross, center;* C *The "beau relief," Temple of the Jaguar, right.*

on the interior walls of the Palace; seven of the exterior piers from the Palace and Temple of the Inscriptions; an interior stucco relief, now gone, showing a figure seated on a double-headed jaguar throne; tablets from the sanctuaries of the Group of the Cross; two hieroglyphic panels from the open passageways beneath the Palace; and the right leg of the throne in House E (figs 10A, B, C, and see fig. 12A). It was an astonishing achievement in both perseverance and extraordinarily fine draftsmanship. It is difficult to imagine the adverse conditions facing Armendáriz during those three weeks in the debilitating heat of a tropical spring, in the half-lit interiors where the largest sculptures were, and having to contemplate and draw on paper dampened with humidity and perspiration the stupefying details carved by an unknown people in an unknown time. For this, plus the extraordinarily high quality of his production, Armendáriz emerges as the first true hero in the visual documentation of Palenque.[19]

As the recording of Palenque began in earnest, so did speculation about the builders of the mysterious houses of stone. In a manuscript of 14 June 1787, a mere ten days before del Río made his report to Estacharía, one

Vicente José Solórzano of Yajalón stated his opinion: the Indians themselves had built both Palenque and Toniná. This precocious conclusion would not reach print for another two centuries.[20]

Dupaix and Castañeda Visit the Ruins

Nearly two decades passed before the next expedition to the ruined city. In 1804, Charles IV of Spain, influenced by the powerful recommendations of Alexander von Humboldt and other respected scientists, issued an order to make and gather exact drawings of any and all ancient buildings and monuments that would contribute to the knowledge of the history of New Spain in general. This endeavor was to concentrate on the ruins of Mexico. For the task, the viceroy of New Spain chose retired Captain of Dragoons Guillermo Dupaix, who had been stationed in Mexico since 1791. Dupaix chose José Luciano Castañeda to be expedition artist.

Between 1805 and 1809, Dupaix led three separate expeditions among the ruins of Mexico. The first two covered much of Mexico's central highlands and the Oaxaca Valley. The third took the group along the trail eastward, into the Guatemalan province of Chiapa, up the escarpment to Ciudad Real, then north, overland via Ocosingo and Toniná to Santo Domingo de Palenque. The 80-km (50-mile) trek from Ocosingo to Santo Domingo took a full eight

days on a trail that wound through mountains, an area "scarcely passable by any other animal than a bird." Pausing briefly in the town, Dupaix, his men, and pack mules entered the ruins on 10 January 1807.[21]

In three weeks, while Dupaix set his descriptions and observations to paper, Castañeda recorded his version of Palenque in 27 drawings, among them ten stucco piers, the monumental reliefs from Patio A of the Palace, and three hieroglyphic panels. The rest depict buildings and floor plans, cross sections of the Palace, and views of the bridge, the aqueduct, and other features at the site (fig. 11).[22]

Completion of the third Dupaix expedition in 1809 marks the end of the period of discovery, the last of the earliest noteworthy attempts to record the marvels of Palenque for the outside world. However, the results of the labors of Calderón, Bernasconi, del Río, Armendáriz, Dupaix, and Castañeda would not reach print in usable form for more than a decade as other events that would profoundly affect relationships between Europe and the Americas – and the pace of scientific investigation and publication as well – were unfolding.

Who Drew What, and When?

Napoleon's invasion of Spain and the abdication of Charles IV in 1808 provided the political setting for the patriotic movements that culminated in independence for Mexico in 1821, Guatemala in 1822, and most of Spanish America by 1825. Chiapas – and with it Palenque – became part of Mexico in 1824.[23] The sudden debut of the new nations, previously unknown outside the Spanish empire, created an unprecedented interest in Europe and the United States. It was also during this period that the history of the two existing sets of Palenque drawings, the one that Armendáriz finished shortly after the 1787 expedition, and the other that Castañeda completed at least two decades later, becomes confused.

First of all, certain readily identifiable sculptures, among them the carved throne leg from Palace House E and two hieroglyphic panels from

11 *José Luciano Castañeda's rendering of the east side of the Palace as it appeared in Lord Kingsborough's* Antiquities of Mexico, *1830. This view greeted the earliest visitors who took the trail from the settlement of Santo Domingo de Palenque.*

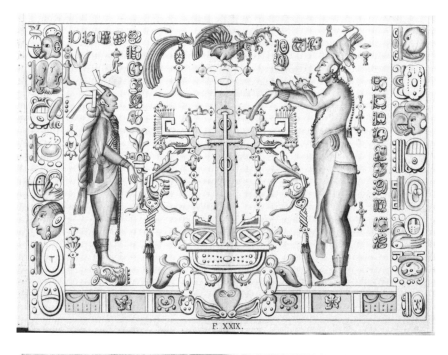

F. XXIX.

12 *Armendáriz's (above) and Castañeda's (below) renderings of the Tablet of the Cross.*

the "subterranean" chambers below, had been taken from Palenque 20 years before Castañeda arrived on the scene, so he could not have seen them there, much less drawn them! Second, there is the matter of the two artists' renderings of the tablet in the Temple of the Cross. When Armendáriz drew the panel, he succeeded reasonably well in rendering the great central scene – two figures facing inward toward the complicated cruciform motif that gave the building its name – and the short rows and columns of hieroglyphs within it. As for the two vertical panels of 100 glyph blocks each that flank the central scene, Armendáriz for whatever reason simply represented each panel as a column of eight glyphs, apparently chosen at random and grotesquely enlarged to fill the vertical space.

Castañeda's drawing of the same panel, done 20 years later, duplicates the Armendáriz rendering in all details, including the sequences of the enlarged glyphs that Armendáriz had inserted at random (fig. 12). An examination of all "Castañeda" drawings of Palenque, in fact, indicates that Castañeda copied as many as 14 of the Armendáriz renderings.[24] The story behind these first illustrations of Palenque would be of little more than passing interest except for the fact that soon after the Dupaix expedition these images began to appear in print.

Palenque Reaches Print – in an Unfortunate Way

Alexander von Humboldt was the first to publish a recognizable illustration of Palenque. Based on the Armendáriz-Castañeda rendering of Pier E of Palace House A, the Humboldt illustration appeared in 1810 as a full-page plate in the monumental folio of *Vues des Cordillères*, the illustrated narrative of the famed scientist's travels through Spanish America with the French botanist Aimé Bonpland (fig. 13). Humboldt obtained the drawing from the Mexican botanist Miguel Cervantes, who likely found it in the archives in Mexico City, where the reports of the Dupaix expedition ended up, or perhaps from Castañeda himself. Whatever the source, the relevance of this image to the story of Palenque was all but nullified by a crucial misidentification: Humboldt's caption identifies the image as a "Mexican relief found in Oaxaca"![25]

The period following Mexican independence in 1821 and the formation of the Federated States of Central America soon afterward saw interest in those nations and regions, initially triggered by the prodigious writings of Humboldt and others, grow rapidly. On 2 November 1822, perhaps spawned by this new interest in the former Spanish colonies, a remarkable volume appeared on London bookstalls. It bore the ringing title, *Description of the Ruins of an Ancient City Discovered near Palenque in the Kingdom of Guatemala, in Spanish America.* It stands as the earliest publication devoted solely to a Maya ruin.

Published by Henry Berthoud, the thin quarto volume – it is hardly more than two cm (¾ inch) thick – contains a full translation into English of del Río's 1787 report on Palenque, along with *Teatro Critico Americano* by Paul Felix Cabrera, an Italian lawyer and antiquarian who lived in Guatemala. Cabrera's gloriously ponderous and wide-ranging essay argues at great length on the origins of the Native Americans among the worshippers of Votan, Osiris, and other Old World heroes and gods.

The illustrations form the most important part of the book. Their source is unknown, as is the certain identity of the Englishman credited with transporting them and the two manuscripts from Guatemala to London.[26]

The mystery of the drawings lies in the makeup of the set: in neither order nor number do the 17 drawings correspond with the figure citations in the accompanying text, where del Río was naturally referring to the

13 RIGHT *Humboldt's misidentified plate of Palenque, 1810, based on a Castañeda copy of an Armendáriz original (compare with figs 10A and 14A).*

14 OPPOSITE *Waldeck's 1822 engravings, after Armendáriz-Castañeda originals.*
A *A Palace pier, left;* B *The relief in the Temple of the Jaguar, right (compare with figs 10C and 15A).*

30 figures that Armendáriz had made for him in 1787. The most probable explanation is that all 17 plates derive from an abridged set of Castañeda's drawings of Palenque. Of these, 15 appear to be based on his direct copies of 15 Armendáriz originals, plus two of Castañeda's own works: the floor plan of the Palace and a curious brass medallion, clearly non-Indian in origin.[27]

Still another generation of change in the Palenque drawings took place in 1822 during the preparation of the printing plates to accompany the del Río report. This was the work of the flamboyant Jean-Frédéric Maximilien de Waldeck, a self-styled "count" then in his mid-fifties with some notoriety as an artist, traveler, and avid antiquarian. Whereas Castañeda had merely copied Armendáriz's drawings without much change in style, Waldeck, perhaps unconsciously, re-touched the images by adding embellishments such as fine-line suggestions of musculature and details of costume and ornament, all of which gave the figures depicted in the final plates a look that was more classical Roman than Classic Maya (fig. 14). In 1822, however, the quality of the illustrations was of little concern. What really mattered was that these were the very first images of Palenque art to reach the general public. Even so, reception of the volume was at first only faintly favorable, due perhaps to a negative review in London's *Literary Gazette*.[28] Among his comments "upon a certain mass of ruins in New Spain," the reviewer (perhaps after wading through Cabrera's text!) labels the volume as "obscure, and in parts unintelligible." Interest in Palenque nonetheless

increased over the next decade, with two German editions of the work appearing in 1823 and 1832.[29] In 1827, eight of the illustrations from the 1822 volume reappeared in David Warden's short work on American antiquities linking the ancient Indian earthworks of Ohio and the ruins of Palenque.[30]

Up to now, our history of research at Palenque has dealt mainly with archival records and other manuscript sources that remained largely unpublished for decades, even centuries, after their creation. With the 1822 publication came a whole new period in the story of research, one in which the cadence of publication began to cater more and more to those interested in the ancient American past. Between 1829 and 1848 there appeared what is surely the largest, most sumptuous work ever published on ancient America – the *Antiquities of Mexico*, by Edward King, Viscount Kingsborough (known as Lord Kingsborough).[31] First son of an Irish Earl, Lord Kingsborough was obsessed with the belief held by many of his contemporaries that Native Americans had descended from the biblical Lost Tribes of Israel. In preparing his great work, Kingsborough cast his net far and wide for any material that he thought might support his thesis. Among his catches were the reports of the three Dupaix expeditions and Castañeda's complete corpus of images.[32] Among the Palenque illustrations published, as many as 21 were new to the readers; the rest, as we have seen, had already appeared in print in London in 1822, including the persistent medallion!

Castañeda's images survived Lord Kingsborough's engravers reasonably well, save for gratuitous over-elaboration of the artist's view of the Palace and a few other distortions. Thus the second published version of the remains of Palenque made its debut. Sadly, the prohibitive cost of purchasing a set of the *Antiquities of Mexico* and the relatively small number of sets issued severely limited public access to the work.[33]

The Count, the Eccentric, and the Enthusiast

By the 1830s an increasing awareness of aboriginal American remains in general, and Palenque in particular, began to draw visitors. Among the first of note to arrive in Palenque was the peripatetic 66-year-old Waldeck, the colorful artist who had made the lithographic plates for the 1822 London

(*Above*) Palenque artifacts collected in 1787 by Antonio del Río in the Museo de América, Madrid, *c.* 1882. Heinrich Schliemann, famed discoverer of Troy, is seated left; and museum director Juan de Díos de la Rada y Delgado, right. The collection, notable as the earliest documented assemblage related to the Maya, remains available for study to this day.

2 (*Below*) Désiré Charnay's published view of Palace House C, 1885, indicating the bas-reliefs that covered its piers and platform as well as the "seven enormous heads" that decorated its upper frieze. Such wood engravings, based largely on photographs and casts that Charnay laboriously made at Palenque early in 1881 under a continuing winter rain, provided readers with views of many buildings and other features that earlier visitors had failed to record (see plates 19A and 19B).

3 (*Above*) Alfred Maudslay's composite photograph of the Tablet of the Cross, including the right-hand slab, then at the Smithsonian Institution in Washington, D.C., and the damaged central slab, photographed by Charnay as it lay in the nearby forest and later removed to Mexico City. This image, first published in October 1897, typifies the high standards of documentation that characterize all of Maudslay's work.

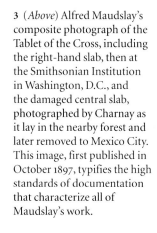

4 (*Left*) Maudslay's photographs of four of the stucco piers of the Temple of the Inscriptions. To obtain these, vegetation had to be cut, scaffolding built, and the reliefs themselves cleared of black fungus, then carefully cleaned to reveal the original carving and any intact paint. For the publication of these monuments Maudslay added Miss Annie Hunter's meticulous drawings of each one (see fig. 24).

5 Workers in the East Court of the Palace, 1891. Here, Maudslay's crew has cleared the courtyard of dense vegetation, revealing the front of House C and preparing it for documentation. Barely visible in the near distance are the overgrown remains of the Tower; in the right distance, the doorways of the Temple of the Inscriptions.

8 (*Below*) José Cabrera of Palenque town holds two of the magnificent stucco glyphs from the *Templo Olvidado*, a building in deep forest west of Palenque's Central Group. First reported in 1926 by Frans Blom, the building was later excavated by Heinrich Berlin, whose fascination with its unusual glyphs ultimately led to his extraordinary career in epigraphy (see fig. 46).

(*Opposite, above and below, and above, left*) The ruins of Palenque as they appeared in 1942, barely visible with their covering of vegetation. Excavation and consolidation of the Palace and its Tower, above, had begun eight years earlier under the direction of Miguel Angel Fernández. Among his discoveries: elegant stucco reliefs (below, left) that flanked the grand stairway on the north side of the massive platform supporting the Palace (see fig. 72).

(*Below*) The Tablet of the 96 Glyphs soon after its discovery by Miguel Angel Fernández. Workmen discovered the piece whole although face down in the rubble near the base of the Tower but, unaware that it was carved, broke it up with their picks for easy removal. Thanks to the clean breaks in the fine limestone, the tablet has now been restored to near its pristine state (plate 29). It proved to be an important key in reconstructing Palenque's king list.

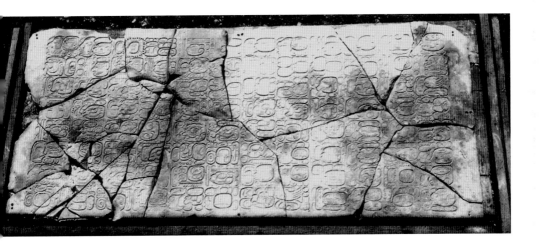

9 (*Below*) Large ceramic incense burner stand excavated near the Temple of the Foliated Cross. Scores of such objects have been excavated at Palenque, especially from the terraces in the Group of the Cross. Their elaborate modeling and appliqué decorations represent a variety of gods and elite personages, in this instance the jaguar god of fire and the underworld, a symbol of the night sun.

10 (*Above*) One of nine stucco relief portraits on the wall of Pakal's tomb chamber that depict the dead king's ancestors and royal predecessors. This one portrays the early queen Ix Yohl Ik'nal in the elaborate costume of royalty, who also appears on one side of Pakal's sarcophagus (see fig. 39c).

11 (*Right*) The Dumbarton Oaks tablet, showing a young K'inich K'an Joy Chitam who dances in the guise of the rain god, Chahk, flanked by his mother and father, Pakal, at right. The stone panel was illicitly removed from an unknown temple near Palenque in the mid-20th century.

12 Temple XIX's limestone panel, depicting K'inich Ahkal Mo' Nahb in an elaborate feathered dance costume representing an enormous bird's mouth. Two priests kneel at his side, helping to support the cumbersome outfit. The limestone relief originally decorated an interior pillar of the temple. Though incomplete, this panel preserves in intricate detail the superlative talent of Palenque's sculptors and ranks as one of the great masterpieces of ancient American art (see plate 34).

publication. Waldeck appeared at Palenque in May 1832, built a pole-and-thatch house near the base of the Temple of the Cross, and moved in with a local girl.[34]

Waldeck lived at Palenque for more than a year – the "Temple of the Count" is named after him – and during that time he made many drawings, not only of the sculptures and the hieroglyphic texts at the ruins, but also of people and scenes in the town of Santo Domingo.[35] Judging from existing drawings and paintings, Waldeck's archaeological illustrations of Palenque range from the highly competent to the absurd, from carefully measured line renderings of figures and hieroglyphs to elaborate fantasies featuring grotesque elephant heads. In many instances, he used evocative views of Palenque architecture and landscapes as romantic settings for later paintings and lithographs. Perhaps Waldeck's most famous rendering is that of the now-destroyed "Beau-relief," an apparently magnificent sculpture in stucco that once graced the Temple of the Jaguar, and that Waldeck carefully drew before he destroyed the figure (figs 15A, B). Fortunately, Armendáriz had drawn the same relief almost a half century earlier (see fig. 10c)!

In the meantime, another actor had entered the ongoing drama of Palenque research. Constantine Samuel Rafinesque was born in Constantinople in 1783. His early adult years were passed in the United States and Italy, particularly Sicily, followed by his permanent settlement in the United States in 1815. By any conceivable measure, Rafinesque was a remarkable human being. Perhaps the most telling glimpse of the man appears in his own words: "Versatility of talents and professions is not uncommon in America; but those which I have exhibited…may appear to exceed belief; and yet it is a positive fact that in knowledge I have been a Botanist, Naturalist, Geologist, Geographer, Historian, Poet, Philosopher, Philologist, Economist, Philanthropist…by profession a Traveller, Merchant, Manufacturer, Collector, Improver, Professor, Teacher, Surveyor, Draftsman, Architect, Engineer, Pulmist, Author, Editor, Bookseller, Librarian, Secretary…and I hardly know myself what I may become…."[36]

Also by his own account Rafinesque had read a thousand volumes by his twelfth year; by the age of 16 he had studied 50 languages and remained an insatiable reader throughout his life. By the age of 40 Rafinesque had read, among many other things, Humboldt in French and many, if not most, of the histories of New Spain, including Diego López de Cogolludo on Yucatán and Villagutierre de Soto-Mayor on the conquest of Guatemala – in Spanish, of course. Not surprisingly, Rafinesque's frenetic pursuit of knowledge led him to del Río's illustrated description of Palenque, then recently published. There for the first time he saw Maya hieroglyphs, and was apparently spellbound (see figs 16 and 17).

On New Year's Day 1827, Rafinesque penned a letter to the prominent philologist of the time, Peter Duponceau of the American Philosophical Society in Philadelphia. As was customary during this period, this was "sent" through a local newspaper, in this instance *The Saturday Evening Post*, which published it two weeks later. In it Rafinesque speaks of the hieroglyphs at Palenque, which he calls by the name Otolum, after the nearby river, in order to distinguish the ruins from the town: "These OTOLUM characters are totally different from the Azteca or Mexican paintings...and also from every other mode of expressing ideas by carving, painting, or [Inka quipus]. They appear besides to belong to a peculiar language, distinct from the Azteca, probably the Tzendal (called also Chontal, Celtal, &c.), yet spoken from Chiapa to Panama, and connected with the Maya of Yucatan."[37]

Throughout 1828 and 1829, Rafinesque corresponded frequently with antiquarian (and harbor master) James H. McCulloh of Baltimore, Maryland. At this time McCulloh was engaged in revising his 1817 *Researches on America*, and Rafinesque's speculations on Maya hieroglyphic writing at Palenque interested him greatly – so much so that McCulloh's new and greatly expanded 1829 work, *Researches, Philosophical and Antiquarian, concerning the Aboriginal History of America*, devoted ten pages to the topic. In his discussion, McCulloh drew upon what he considered to be the best of the available literature, including Rafinesque's letters, to create what stands as the earliest serious discussion of ancient Maya writing in print. In his book McCulloh raises the hand of caution against most of Rafinesque's torrent of speculation, but accepts and expands upon one crucial link that we now take for granted – that the hieroglyphs of Palenque and the Dresden Codex (at the time this was the only known Maya book and had survived in Dresden's Royal Saxon library) which Rafinesque had seen in Humboldt's

15 *Waldeck's drawings made at Palenque during his residency in the early 1830s.* A *Perspective rendering of the relief in the Temple of the Jaguar, left.* B *The same relief as it appeared in 1942, after its partial destruction, right.*

1810 publication, and which McCulloh tied to Peter Martyr's description of the books of Yucatán – were *both* products of the Maya. As sole illustration for this decisive and determining conclusion, McCulloh uses the column of ten glyphs – as we will see later, there were actually 15 glyphs in that column – from the 1822 Armendáriz-Castañeda-Waldeck illustration of the Tablet of the Temple of the Cross (fig. 16). To our knowledge, this is the first illustration of Maya hieroglyphs to be published in the Americas.[38]

In April 1831 Juan Galindo, governor of Guatemala's District of Petén, visited Palenque and produced a few drawings of stucco glyphs, some of which he removed. Galindo, a versatile man – soldier, geographer, and diplomat – was also dubbed "enthusiast" by one authority who suggests "it would not be grotesque to call him the first archaeologist in the Maya

16 RIGHT *The first American publication of Maya hieroglyphs – by James McCulloh in 1829, showing a column of ten from Waldeck's 1822 engraving of the Tablet of the Temple of the Cross (see fig. 17).*

17 BELOW *Waldeck's engraving of the Tablet of the Cross, based on the Armendáriz–Castañeda original (see fig. 12). The ten hieroglyphs that so captivated Rafinesque appear in a column immediately behind the standing figure on the right.*

field," for Galindo reached two important conclusions – first, that the hiero-glyphs at Palenque were part of the same system as those he had seen on his frequent visits to Copán; and second, that the individuals depicted in the Palenque sculptures were physically identical to the local Maya.[39]

Early in 1832, Rafinesque began issuing the quarterly *Atlantic Journal,* and *Friend of Knowledge,* a short newsletter to which he was virtually the sole contributor. In the first issue – only eight were completed – Rafinesque writes to "Mr. Champolion" [sic], the famed scholar who as a youth had successfully deciphered the ancient Egyptian hieroglyphic inscriptions, recapitulating his own interpretations of the hieroglyphs of Otolum (Palenque) that had appeared earlier in The *Saturday Evening Post.* The texts at Palenque, Rafinesque stated, fell into his category of "alphabetical symbols, expressing syllables, not words." Unfortunately, the great Egyptologist died as Rafinesque sought to contact him.[40]

In 1834, nearly a generation after the end of Dupaix's third expedition, Dupaix's own account, along with Castañeda's illustrations, finally reached print in a publication devoted solely to these three important early journeys of exploration. *Antiquités Mexicaines,* published in Paris under the editor-ship of H. Baradère, repeated the Castañeda images of Palenque published earlier, and with the distortions mentioned above, by Kingsborough.[41] This time, however, those who prepared the plates for printing added even more "improvements," such as reconstructing the east façade of the Palace while moving the Tower to a more central position. At the same time, all three images of the sculptures in the Temple of the Cross were shown in reverse![42]

With this publication, results of the two major expeditions to Palenque were now in print in three separate works. Of those, two appeared as lavish and costly productions, far out of reach of all but the wealthy antiquarian. Despite this, word of Palenque was beginning to filter through to the public press in the form of various articles and communications dealing with "American antiquities." These had begun in 1827 with Rafinesque's prolific correspondence through newspapers. By 1834 papers in New York had taken up the cause: in November 1833, *The Knickerbocker* published a local lecture on Palenque by Samuel Akerly, which incorporated data Akerly had obtained from Waldeck, and one Dr. François ("Francisco") Corroy of

Tabasco, himself a frequent visitor to the ruins, judging from his graffiti on the walls of the Palace, noticed by later visitors.

In the United States, public interest in distant Palenque reached its first peak between December 1833 and March 1834 when the *Family Magazine, or Weekly Abstract of General Knowledge* in New York, perhaps inspired by the *Knickerbocker* piece, ran installments of del Río's report on Palenque and Cabrera's *Teatro Critico Americano* – both taken verbatim from the 1822 London publication. Five of the installments carried full-page illustrations from the same work.

During this same period, Rafinesque's work appeared again and again, most often illustrated by the now familiar glyphs from the Temple of the Cross at Palenque, in a perennial anthology of natural and historical curiosities entitled *American Antiquities, or Discoveries in the West*, by Josiah Priest, an Albany, New York, harness-maker and carriage fitter turned "author." The final publication of Rafinesque's musings on the hieroglyphs of Palenque appeared in 1843 as an appendix to Benjamin F. Norman's *Rambles in Yucatan.*

On 4 April 1836 an itinerant eye surgeon, Edward FitzGerald, arrived at Palenque, apparently for the single purpose of describing Palenque for Lord Kingsborough. He did so in the form of a 3,000-word letter dated 17 April. In it FitzGerald describes the countryside, the forest, and the site – and all the structures he mentions are immediately recognizable. Occasionally, however, FitzGerald grossly exaggerates measurements, giving, for example, 200 feet as the Palace platform height! He also mentions the ancient quarry, from which many of the stones used to build Palenque came, and closes with some unkind words about Waldeck's removal of artifacts from the ruins.

FitzGerald also mentions having talked with Waldeck in Mérida, where the irrepressible 70-year-old count was teaching drawing. Waldeck, typically, had warned FitzGerald of an unusual creature that lived in the ruins: "Mr. Waldeck's snake is 45 or 50 yards long, beautifully speckled, & has its cave near the ruins of the Palace. I asked one of his guides who had been his servant if he had seen this enormous serpent, & he told me it was true & just as Mr. Waldeck had described."

Knowing full well that Lord Kingsborough was Waldeck's key sup-porter, FitzGerald proceeded to take verbal revenge on the old artist, who was at this time in Mexico City defending himself against charges of remov-ing relics from Palenque by writing to the viscount: "Your Lordship will do well to receive Mr. Waldeck's drawings, disbelieving all he says about snakes as he deals so much with the marvelous that few now believe him tho' he should speak the truth." Toward the end of his letter, FitzGerald makes a strong recommendation: "A good Draftsman to be sure would find much to employ his pencil [here]."

In the meantime Waldeck, having survived both his legal ordeal and FitzGerald's gratuitous appraisal, turned attention to his first major publi-cation on the Maya – the impressive *Voyage pittoresque et archéologique dans la province d'Yucatan*. Of its 22 plates, most are devoted to romanticized images of Uxmal. Only one pertains to Palenque – a poor re-rendering of the very same "astronomical relief" over an interior doorway in the Palace that he had engraved for the del Río and Cabrera volume 16 years earlier. This, he stated, was simply to announce, in effect, a future book on Palenque. Waldeck dedicated this work to "le Vicomte de Kingsborough" who had died the year before, at the age of 41.

In 1839, John Delafield's *An Inquiry into the Origin of the Antiquities of America* drew indiscriminately upon a hodge-podge of data to present virtually all previous speculations offered to date on the Old World origins of the ancient Americans. To make his point, the author showed the three figures from Humboldt's wrongly captioned Palenque illustration of 1810.

With the appearance of the works of Waldeck and Delafield, the first major era of exploration at Palenque drew to an end. Despite his lack of accuracy in showing a true vision of the Maya ruins, no one can deny the great effect that Waldeck's images of Yucatán had on an eager public. While Delafield's work thankfully passed into relative obscurity, Waldeck's effort endured somewhat longer.[43] Soon it would help inspire two readers who would lead the ancient Maya remains into the next period of research – an era that would see the beginning of the accurate documentation of Palenque and the other lost cities and monuments that had so long lain hidden from the outside world.

CHAPTER THREE

Visitors Spread the Word

Not only men like leaves may fall,
But the whole nation sink, and all
Be lost – extinct this race of man;
Like Palenque, or like Copan[1]

Early in 1839, three friends occasionally gathered at Bartlett and Welford's fashionable antiquarian bookstore at Number 7 Astor House, New York City. John L. Stephens had recently published two popular travel works; his *Travels in Arabia Petrea and the Holy Land* was currently enjoying unprecedented sales. His companion in these meetings was the 40-year-old English architect Frederick Catherwood. The two had met in London a few years before, when Stephens, en route to New York from his sojourn in the Holy Land, attended Catherwood's lecture on the "Panorama of Jerusalem," a spectacular painting based on his drawings. Friendship between the two had grown, particularly after Catherwood moved his architectural practice to New York, where he opened another panorama.[2]

The third person involved in these get-togethers was John Russell Bartlett, bibliophile, bibliographer, author – and senior partner in the bookstore. At that time, Bartlett probably knew the world of books and publishing as well as anyone in the United States, and he had naturally followed Stephens's recent publishing success with high interest.[3]

"One day in my office," wrote Bartlett in his journal, "I said to [Stephens], 'why do you not undertake the exploration of Yucatán and Central America?' I invited him to come to my house where I showed him Waldeck's work on Yucatán…which I had just imported from Paris…Mr.

Stephens said he had never heard of these remains [Uxmal] but he would be glad to know more about them."[4]

By the middle of the year, Stephens had read not only Waldeck's work, but also the 1822 illustrated report on Palenque, and Galindo's description of Copán as well. He and Catherwood gazed in growing astonishment at the 1834 folio of Castañeda drawings. By mid-summer, their minds were fixed on the three places whose names kept cropping up in the accounts – Uxmal, Copán, and Palenque. Stephens and Catherwood soon had a plan: they would travel together to Central America and see these wondrous things for themselves. Then chance stepped in.

President Martin Van Buren had only recently appointed one William Leggett as minister to Central America, but Leggett died before being able to embark on the assignment. Stephens, whose politics, as Bartlett put it, "were the same as Mr. Van Buren's," applied for the position, and got it. Stephens's mission was to see if a government had emerged from the civil war in the area and, if it had, to make contact with it on behalf of the United States.[5]

On 9 September 1839, Stephens and Catherwood signed a contract of agreement regarding their search for the ruins and publication of a book about their endeavors. In return for expenses plus $1,500, Catherwood agreed to accompany Stephens and make all necessary drawings of "Palenque, Uxmal, Copán, and such other ruined cities, places, scenes, and monuments as may be considered desirable by the said Stephens." Stephens retained control of all rights pertaining to the publication of and products resulting from the expedition.[6]

On 9 October the two men sailed from New York on the brig *Mary Ann*, docking in Belize City, British Honduras, three weeks later. A few days later, after the round of official hospitality to celebrate Stephens's diplomatic mission, the pair set out on the first major expedition since that of Dupaix to seek the mysterious ruined cities.

Hardly had Stephens and Catherwood left Belize City than a second expedition departed – one hastily put together by Patrick Walker, assistant to the superintendent of British Honduras, and Lieutenant John Caddy of the Royal Artillery. Caddy had met Stephens and Catherwood on their arrival and learned of their plan to visit Palenque, not directly, but by way of

Copán, which lay in the opposite direction. As soon as the American team left town, Walker and Caddy, apparently irked that the two might reach Palenque ahead of Britons, made plans to get there first. By going due west along the Belize River and across Guatemala's Petén, they arrived a full two months ahead of Stephens and Catherwood. Unfortunately, the two Englishmen appear to have had little real interest in anything but winning the race – in Walker's request for official approval of the trek, he misspelled their destination as "Polenki"! Partly as a result of this, but mostly because Stephens's and Catherwood's effort soon eclipsed their own, the report of the Walker-Caddy expedition, including a few evocative drawings of architecture, remained unpublished for more than a century and a quarter.[7]

An Epochal Visit

In May 1840, six months after leaving Belize City, Stephens and Catherwood arrived at Palenque and took up residence in the sheltered east corridor of the Palace, where they found the graffiti left by the British team who had already come and gone, along with others.[8] Fortunately for the Palenque drawings, months earlier Catherwood had passed through a "baptism of fire" at Copán, where by sheer determination and the aid of a *camera lucida*, he had begun to master the intricacies and lines of Maya sculpture.[9]

In the course of several weeks at Palenque, and despite illness and misery "beyond all endurance" wrought by swarms of insects and torrential rains, Catherwood produced the best renderings of the site and its individual buildings and sculptures yet achieved (figs 18, 19, 20, and 21). Even so, it is clear from the published lithographs and engravings – the original drawings are lost – that some of his Palenque work is not quite up to Catherwood's usual high standards. This is not surprising, given the artist's dreadful state of health and the miserable working and sleeping conditions at the ruins.[10]

For the Temple of the Inscriptions (Stephens calls it "Casa No. 1") Catherwood presents a straightforward view of the tree-covered structure, followed by careful and excellent renderings of the stucco reliefs on the four piers. And, as a monumental testimony to his doggedness in the face of adversity, the architect drew in astonishing detail each and every visible

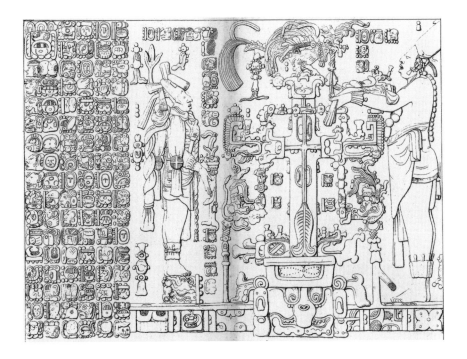

18 ABOVE *Catherwood's drawing of the Tablet of the Temple of the Cross ("Casa No. 2"), showing only the left and central panels present in the wall.*

19 BELOW *Catherwood's rendering of Palace House A from the East Court.*

20 RIGHT *Catherwood's rendering of the Temple of the Sun plan and elevation showing the sanctuary depicted in fig. 21, below.*

21 BELOW *The inner sanctuary of the Temple of the Sun, as drawn by Catherwood. The artist, believing the jambs removed to town to be from the Temple of the Cross, erroneously "restored" them here (see fig. 26).*

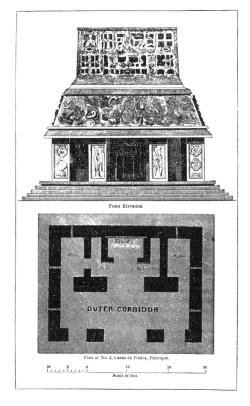

Front Elevation.

Plan of No. 3, Casas de Piedra, Palenque.

glyph block of the 640 that covered the three huge hieroglyphic panels inside the building.[11]

Thirty-one of Catherwood's Palenque drawings were converted to engravings (with final approval by the artist) for Stephens's two Central America volumes. These included plans, elevations, and general views of the Palace and other major buildings, as well as detailed views of scenes on eight stucco piers, and seven bas-relief tablets, including four sanctuary jambs (figs 20, 21). Among the latter were two that Stephens discovered decorating a private home in the village! Later it was found that both belonged to the Temple of the Cross, not the Temple of the Sun as Catherwood thought and erroneously reconstructed on paper.

More than any other ruin of the many he had seen, Palenque led Stephens to conclusions as astute as they were grand, even rhapsodic. Near the end of his Palenque stay, he sat on the ruined steps of the Temple of the Cross and wrote:

> In the midst of desolation and ruin we looked back at the past, cleared away the gloomy forest, fancied every building perfect, with its terraces and pyramids, its sculptured and painted ornaments, grand, lofty, and imposing, and overlooking an immense inhabited plain; we called back into life the strange people who gazed at us in sadness from the walls; pictured them, in fanciful costumes and adorned with plumes and feathers, ascending the terraces of the Palace and the steps leading to the temples.... In the romance of the world's history nothing ever impressed me more forcibly than the spectacle of this once great and lovely city, overturned, desolate, and lost; discovered by accident, overgrown with trees for miles around, and without even a name to distinguish it.[12]

A Publishing Triumph

On 31 July 1840, Stephens and Catherwood docked in New York, successful travelers returned safely from a dangerous and unknown land. One poignant event briefly interrupted these giddy days of celebration. Rafinesque, the man dubbed "the eccentric naturalist" by John James Audubon, and the publisher of precocious conclusions on the hieroglyphs of "Otolum" less than a decade earlier, wrote to Stephens, reminding him of the priority of those discoveries and urging him to acknowledge them. Stephens apparently did so, but his letter never arrived, for Rafinesque had died. "Even as the mailman was seeking to deliver Stephens' letter," reports Stephens's biographer Victor von Hagen, "Rafinesque's friends were lowering his cadaver out the window to save it from sale to the local medical school...to pay for his arrears of rent."[13]

Stephens's two-volume *Incidents of Travel in Central America, Chiapas, and Yucatan* came off the presses of Harper and Brothers in New York on 25 June 1841. It held nearly 900 pages of lively adventure, astute observation, and sober reasoning. The combination, with Catherwood's illustrations, took the American public by storm. In just three months Harper and Brothers went back to press 11 times, printing 20,000 copies (at five dollars a set) to meet the need. "Bartlett & Welford, booksellers," noted the New York diarist Philip Hone, "told me that [Stephens] had already cleared $15,000.00 by his latest work."[14]

Reviews of the work and its 77 engravings – nearly 40 per cent depict Palenque – were both numerous and favorable. "Mr. Catherwood's drawings are so distinct, so perfect," one wrote, "that...reflecting in the proportion of their parts such exact likenesses of the original that even Mr. Stephens thinks it useless to add to them any explanations." And Edgar Allan Poe, after a few grumpy comments about Stephens's "unprofound" reflections – Poe apparently had not been given a copy, but had perused the work – acknowledged that "the work is certainly a magnificent one – perhaps the most interesting book of travel ever published." Word was out.[15]

On 23 February 1841, the *Republican Compiler*, a newspaper in Gettysburg, Pennsylvania, breathlessly reported the existence of "the vast and wondrous ruins of an ancient world-forgotten city, near the present village of Palenque." Quoting a Belize City newspaper, the reporter continues, "what can more astonish the human mind than to hear that the deserted ruins of a city have been discovered, equal in size to three modern Londons [but see below]; and that, too, built of materials, the immensity and durability of which appear almost fabulous to modern architects?"

Another commentary, printed only a week after *Incidents of Travel* was published, foretold future visits to the ruined city: "Hereafter it may become fashionable to visit Copan, and 'as easy as lying' to run down to Palenque. Pic-nic parties may be viewed 'seated in the pleasant shade' of those trees which have overgrown the ruins of the former, and nice young men be observed squinting through eye-glasses at the hieroglyphics on the crumbling walls of the latter." [16]

A few months later, the *New York Tribune* reported on a lecture Stephens gave at New York City's Stuyvesant Hall as "well worth the dollar it cost us." Stephens took the occasion to correct "the absurd story that they found the ruins of Palenque three times the size of London…. All that has been explored does not cover an area larger than our Park or Battery." "The Hall," continued the piece, "was crowded with an intelligent and deeply interested auditory."

Powerful Tales and a Vulnerable Public

In 1841, the same year that Stephens's Central American travels took the public by storm, another book appeared in London. Charles Mackay, Scottish poet and journalist, wrote of the collective public compulsion to accept as truth the more powerful fantasies and myths of the time:

> In reading of the history of nations, we find that, like individuals, they have their whims and their peculiarities; their seasons of excitement and reck-lessness, when they care not what they do. We find that whole communities suddenly fix their minds upon one object, and go mad in its pursuit; that millions of people become simultaneously impressed with one delusion, and run after it, till their attention is caught by some new folly more capti-vating than the first. [17]

The famed showman Phineas T. Barnum knew well what Mackay was talking about, and would not be outdone in seizing the opportunity for publicity and profit. In the success of Stephens's Maya travels Barnum saw wonderful possibilities, and from his fertile mind emerged a scheme. He hired two diminutive – each was just over 1 m (3 ft) tall – Salvadorians, Maximo and Bartola, to pose as "Aztec children" (fig. 22). Then he drew upon the Stephens narrative (which in most cases he credited to John L. "Stevens" and a mysterious "Pedro Velazquez") and constructed a sensational account of a lost and living jungle city called "Iximaya," and the "Active, Sprightly, and Intelligent Little Beings" that had been taken from there. Barnum illustrated this narrative of Iximaya with images lifted directly from Catherwood's published Palenque work (fig. 22). Following their premiere appearance at Barnum's New York Museum, the Aztec Lilliputians journeyed abroad. In London, they were granted an audience with Prince Albert – a living testimony to the immense impact Stephens and Catherwood, and the intrigue of lost cities, had on popular culture in the decades following their epochal journey.[18]

Barnum's contribution to the Palenque story was neither the first nor the last to capitalize on public attraction to a good story, however false, convincingly told. We have seen how, in the absence of evidence to the contrary, early writers on ancient Palenque, from Cabrera to Waldeck and beyond, saw the origins of the city in the Egyptians, Romans, Greeks, the Lost Tribes

22 *P. T. Barnum's exhibition of the "Aztec Lilliputians of Iximaya." Title page of the pamphlet announcing the New York show, left; the "children" Maximo and Bartola as depicted in the French edition of the pamphlet, below.*

of Israel, or other civilized poeples of the Old World.[19] It was simply inconceivable that the Native Americans themselves, customarily relegated to the stereotypical category of "primitive (albeit noble) savages," could have built Palenque, or for that matter the ancient mounds and complicated earthworks of Eastern North America.[20] According to one pamphlet, which went through at least 17 printings between 1841 and 1847, Palenque, the "Thebes of America," was "sixty miles in circumference… [with] a population of three million."[21]

This attitude began to fade slowly in the wake of the publications of John L. Stephens and other serious observers during the mid-19th century, such as Stephens's colleague, historian William Hickling Prescott, whose sober and considered treatment of the Spanish conquest of the Aztec empire, published in 1843, found a huge readership.[22]

Despite the encouraging beginnings in Stephens's relatively dispassionate observation, Palenque continued to be a primary magnet for declarations ranging from sincere but hapless science to what seems, in retrospect, to be downright fraud and publicity seeking. For example, in 1879 the Placerville, California, newspaper carried a "thrilling recital" from the pen of "Dr. Loeder Von Herbet" describing Palenque sculptures as depicting "the trip [from Egypt] across the ocean in immense canoes…with slaves represented in the act of rowing." This is not all. Dr. Von Herbet also writes of his amazing visit the year before to Palenque, where nearby he found many mummies, some of which, according to a medical colleague in Berlin, had apparently been "*embalmed alive*"![23]

Even today, unsubstantiated beliefs and speculations about ancient America in general and, it seems, Palenque in particular, continue to bring us an almost uninterrupted parade of ancient astronauts, wandering tribes, and refugees from sunken Atlantis. In 1969 Erich von Däniken's *Chariots of the Gods?* proposed, among many other things, that the scene carved on the sarcophagus lid in the Temple of the Inscriptions at Palenque depicted an ancient alien at the controls of a flaming rocket lifting off another planet. Another opinion, based on the very same scene turned sideways, confidently declares that it shows an early (uneasy?) rider on a motorcycle. Still another individual counters this, claiming instead that the complex sculpture is none of the above, but rather a map of Lake Titicaca, on the Peru-Bolivia border far to the south.[24] With these examples as cautionary tales not to be mentioned again in these pages, it is now appropriate to return to our main story of the human visitors to Palenque in the middle and late 19th century.

French Explorations and the New Technology

Not long after the two expeditions to the Maya area by Stephens and Catherwood, the French initiated explorations in Central America – and at Palenque.[25] Naturalist Arthur Morelet visited the ruins for a fortnight in 1847, lodging as his predecessors had done in the eastern hall of what he correctly called "the vast parallelogram" of the Palace. While the romantic ambience of Palenque briefly captivated him, Morelet found the remains quite unremarkable, with their "appeal to the imagination instead of to the remembrance." And even as he deplored the obvious destruction wrought by those who had preceded him to Palenque, he found that the ruins "deeply impress us with the nothingness of humanity, and the vanity of man's attempts to perpetuate his own glory." Despite this glum and bleak view, Morelet at least issued a qualification: "But I think it will be well to await the coming of a second Champollion to furnish us with a key to the American hieroglyphics." On leaving Palenque, however, the naturalist extolled the site as a place of leisure enjoyment for the "fashionables of Santo Domingo" during the "fine season."[26]

Meanwhile, a new process for recording visual reality in a portable medium had come into being. On 19 August 1839, even as Stephens and Catherwood were preparing for their epic journey to Maya country, a French artist, Louis-Jacques-Mandé Daguerre, published details of the process he and his collaborator Joseph Nicéphore Niépce had created the "Daguerreotype," an image captured on thin copper plates coated with silver and "developed" with iodine gas.[27] Within a decade, this ancestor of the modern photograph had forever changed the way people made lasting and accurate images of the visible world, be they family portraits, landscapes – or ancient ruins. By 1860, with the development of easier

23 *Charnay's 1861 photograph of the central slab of the Tablet of the Cross, abandoned on a trail near the temple.*

negative-positive techniques and the process involving glass plates coated with a light-sensitive emulsion, photography moved into the field.[28] Despite cumbersome equipment and the need of various chemicals, plus the intensive labor it demanded under difficult conditions, the medium quickly became a necessity for serious travelers and explorers.

The energetic French traveler Désiré Charnay was the first to take expeditionary photography to the Maya area. In 1860, he spent nine days at Palenque, and despite discouraging conditions and what he considered indifferent results, published some important photographs of the site and its sculptures. One of his most important images showed the middle slab of the tablet from the Temple of the Cross, the part containing the main scene. Charnay had discovered it where Catherwood had seen it earlier, near the road leading to town, ignominiously covered by mud and debris. He cleaned it again, had it lifted into better light, sideways but stable, and made the first known photograph of the important stone (fig. 23).[29]

In 1866, the 100th year of his life, Waldeck made the last of his sporadic appearances in the saga of Palenque just as the French cleric-scholar E. C. Brasseur de Bourbourg published a large and grandiose summary of Palenque's discovery and history. To illustrate the lavish work, Brasseur used 57 images of Palenque supplied by Waldeck, many based on renderings made at the ruins more than three decades earlier. These views, while often lovely and evocative, show romantic views of Palenque architecture along with images of Maya life in the 1830s, but add little in the way of useful information about the ruins.[30]

From 1875 to 1877, a decade after the Brasseur-Waldeck collaboration, the Mexican historian Manuel Larrainzar published his remarkable *Estudios sobre la historia de America, sus ruinas y antiqüedades*. A third of this labored and laborious work – its five volumes contain nearly 3,000 pages – deals with Palenque, as does every one of its 37 plates, taken directly from Stephens's 1841 work. This emphasis may have derived from Felipe Larrainzar, Manuel's brother, who visited Palenque in 1856 and was impressed by the Temple of the Inscriptions – which he called the "House of the Judges," believing the "characters, in small repeating blocks" on the three tablets to be "phonetic writing" containing nothing less than the laws of ancient Palenque. This interpretation of the building soon entered local Palencano folklore as the "house of laws."[31]

The photographing of Palenque slowly increased in the wake of the issuing of Charnay's 1863 folio of views at various Maya sites.[32] In the summer of 1877, the Austrian expatriate Teobert Maler appeared at the ruins for the first time and made a series of excellent images of the Cross Group, including a spectacularly clear view of the bas-relief tablet in the Temple of the Foliated Cross and various parts of the Palace complex. It is likely that this visit to Palenque inspired Maler to devote the rest of his field career to the photographic documentation of Maya sites.[33]

Removing the Record

While the ever-increasing visitations to Palenque continued to add more and more to the accumulating record of the remains, they also saw an increase in the removal of objects from the ruins. As we have seen, such activity began in earnest with del Río in 1787, but he was following royal orders and directed the pieces removed to a place where they are still available for public inspection – not bad, indeed quite commendable, for an "archaeologist" of two centuries ago. Less forgivable in retrospect are some of the actions of later visitors such as Waldeck, who purposely destroyed part of the famed "beau relief" after he drew it, or those who actually pried relief sculptures from ancient walls where they had been safe and untouched for more than a millennium.

The story of what happened to the three great sculptured slabs of limestone that originally formed the great bas-relief tablet on the rear wall of the Temple of the Cross effectively shows what can happen to an important relic of the past. When Dupaix and Castañeda saw the tablet in 1807, it was apparently whole and still imbedded in the temple wall. In 1840, however, Stephens and Catherwood found only the left-hand slab in place; both the middle and right-hand slabs were missing. The larger middle panel was soon located beside the road – the same spot, as noted above, where Charnay saw it. Catherwood then drew it and, on paper, joined its image to that of the left-hand slab (see fig. 18, above). As for the missing right-hand slab, Stephens notes only that it must have been "unfortunately, altogether destroyed…most of the fragments have disappeared."[34]

We now know that the missing right-hand slab of the Tablet of the Temple of the Cross, in many fragments, somehow reached Charles Russell, consul of the United States stationed at Laguna (now Ciudad del Carmen, Campeche), around 1840, the very time of Stephens's visit to Palenque. Russell, in turn, shipped the fragments to Washington, where they arrived in early 1842.[35] There the pieces were accepted by the "National Institute for the Promotion of Science" and, joined together, were exhibited with other materials at the United States Patent Office. In 1858 they were transferred to the care of the Smithsonian Institution in Washington, D.C.

In 1863 Joseph Henry, Secretary of the Smithsonian, charged one of his staff, George Matile, with the making of a cast of the old carving. Fortunately, Matile had read Stephens and, remembering the engraving, immediately recognized the Smithsonian tablet as the missing right-hand piece (plate 3).[36] By 1879, this important piece of a Palenque puzzle was "solidly framed" and on exhibit, where it attracted "considerable attention on the part of the numerous visitors."[37]

That same year, Charles Rau published his valuable history and analysis of the Tablet of the Temple of the Cross. There he employed for the first time the now-routine method of designating individual glyph blocks, labeling columns with letters and rows with numbers. Soon, astronomer Edward Singleton Holden, professor of mathematics at the U. S. Naval Observatory in Washington, D.C., had his turn with the tablet. With the works of Stephens and Rau at hand, Holden compared sculptures from the Maya area with Aztec art and, more importantly, produced a systematic structural analysis of sign positions within individual Maya glyph blocks at Palenque and Copán. This allowed him to confirm Galindo's impression that the two places shared the same writing system.[38]

In 1880 Charnay, who had traveled to Madagascar, Chile, Argentina, Java, and Australia since his last visit to Mexico, returned. This time he had the financial support of the New York tobacco magnate Pierre Lorillard IV, several American institutions, and the Trocadéro Museum (a predecessor of the present Musée de l'Homme) in Paris.[39] Charnay explored in Mexico's central highlands for the better part of the year, even excavating in Teotihuacan's "ocean of ruins" and amid the remains of Tula of the Toltecs. In January 1881 Charnay returned to Palenque for just over a month, obsessed with the idea that it was Toltec in origin, perhaps the legendary Tollan itself, built not as the seat of an empire, but rather as a holy place of pilgrimage. Although the "Palenque jinx" that had hindered his earlier photographic endeavors at the site again plagued Charnay, he made many useful and detailed observations of the architectural features. In the Temple of the Inscriptions, he paid particular attention to the curious floor composed of superbly cut flagstones. It is even possible that he noticed the beginning of the interior stairway in the interior hall of the building, an area perhaps disturbed by del Río's zealous exploration almost a century before.[40]

Charnay also made molds of Palenque's main bas-reliefs, using the laborious "wet-paper" method, which involves pressing six saturated layers of special paper into every detail of the carving and at the appropriate time carefully removing them for the final drying. Toward the end of his visit, a fire of unknown origin destroyed all the molds, forcing Charnay to repeat the entire process. In 1883, the Trocadéro Museum in Paris made casts from Charnay's molds for the Smithsonian Institution in Washington, D.C., where they went on exhibit in early 1883. "The greatest number of these," stated the *Washington Post*, "came from Palenque, where were situated three temples, that of the Cross, the Sun, and the Inscriptions."[41]

In 1884, not long after this exhibition of Charnay's Palenque casts and perhaps as a result of the widespread publicity of the event, the large middle slab of the Tablet of the Temple of the Cross that had lain so long in the mud at Palenque was moved to Mexico's Museo Nacional de Antropología, where it would eventually be joined with its partners.

The Golden Season of Documentation

From 1881 to 1894 the English explorer Alfred Percival Maudslay, inspired by ancient carvings he had once seen at the ruins of Quiriguá, Guatemala, made a series of epic journeys through the Maya area with the sole purpose of documenting the ruins. Early in January 1891, Maudslay and surveyor Hugh W. Price, along with their equipment and a team of men recruited from Santo Domingo and nearby Tumbalá, arrived at Palenque.

The task of directing the clearing of the ruins of the forest, which Maudslay described "as heavy as any I have seen in Central America", fell to local expedition member Benito Lacroix, who accomplished the seemingly impossible task despite occasional torrential rainfalls and a highly unpredictable labor force. "For a few days," Maudslay recalled later, "we actually had as many as fifty men at work, and during the next week we were left without a single one."[42] At this pace, it took nearly three months merely to clear enough forest to permit the photographing and mapping of Palenque's central groups.

In mid-March 1891 the team was hard at work. With Price's help, Maudslay laboriously cleaned the encrustations, some of them six inches thick, that coated many of the stucco reliefs. Later, while Price surveyed, Maudslay lugged his cumbersome large-format camera equipment from place to place, photographing the buildings and the cleaned reliefs (plates 4 and 5). With the expert help of Gorgonio López, his brother José Domingo, and son Caralampio from Guatemala, who had mastered the process at other sites, Maudslay made wet-paper molds of the stone and stucco reliefs. On one occasion reminiscent of Charnay's disastrous episode, an unusually severe torrent of rain transformed three weeks' worth of precious molds into a sodden mass, and the tedious work had to be repeated. The mapping operation progressed more smoothly. In a month Price surveyed the entire site center and made detailed floor plans of the Palace and other structures. The result of his effort still stands as "one of the most accurate maps ever produced on Palenque."[43]

One of the more intriguing finds made during the Maudslay-Price survey of Palenque occurred in a small, almost totally ruined set of structures immediately north of the Temple of the Sun, now known as Temples XIV and XV. At the northeast end of Temple XV, Maudslay describes a set of three once-sealed "sepulchral chambers," reached from above by means of a stone staircase. In the middle room lay a sarcophagus made of thin stone slabs coated with stucco on the outside and red powder smeared on the inside. Unfortunately, by the time Maudslay saw it, this tomb had been emptied.

What Maudslay and Price accomplished at Palenque, along with the meticulous drawings made (at actual reproduction scale with hardly a blemish) by Miss Annie Hunter from the casts produced from Maudslay's paper molds, appeared between April 1896 and January 1899 as part of Maudslay's "Appendix" to the 73-volume *Biologia Centrali-Americana* (fig. 24).[44] The achievement of Maudslay and his colleagues stands as a unique milestone in the publication of American archaeology, a work perhaps even more useful today than it was a century ago.

Four years after Maudslay's departure, another important visitor, William Henry Holmes, appeared at Palenque. He was an American anthropologist, archaeologist, artist, and geologist, then curator of anthropology at the Columbian Museum of Chicago (now the Field Museum). Holmes concentrated on the architecture of the site, and in four days produced a vast amount of detailed data on the construction of the Palace and surrounding

24 *The west sanctuary jamb of the Temple of the Cross, as drawn by Miss Annie Hunter from Maudslay's casts and photographs.*

buildings, as well as a spectacular panorama of the entire central zone. Holmes' work, as he gratefully acknowledged, was made at least somewhat easier by the clearing that Lacroix had accomplished for Maudslay four years earlier – and by Maudslay's continuing generosity in sharing photographs and other material.

Holmes's study is acknowledged as one of the most valuable ever produced on the architecture of Palenque by virtue of his flawless draftsmanship in the presentation of construction features and cutaway renderings of major buildings. Holmes also cautiously ventured some thoughts on the function of Palenque's buildings. Some, he prophetically suggested, "may have been erected to do honor to some ruler or religious official whose remains occupied a vault in the body of the pyramid…" This idea was rooted in Holmes's knowledge of earlier discoveries by del Río and others of burials within buildings and pyramids at Palenque. Aside from the tantalizing mention of the chambers by the north side of Temple XIV, which Holmes had recorded and quoted (as noted above), he also had the detailed account of another visitor, Edward H. Thompson (later famed as the explorer of the Sacred Well at Chichén Itzá), who had explored other tomb chambers holding small stone "burial-cases" in the same area, apparently built into the base of the pyramid of the Temple of the Cross. On top of one such sarcophagus Thompson found a broken figurine and other offerings. Inside lay two badly preserved skeletons.[45]

Expedition of Good Intentions

At the time of Holmes's visit, Marshall H. Saville of the American Museum of Natural History in New York was planning the "expedition of expeditions" to Chiapas. It would take place during the winter of 1897 to 1898 in collaboration with engineer H. C. Humphries, with financial backing from the wealthy American bibliophile, author, and antiquarian Joseph Florimond, duc de Loubat.[46] As his objective, Saville chose the ruins of Yaxchilan and nearby sites in the Usumacinta Valley. The project had the official blessing of the Mexican government.

"The expedition," recalled Saville later, "had probably the most complete equipment for prosecuting archaeological work ever sent to tropical Mexico or Central America up to that time, including several tons of special paper purchased in Spain for making molds of sculptures." Problems, however, began almost immediately, when Leopoldo Batres, Mexico's inspector of ancient monuments, who was to accompany Saville and Humphries, was delayed for more than a month in Mexico City. When the group finally arrived in Chiapas, Batres, apparently concerned that Yaxchilan might lie within Guatemala – the site occupies a nearly closed meander loop on the river, which is the international border – refused to go there. Saville was obliged to change plans, and the entire operation and its many tons of equipment moved toward Palenque.

"Owing to constant rains," wrote Saville, "the road from Monte Cristo [the present Emiliano Zapata] on the Usumacinta River, to Santo Domingo de Palenque was almost impassable. After getting the outfit to the ruins," he continues, "Batres refused to take up his abode there, and remained in the village, making only one or two trips to the ruins during the six weeks the expedition remained in Chiapas."[47]

The rains kept coming, and lack of cooperation made labor so scarce that not even a cook could be hired. As a last straw, Humphries became ill and had to abandon the project for good. On 4 January, after barely a month at Palenque, Saville departed in disgust, only to have to spend nearly three weeks in Monte Cristo, waiting for the river boat to take him away![48] On this note of sad exasperation, the 19th-century exploration of the ruins of Palenque came to a close.[49]

An Important Visit

In February 1909, at the invitation of Batres, the distinguished Justo Sierra Méndez, Mexico's minister of public instruction and fine arts, made a short but important visit to Palenque, where a comfortable camp had been set up in House C of the Palace, where Maudslay had stayed.[50] Sierra Méndez was no stranger to the Maya area. Born in Campeche, he was the son of the statesman and poet Justo Sierra O'Reilly, who, in 1848, had produced a Spanish edition of Stephens's travels.[51]

For Palenque, Sierra Méndez's visit resulted not only in widespread publicity, but also in the final step in the reunion of the three slabs of the Tablet of the Temple of the Cross. Two were already in Mexico City: the Smithsonian Institution had returned the right hand slab the year before – a gesture suggested by American archaeologist Zelia Nuttall and facilitated by Theodore Roosevelt's Secretary of State, Elihu Root. Well aware from the press coverage of the transfer that two of the three parts of the tablet were already in Mexico's Museo Nacional de Antropología, Sierra Méndez arranged for the only remaining slab, the left-hand portion of the tablet, to be removed from the rear wall of the Temple of the Cross, which seemed the right thing to do at the time, and reunited it with its companion stones in Mexico City – a relatively happy ending to what otherwise would have been a tragic loss to the study of world art and archaeology.[52] A cast of the whole has since replaced the original in the Temple of the Cross.

The period between 1840 and 1910 witnessed a revolution in the documentation of Palenque, and, indeed, in the Maya area as a whole. And even as the number of reports from the field increased, another very different but extraordinarily important body of data was beginning to emerge from the libraries and museums of Germany, Spain, and France – the pictures and hieroglyphs on the paper of three ancient Maya accordion-fold books, or codices, that had lain for centuries in Dresden, Madrid, and Paris.[53]

As we saw above, the early publications of the Dresden Codex as an "Aztec manuscript" by Humboldt and Kingsborough had provided both Rafinesque and McCulloh with their basic evidence for connecting the hieroglyphs in the accordion-fold book to the texts carved on the Palenque tablets as published by del Río.

Working half a century later, from 1880 to 1896, Ernst Förstemann, head of Dresden's Royal Saxon Library, found the manuscript in the institution's collection, where it had rested since an earlier librarian had purchased it in a Vienna flea market in 1739. Förstemann carefully photographed this mysterious document and began a systematic page-by-page study of its content. By 1900, with the data recorded by means of ordered numbers using bars (fives) and dots (ones) in the Dresden Codex, supplemented by Maudslay's photographs and drawings of the hieroglyphic texts at Palenque and Yaxchilan, Harvard University's publications on the monuments of Copán, and Maler's photographs from the Usumacinta Valley, Förstemann had cracked the ancient Maya calendar system and the pattern of its glyphic notation.[54]

In 1897, Förstemann turned his attention to the Tablet of the Temple of the Cross. Using Rau's innovation of using letters and numbers like map coordinates to label the rows and columns of glyph blocks, he employed his own discovery of the time period glyphs to confirm, once and for all, what Rau, Cyrus Thomas, Maudslay, and others had concluded: that lengthy inscriptions such as this, and indeed most Maya texts, should be read in order from left to right and down, two columns at a time. At the same time, Lewis W. Gunckel, another largely unsung hero of Maya epigraphic studies, reached the same conclusion from the same tablet and other inscriptions.[55]

In 1905, American journalist Joseph Thompson Goodman, who had met Maudslay in 1893, proposed a correlation of the ancient Maya and modern Christian calendars that, with minor modifications, still works to the satisfaction of most researchers today.[56] As a consequence of the genius of this part-time Maya calendar enthusiast, and for the first time since Palenque's abandonment, people could read the dates carved in stone by the builders of the ancient city.

In 1909, a photographer, George Constantine Rickards, visited Palenque and soon afterward published an album with 33 excellent photographs of the ruins.[57] In his brief introduction, Rickards remarks, "even to the ordinary traveler [the ruins] have a wonderful fascination which is hard to overcome." Then he makes an urgent plea for the scientific exploration of the city. Rickards was probably unaware that, even as he wrote, and while the

25 *The overgrown Palenque Palace, c. 1905, with William David Plant and Jeanne Jenkins Plant, owners of the Finca San Leandro and parents of Karena Shields, standing in the Tower (see note 49).*

ruined buildings quietly yielded once more to the waiting forest (fig. 25), a plan for the archaeological investigation of Palenque had already begun to be formed in Mexico City.

CHAPTER FOUR

Archaeology Comes to Palenque

*I have had the good fortune to realize a dream of the archaeologist:
to work in Palenque and to make an important discovery. An eternal
link unites me with this marvelous place.*

ALBERTO RUZ LHUILLIER[1]

Despite the turbulence of the decade that witnessed World War I and the Mexican Revolution of 1910 to 1917, the idea of the scientific exploration of Palenque and other Mexican ruins began to grow. On 20 April 1909, only two months after his visit to the ruins, Sierra Méndez approved the establishment of the Escuela Internacional de Arqueología y Etnología, a center in Mexico City for students from Mexico, France, Germany, and the United States. The by-laws were signed in September 1910; Eduard Seler of Germany, the founding scholar of Mesoamerican iconographic research, was elected director for the first year.[2]

Seler's visit to Palenque with his wife Cecilia the following spring immediately inspired him to attempt the interpretation of the complex images and inscriptions at the site. With Maudslay's work at hand, Seler brought together a dazzling array of iconographic evidence, mainly from the central highlands of Mexico, to bear upon the sculptures at Palenque. His detailed analyses, while modified by later interpretations carried out in the light of more available data, stands as the first attempt to place Palenque art and iconography into the greater context of Mesoamerica.[3]

The Escuela Internacional closed in 1920, ending the first ambitious plan for unifying the international community of scholars in the quest for scientific anthropology in Mexico.[4] Its functions and activities passed to the

Universidad Nacional de México (now the Universidad Nacional Autónoma de México, or UNAM), where Herman Beyer taught. Beyer had a distinguished career which began in 1910 with archaeological and iconographic research and publication in various local scientific journals.[5] Beyer's student, 24-year-old Alfonso Caso Andrade, was just beginning a remarkable career that earned him the recognition of Ignacio Bernal – no slouch himself – as "probably the best [archaeologist] Mexico ever had."[6] With the likes of Beyer, the young Caso, and their colleagues, plus the new outlets for rapid publication, Mexican archaeology had come of age by 1920. While most of the fieldwork of the time concentrated on Teotihuacan and other well-known sites in the general area of Mexico City, attention was slowly turning eastward, toward the Maya area, where Americans had already begun to work.

Frans Blom and the Beginning

If one had to choose a date for the beginning of the modern scientific investigation of Palenque, it might well be 14 December 1922, when a 29-year-old Dane, Frans Blom, arrived at the site. Blom had followed his fondness for adventure from Copenhagen to Mexico in 1919, where he worked in the oil fields of Tabasco State. There he became fascinated by Maya ruins in the locality, among them, Tortuguero. Later, while recuperating from malaria in the capital, and witnessing Aztec sculptures coming to light almost daily from excavations in Mexico City's great central plaza, his future course was set. In Mexico City he met the influential American archaeologist Nuttall, who introduced him to Manuel Gamio, founding director of Mexico's Dirección de Antropología and the most respected archaeologist in the country.[7] Impressed by Blom's drawings and notes on Tortuguero, Gamio quickly hired the young student and, late in 1922, gave Blom his first real job in archaeology which was to examine the ruins of Palenque thoroughly, and to make recommendations for the conservation and future investigation of the site.

The early 1920s proved to be a key period in the refinement of archaeological field methods in both central Mexico and North America. Gamio had just completed his monumental study of the ruins of Teotihuacan, the ancient metropolis not far north of Mexico City. Nuttall had recently studied the layered sequence of potsherds and figurine types from the lava deposits at Coyoacán. Others, also inspired by the brilliant and innovative stratigraphic analyses of sites in the North American Southwest by Danish archaeologist Nels Nelson and similar work by the European-trained geologist Jorge Engerrand, had begun to read the layers of prehistory at Santiago Ahuitzola, Coyotlatelco, and other central Mexican sites.[8]

In the meantime, the archaeological investigation of ruins in the Maya lowlands was well underway. Beginning in the 1890s, while Maudslay was documenting Palenque, George B. Gordon and colleagues from Harvard University's Peabody Museum of Archaeology and Ethnology spent more than a decade excavating and reconstructing at Copán: in 1910 and 1911, Raymond E. Merwin, another Harvard investigator, worked out the architectural and ceramic sequence at Holmul, in Guatemala's District of Petén. And in 1913 Herbert Spinden published his pioneering *Study of Maya Art*. The following year Sylvanus G. Morley persuaded the Carnegie Institution of Washington D.C. to begin a long-term program of archaeological fieldwork throughout the Yucatán Peninsula, and in 1920 Morley published his monumental work on the dated inscriptions at Copán.[9]

It is also interesting to note that when Blom arrived at the northern base of the Palenque Palace in the late autumn of 1922 exactly 100 years had passed since del Río's illustrated report was available on London bookstalls. Having taken the old trail that ended at Palenque's main structure, Blom found himself in what he called "a fairy tale palace beyond description." His first task, however, was to clear the forest growth, and he approached it with great reluctance:

> Truly, I walked around for days and couldn't do a thing. Right and left were the old temples, settled in the world's most beautiful forest. Lianas and orchids and other tropical verdure was covering one and all of the buildings. AND – dam[n] it – it was my orders and my job to tear down all that floral beauty.... There were the temples and the palaces, and every one of their rooves [sic] were covered in a solid carpet of wild pink begonias.... With every machete slash my heart was bleeding.[10]

Despite Blom's reservations, he performed the necessary clearing, except for those trees whose roots were actually holding structures together. Then he ordered the cut logs to be saved for lumber for the eventual construction of buildings to house guardians, a museum, and a laboratory. Over the next three months, Blom expanded Maudslay's map beyond the central ruins, while carefully examining each structure he saw and improvising repairs where needed. He also made floor plans, and drew hieroglyphic texts and other features of the site that supplemented the data already in hand. The lengthy illustrated report he submitted to Gamio emphasized the great need to consolidate the roof crests of the buildings in the Cross Group – the Temple of the Sun in particular, for it had recently been struck by lightning and was in danger of complete collapse. He also advocated the cleaning and waterproofing of all extant roofs. Foreseeing a future of increased activity at Palenque, Blom assigned roman numerals to prominent but yet-unnamed buildings, and strongly recommended that they be labeled "to avoid confusion in future descriptions of the ruins." With the practical foresight born of his long field experience in Tabasco, he also emphasized the need for a road between Monte Cristo and Palenque to replace the narrow trail and reduce the expense and delay involved in transporting material to the site.[11] Blom's exhaustive 1923 report on Palenque joined another extraordinary document in Mexico's archaeological archives – Eduardo Noguera Auza's thorough compendium of the works pertaining to the discovery and exploration of the site up to 1921 (it was later updated to cover the period up to 1926), accompanied by excellent architectural drawings after Holmes and other data.[12]

Blom returned to Palenque in 1925, this time accompanied by ethnologist Oliver La Farge and a small mountain of field equipment. They had come from New Orleans to Veracruz, Tabasco, and Chiapas as the "First Tulane University Expedition to Middle America," and on 12 May they entered Palenque. To Blom's delight, Leandro the caretaker had discovered and carefully saved three fragmentary tablets bearing hieroglyphs or parts of figures, all from the Group of the Cross. Leandro's good instincts almost certainly prevented the theft of these sculptures. However, Blom and La Farge also noticed signs of recent digging in several floors. Leandro explained that only a few weeks before, a crowd from Tila led by the

26 *Sculptured panels from the Temple of the Cross in the church façade, Santo Domingo de Palenque, 1917. Close-ups, below, show the jambs still in the façade in 1942.*

Reverend Eleazar Mandujano and seven friends, including one Carmen Ayanequi, had descended the mountain trail with an entourage of 30 companions and a band of musicians. The festive group proceeded to make camp among the buildings, Leandro related, and while some diverted the custodian, others had made the excavations.

"We found waste scattered all around," recalled the anthropologists. "Even the fair Doña Carmen, the lady love of the priest, had left a strip of intimate lacework on the floor. When they left, they took with them four objects belonging to the local museum. Fortunately Leandro discovered this in time and telegraphed Salto de Agua, where the priest was arrested and held prisoner until the objects were returned."[13]

The episode of the "holy and learned padre" (Blom's term), however trivial and amusing it may seem, reminds us of an important issue: the removal of art and artifacts, whether by archaeologists, art thieves, or curio seekers, from Maya sites in general and from Palenque in particular. We have already seen the tangled history of the Tablet of the Cross as a sobering example of the near-loss of a crucial piece of Palenque's precious past. Another such case involved the sculpted reliefs from the same building. As we noted in Chapter 3, Stephens saw the reliefs in a private home in Santo Domingo, but when Blom arrived, he found them proudly flanking the front door of the church (fig. 26). Such episodes only underscore what Blom and his colleagues recognized as the highest priority at Palenque – the need for conservation.

The Founding of INAH

The actual archaeological investigation and consolidation of Palenque began in 1934 under the direction of Miguel Angel Fernández and continued sporadically through nine more seasons. Major work focused on the Palace, and excavations around the base of the Tower revealed the remarkable Tablet of the 96 Glyphs (plate 29). Its discovery, however, was marred by misfortune: workers uncovered the slab face down in the rubble and, believing it to be part of the fill, broke it into smaller pieces for removal. On a more fortunate note, when Fernández and his crew further cleared the area they encountered the carefully constructed toilets and drains that had served the Palace.[14]

Early in 1939, President Lázaro Cárdenas, who had visited Palenque in 1934 and many times afterward, signed the act that created the present Instituto Nacional de Antropología e Historia (INAH) which replaced earlier government agencies. It was made responsible for the exploration of archaeological zones, conservation and restoration of archaeological and historical monuments and artifacts, and the publication of findings.[15]

In 1940, 25-year-old Heinrich Berlin, who had come from Germany to the Mexican capital five years earlier, joined the Palenque team. He began by overseeing the consolidation of what remained of the Tower, which due to its height was unusually vulnerable to destruction by trees growing out of cracks in its masonry. Soon, Berlin was helping to supervise excavations at the *Templo Olvidado*, a well-preserved vaulted building in the forest almost a kilometer west of the Palace. There he also analyzed the stucco date glyphs, some of which Blom had reported on his visit to the structure in 1926 (plate 8). This was the beginning of Berlin's long career in epigraphy.[16]

Fernández, meanwhile, had the two sculptures taken from the town church façade and restored to their original places in the Temple of the Cross, a full century after they had been removed. He also effected the consolidation and reconstruction of the roof crests on the Temples of the Cross and Foliated Cross, as well as the platform of the Temple of the Sun and many of the buildings in the Palace.[17]

During the 1939 season yellow fever felled Fernández and slowly his health began to falter. In 1945 Berlin helped transport him from Palenque strapped on the back of a horse, very much as Catherwood had departed the site a century before. Fernández's death shortly afterward ended the first decade of intensive archaeology at Palenque.[18]

Alberto Ruz Lhuillier

Following the death of Fernández, leadership of INAH's program of excavation and reconstruction at Palenque fell to Alberto Ruz Lhuillier. Ruz brought to Palenque the specific goal of establishing a complete archaeological chronology based not only upon dates recorded in the hieroglyphic texts, but also on architectural and ceramic sequences. A related aim was to determine the date and nature of the earliest occupation of Palenque and thereby to see how the place related to other areas of Mesoamerica. Or, as Caso, referring to Mesoamerica's earliest civilization, jokingly ordered Ruz as the latter departed for his first season, "Discover us another Olmec underneath one of those Palenque temples!"[19]

The 1949 season saw intensive excavation in several areas of the site. Under Ruz's supervision, Jesús Núñez Chinchilla worked in Palace House A–D, the northern portion of the complex, where he quickly discovered that the entire central dividing wall had fallen as a unit. Careful excavation of the center part soon revealed three great slabs face down, where they had fallen forward with the collapsing wall.[20] The slabs formed the important sculpture now known simply as the "Palace Tablet," the relief that Merle Greene Robertson calls "the most beautiful of all Palenque stone tablets (plate 17)."[21]

In the meantime, artist Augustín Villagra recorded the columns and rows of flower-like elements and other motifs painted on the front façade of House E – a unique set of some 150 images whose significance has challenged scholars ever since Seler published them in 1915 (plate 18B).[22]

While all this was going on in the main portion of the ruins, construction of the road from the train station north of town to the ruins, begun after the visit of President Miguel Alemán in 1950, was nearing its end. Just inside the final loop of the last sweeping curve leading to the site center, and only 300 m (980 ft) northwest of the Temple of the Inscriptions, the road crew accidentally cut into the corner of an ancient platform and the edge of a collapsed building. Excavation of the structure, known prosaically as "Building A" in "Group IV" on the Palenque map, yielded another three-slab panel, the so-called Tablet of the Slaves, which appeared in place on the rear wall of the second level of what had been a two-story vaulted building (see figs 73 and 74).[23]

In 1951, in a program of cooperation between INAH and Columbia University, New York, Robert and Barbara Rands meticulously examined Group IV. In a relatively small area of the plaza fronting Building A, they located and recorded 13 burials, many of them superimposed upon others, and most lacking accompanying grave goods – a "cemetery" pattern that differed markedly from previous findings of individual burials at the site. Second, and most important, these excavations in Group IV initiated the Rands' brilliant professional careers, devoted almost entirely to the establishment of a ceramic chronology that, with continuing refinements, still serves as a principal measure of time and culture change at Palenque and among its neighbors, near and far.[24]

Ruz's search for chronological data about Palenque's deep past led him to the Temple of the Inscriptions: by virtue of its size – it was even larger than the Temple of the Cross – this single building and its platform seemed to offer the best opportunity for finding buried earlier structures and their associated ceramics.[25]

In 1949, Ruz began to explore the base of the gigantic stepped platform supporting the Temple of the Inscriptions, peeling away the rubble to reveal the evidence of the history of its construction. This work continued for the next three seasons and beyond and, as we noted in Chapter 1, resulted in the discovery that astonished the archaeological world.

The great platform, Ruz discovered, had been built in three distinct stages. The earliest consisted of a regular rectangular platform about 50 m wide and 40 m deep (164 x 131 ft) that the architects had situated by the base of the mountain slope immediately southwest of the Palace. It rose in eight steps to a height of 20 m (66 ft) and featured a stairway on its north side. The whole faced about 15 degrees east of magnetic north.[26]

On the summit of this great platform stood the temple itself. It rested on a thick basal molding, or plinth, that, in effect, formed a ninth step of the whole platform. The building, about 24 m (79 ft) long and 8 m (26 ft) deep, held two parallel ranges of rooms. The front room ran the full length of the building; the back was divided into three parts, a long central room with two small flanking chambers. The north, or front, façade of the temple held five doorways flanked by the six piers of about equal width that defined them. Above these rose the superior molding, and the long centerline of the roof held the remains of a hollow masonry crest (fig. 27, plate 20).

The second stage in the building of the platform was defined by additions of tall sloping steps, or zones, to create three high steps where there had been eight. The original corners, however, were left as they were, in eight steps. The third stage of construction saw the widening of the lower portion of the front stairway and the adding of balustrades.

The chronological data that Ruz sought in the pottery he found in the fill of the platform were somewhat disappointing at first, for the material recovered from caches and other areas contemporaneous with the construction appeared to be confined to the Otolum ceramic phase – the Late Classic period. In contrast, earlier pottery fragments seemed to have merely been part of the construction fill brought from other parts of the site. These

27 *The Temple of the Inscriptions in the 1940s, on the eve of its excavation by Alberto Ruz Lhuillier. This view, from the Tower in the Palace, shows the mountain slope behind the structure, against which its great nine-stepped platform was built.*

ceramic data were reinforced by hieroglyphic dates from the temple and related structures, suggesting a very short period, the last part of the 7th century AD, for the building. The conclusion was inescapable: the short period of construction indicated that the architectural evolution of the structure was characterized, not as successive modifications over a long time, but rather as mere stages in a single, relatively short construction project.[27]

While Ruz's main effort continued on the platform, a smaller crew cleared and cleaned the floor inside the Temple of the Inscriptions. Ruz had noticed, as had Stephens, Charnay, Holmes, Blom, and others before him, that it was made up of huge flat stones, not stucco like that of most Maya buildings of this type. Moreover, Ruz also observed that the walls of the back room appeared to extend below the visible floor level. Even more puzzling was an apparent disturbance, a break in the floor, possibly the work of would-be looters, and the curious flagstone edged with drilled holes filled with carefully carved plugs beside the disturbed area. Ruz cleaned the area and expanded the shallow cavity underneath it. There under the rubble and debris appeared a gigantic stone crossbeam and, at the edge of the opening, two stone steps leading downward.[28]

Late in the spring of 1949, Ruz and his team began the long process of clearing the staircase. The effort took three years slowed by both physical and scientific demands. For a start, there was never space for more than two or three workers at a time at the forward end of the descent, where the digging, the heat, and the dim lights powered by a generator shone upon a dim and dust-choked hell where the men chipped away at the wall of stubborn rubble that filled the passage from floor to ceiling. This heavy and cumbersome fill then had to be removed by bucket back up the ever-lengthening passage for inspection and final disposal. At one stage the excavators hope was raised for they thought they had reached the end of the tunnel, only to find a landing where the stairway turned upon itself and continued its descent into the heart of the pyramid. Occasionally their work was interrupted by discoveries of caches within the rubble – offerings of ceramic vessels and human bones, apparent sacrificial victims. Each such find brought a welcome break for the workers while the archaeologists moved in to measure and photograph it in place.

Finally, in June 1952, the excavators reached bottom, 22 m (72 ft) below the level of the floor where they had begun. Here lay a narrow vaulted chamber, apparently empty. But Juan Chablé, the master mason from Yucatán, noticed something unusual: a distinct triangular zone of rubble and mortar on the north wall. Carefully removing this coarse fill, the excavation crew revealed a huge stone of matching shape, set vertically and slightly recessed.[29] Lever poles were quickly procured, and the team slowly pivoted this final barrier just enough to reveal an opening beyond.

In Chapter 1 we briefly witnessed the moment that Ruz first shined his flashlight into the dark void and beheld a great vaulted room glistening like a cathedral of sparkling crystalline limestone. On three of its walls his beam revealed a series of life-size, ornately garbed figures in low-relief stucco. And, almost filling the center of the room, was the wide near edge of a massive slab of richly carved limestone resting upon a great rectangular stone base, also carved with figures and glyphs. Thus, in a glimpse that lasted no longer than about 30 seconds – for the honored visitors he had invited for the occasion were standing behind him with understandable impatience – Ruz knew he had come to the end of his quest. It was Sunday,

15 June 1952, when he and those with him – Eduardo Noguera, director of INAH's Monumentos Prehispánicos division, archaeologists Sáenz and Rafael Orellana, Chablé, and a delegation from Palenque town – first entered the room beneath the Temple of the Inscriptions to share in the momentous discovery.

Ruz presented his initial interpretation of the crypt at the 1952 International Congress of Americanists in Cambridge, England, with appropriate caution. It appeared to be an extraordinarily important ceremonial chamber, he reported, dominated by a large altar on which was depicted what appeared to be a sacrificial victim. Astonishingly, as things soon turned out, this was only the beginning. Some months after the congress, in the fall of 1952, the true purpose of the room came to light. In November Ruz decided to pursue a suggestion of Chablé to drill a small hole into the side of the huge stone to see if it might be hollow. This proved to be the case. Soon the great five-ton slab, now known to be a lid, was raised with automobile jacks set on piles of stone, exposing a small inner lid set flush into the hollow block. Raising it by means of the convenient holes the Maya had used to put it in place, Ruz and his team at long last revealed the reason for the building of the Temple of the Inscriptions, the secret stairway, and the long-hidden chamber. Inside lay the skeleton of a man masked in jade and accompanied by treasures appropriate to the royalty of Classic-period Palenque (fig. 28 and see fig. 59).[30]

The discovery posed two problems for the archaeologists. Firstly, exactly who was this person? They would have to wait a while for the answer to this question. Secondly, how was this remarkable construction built? To Ruz, it was immediately clear that the tomb must have been constructed before the pyramid and summit temple – the five-ton slab could not have been moved down the staircase (not to mention turning the landings!). In Ruz's reconstruction of events, planning probably began around the time of the death of the person in the tomb, perhaps even before. An area of the proper size and orientation was then cleared, excavated slightly below the general level of the plaza, and carefully floored with flagstones. Then the sarcophagus was dragged into its final position, with the great lid nearby, poised to slide over the open coffin of stone. Afterward the crypt walls and vaults rose with

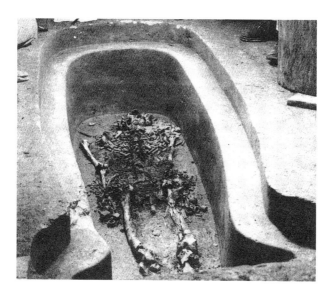

28 *The skeleton of K'inich Janab Pakal as it was discovered in the sarcophagus after removal of its secondary cover, a fish-shaped slab that lay just above the body and below the great carved sarcophagus lid.*

the great bulk of the platform – and its interior stairway. When all that was sufficiently completed, construction of the summit temple took place, with the carving and placement of the sculptures inside and outside the building completing the effort (see figs 53 and 55).

The Hieroglyphs Begin to Speak

Heinrich Berlin's deep interest and extraordinary ability in epigraphy had grown steadily during his 12-year involvement with Palenque and his close friendship with Eric Thompson, then the leading Maya epigraphist. By 1959 Berlin was able to connect the hieroglyphs on various parts of the sarcophagus and, therefore, the sarcophagus itself, to the texts on the great panel upstairs and in other buildings at the site. In doing this work, Berlin became the first to glimpse what he correctly believed were the names of people among the hieroglyphic texts of Palenque and, indeed, the whole Maya area.[31]

Berlin's contribution, in combination with the work of his colleague Tatiana Proskouriakoff, helped greatly in the latter's formulation of the hypothesis that exploded upon the serene world of Maya studies in 1960.[32] It appeared, after all, that the Maya might have recorded their own history, just as Stephens and others had surmised. The next decade passed with diverse contributions seeking to test both the fundamental nature of Maya writing and the presence of history in the texts.

In 1952, even as Ruz was preparing to enter the crypt beneath the Temple of the Inscriptions, a young Russian scholar of epigraphy, Yuri Valentinovich Knorozov, was engaged in publishing his own interpretation of the Maya hieroglyphic system. This was based largely on his reading of the Maya "alphabet" recorded in the famed 16th-century manuscript copy of the *Relación de las Cosas de Yucatán* by Diego de Landa, third bishop of Yucatán. From copies of Landa's drawings, Knorozov, who had never even been to the Maya area, concluded that the various signs used in the Maya script stood for syllables or words that followed certain rules of "spelling" and grammar. Not surprisingly, Knorozov's early efforts contained flaws, and these delayed acceptance of his decipherments. Eventually, thanks to the support of David Kelley, Michael D. Coe, and other Mayanists, the Russian scholar's basic conclusion that Maya writing was essentially phonetic proved to be correct.[33]

In the meantime, back at Palenque, mainly the Palace and the nearby Cross Group, new data were slowly emerging from the rubble as INAH continued its programs of exploration, excavation, and maintenance. During the 1953 season, the Tower reconstruction was essentially finished under the direction of Sáenz, while Ruz continued the analysis of the royal tomb in the Temple of the Inscriptions and INAH artist Hipólito Sánchez Vera drew the carvings on the sarcophagus, its lid, and the stucco figures on the walls of the crypt.[34]

The ensuing seasons saw, among other things, Sáenz's explorations in the Cross Group. At the bases of the platforms of the Temples of the Cross and Foliated Cross he uncovered the first *in situ* offerings of the remarkable effigy incensario supports. Some, more than a meter in height, reminded Sáenz of totem poles (plate 9).[35] Both buildings also yielded sub-floor caches and several burials. Among the most important discoveries of this time were more hieroglyphic texts from the Temple of the Foliated Cross.

Among the new finds revealed by Sáenz were more of the magnificent stucco glyphs fallen from the lengthy inscription that Blom had seen on the rear wall of Temple XVIII in 1923. Berlin had gathered and saved some of these fallen glyphs in 1942 (plate 8). Sáenz not only excavated the rest, but he also carefully made a diagram of *all* the fallen glyphs in their respective locations on the temple floor for use in later reconstruction and interpretation of this important inscription.

At Temple XXI, the base of the staircase yielded a magnificent bas-relief similar to those found by Fernández at the base of the Tower. And, certainly not the least among the findings, Ruz and Sáenz completed their small but crucial excavation verifying that the putative toilets that Fernández had uncovered near the base of the Tower had indeed functioned as units in an ancient Palace bathroom.[36]

With the end of the 1958 season, and the completion of the final consolidation and reconstruction of the Temple of the Inscriptions and many other buildings in the site center, Ruz finished his extraordinary term at Palenque.

The Ruins Restored

Archaeologist Jorge Acosta continued the Palenque effort in the late 1960s and devoted a massive task to the general cleaning and consolidation of the Temple of the Inscriptions, and the structures in line with it to the west. Acosta's reconstruction work culminated in the complete restoration and reconstruction of the monumental staircase running the full length of the western side of the Palace.[37]

At the same time Acosta noted a neglected mound topped by badly damaged remnants of masonry walls. It lay in a seemingly important place in the Cross Group, just north of the Temple of the Sun, and facing the main plaza of the group. On the maps it was referred to as simply as "Temple XIV." Acosta's excavations soon revealed an extraordinary sub-floor cache of eight of the now-famed cylindrical incense stands along with masses of fragments of carved stucco glyphs and ornaments, as well as the pieces of a huge stone tablet. Fitted together, these formed almost all of one of the most important of the great tabular wall panels that contribute to Palenque's fame.[38] In 1974, the new Palenque museum and *bodega*, or storeroom, just northeast of the Ball Court, were dedicated to the purpose of safeguarding objects recovered from the ruins, thus fulfilling Blom's vision from half a century earlier.

In the early 1970s Maya archaeological and anthropological research had an unusually large mass of new data at hand. In archaeology, the results of major field programs by E. Wyllys Andrews IV at Dzibilchaltun, Gordon Willey at Altar de Sacrificios, Edwin M. Shook and William R. Coe at Tikal, and other North Americans were beginning to appear in print, while INAH's mission of investigation continued in the Maya area with excavations by Román Piña Chan at Becan, Victor Segovia Pinto at Kohunlich, and their colleagues at other sites. While all this was happening, Robert E. Smith, Richard E. W. Adams, James C. Gifford, and their colleagues were building on the pioneering efforts of George C. Vaillant and George W. Brainerd by developing new ceramic chronologies for sites in both the northern and central Maya lowlands.[39]

Study of the modern Maya, meanwhile, was coming of age in the monumental study of the Tzotzil Maya of Zinacantan, Chiapas, and other highland Maya groups by Evon Z. Vogt and his Harvard University team, while Robert M. Carmak completed an exhaustive survey of all known sources on the ethnohistory, ethnology, and archaeology of the K'iche Maya.[40]

An important conference held around this time in Cambridge, England, sought to present examples of new and innovative approaches to the study of the Mesoamerican past. The papers selected from the Cambridge symposium for publication ranged in topic from ceramic chronology (on which there were three papers) to analogy based on then-recent ethnographic study (two papers). Among the rest, six dealt with patterns of ancient settlement, one with population, two with trade, and three with the Mesoamerican calendar. Three papers dealt with iconography and, although none dealt specifically with the non-calendrical portions of Maya inscriptions, archaeologist Gordon Willey was encouraged by "the occasional signs of the integration of 'old-style' data, iconography, hieroglyphics, stelae calendrics, and other Mesoamerican 'antiquities', into new problem formations and insights."[41]

On that front, Proskouriakoff's landmark hypothesis of Maya history in the inscriptions was being tested and confirmed: the refinements of Knorozov's phonetic readings by David Kelley, Michael D. Coe, and others were appearing almost too fast for peer-reviewed publication. At the same time, some 30 years after Pal Keleman's revolutionary publication of *Medieval American Art* had begun to reverse the widespread view of all Native American works as "primitive," the efforts of George Kubler and his students were providing full recognition of ancient American art and new ways of analyzing it.[42]

In 1971, an exhibition of Maya polychrome vases and other painted scenes and texts (including the then recently discovered fourth Maya codex) showed for the first time in a single place the dazzling knowledge, talent, and sheer virtuosity of the Maya scribe.[43] Simultaneously, an extraordinarily important project was taking shape in the historic halls of the Peabody Museum of Archaeology and Ethnology at Harvard University. Ian Graham's concept was as obvious as it was brilliant – to record the entire corpus of Maya hieroglyphic inscriptions on stone wherever they might be, by means of photographs and same-scale drawings – and here was the genius of the idea: it was done to a specific set of uniform drafting standards that guaranteed the researcher an impeccable source for epigraphic or iconographic analysis. One wonders why it took so long for Mayanists to recognize this need!

As a consequence of all this, plus the continuing progress in glyphic decipherment and iconography, scholarly attention began to turn toward those Maya sites unusually rich in well-preserved sculpture and hieroglyphic texts, such as Copán, Tikal, and Palenque. Among them, Palenque seemed for some to stand out as a place long overdue for the focus of interdisciplinary scholarship.

The Mesas Redondas

Early in the 1970s a small group of Mayanists and Palenque enthusiasts from the United States, including Merle Greene Robertson (who lived part-time in Palenque town), Gillett Griffin, Peter David Joralemon, and Linda Schele, conceived the idea of holding a periodic meeting of invited scholars at Palenque.[44] Such meetings, they believed, would provide an effective means of addressing the art, iconography, and hieroglyphic inscriptions at the site. And any questions that might arise about details of the sculptures or inscriptions could be answered immediately by visiting the ruins!

In mid-December 1973, the Primera Mesa Redonda de Palenque took place when 28 scholars who had responded to the invitations – 23 from the United States and five from Mexico – plus eight students gathered at the Morales family's La Cañada motel and restaurant complex on the north edge of town. For an entire week, all focused on Palenque, its art, and its hieroglyphic texts, moving from La Cañada to the ruins and back again and again, gathering in between in a small *champa* at La Cañada to hear prepared papers or simply to exchange new ideas, of which there was no short supply.

Among the presentations 11 dealt with iconography, including Joralemon's seminal work on blood imagery in Maya art; three specifically with hieroglyphic texts. The rest treated topics ranging from Griffin's history of the exploration of Palenque to Moises Morales's perceptive summary of Palenque's natural setting. The crowning achievement of this Primera Mesa Redonda took place one afternoon when Floyd Lounsbury, Peter Mathews, and Linda Schele retired to Bob and Merle Greene Robertson's library for several hours. When they emerged, they had constructed a provisional list of Palenque rulers, with dates – the first glimpse of the ruling dynasty that governed the city through its history.[45]

Subsequent Mesas Redondas, held every two or three years, increased in both numbers and scope to embrace the international community. The 20th anniversary of these meetings coincided with the Eighth Mesa Redonda, celebrated in 1993 by 425 participants from 13 countries.[46] With the issuing of the results of that landmark gathering, the Palenque Mesas Redondas achieved a total production of 246 published scholarly papers – more than 2,500 pages in total – of new data and interpretations devoted mostly to Palenque and its world. Since 1993, the Palenque Mesas Redondas, now under the auspices of INAH, has continued the interpretation and, most importantly, the publication of studies of ancient Palenque, and taken both into the 21st century.

If we consider the accurate documentation of Palenque sculpture to have begun with Catherwood in 1840 and matured to near perfection with Maudslay's publication of his photographs and Hunter's drawings a half-century later, we must also recognize the contribution of the indefatigable

Merle Greene Robertson. Throughout the 20-year span of the first cycle of Mesas Redondas, she added another immensely valuable body of data to her inventory of accomplishments by documenting with meticulous detail and color photography and drawings all existing sculptures of the piers, panels, and other works at Palenque.[47] Her achievement stands as one of the most thorough in the long history of research at Palenque and, indeed, in the study of ancient America.

The Discoveries Continue

Excavation, consolidation, and reconstruction, meanwhile, continued with more and more discoveries. In 1993, INAH archaeologist Arnoldo González Cruz uncovered in Group XVI a complex of buildings and platforms just east of the Palace, important new carvings, among them two fragmentary but significant tablets.[48] In his exploration of Temple XIII, next door to the Temple of the Inscriptions, González discovered a vaulted crypt and sarcophagus inside a buried structure (plate 36). In it lay the "Red Queen," the remains of a 40-year-old woman of the 7th century AD, accompanied by a jadeite mosaic mask, and other objects of the precious green stone, including bracelets and a diadem.[49] Powdered cinnabar, red mercury oxide, covered the remains: a common practice in elite burials at Palenque.

While González was making his discoveries, Martha Cuevas García's excavations in the Group of the Cross were continuing to reveal more and more of the unique type of "stacked-portrait" incense burners noted earlier by Sáenz and others in the same area. In 1998, INAH archaeologist Alfonso Morales, himself a native Palencano, began excavating the interior of Temple XIX. There he revealed, among other important finds, the magnificent limestone relief, part of an interior platform, shown in fig. 76 and plate 33, and fragments of a huge and extraordinary stucco panel found nearby in thousands of fragments which Morales and INAH conservators meticulously pieced together (fig. 29). In the summer of 2000, Temple XXI yielded another important discovery when González uncovered an exquisitely carved and once-painted panel which had apparently been made to adorn a throne (see fig. 77).[50]

29 *Conservator Marcia Valle at work on the Temple XIX stucco panel during the final stages of its restoration from thousands of fragments.*

Appropriately, the beginning of the new millennium also witnessed the completion of the accurate mapping of Palenque under the direction of Ed Barnhart and his survey team between 1998 and 2000 (see figs 4, 5, and 7 above). In their map of nearly 1,500 separate structures, one may glimpse the future of Palenque archaeology, for it shows us that less than two per cent of Palenque has actually been explored. And if that were not sufficient to excite future students of Maya archaeology, epigraphy, iconography, and the ceramic arts, it must be noted that one of the structures that lay hidden in the forest until Barnhart mapped it is larger than the Palace![51]

With this background of discovery, exploration, and investigation in mind, we can now move on to another kind of history – that of Palenque itself, which has been teased from the evidence of anthropology, archaeology, architecture, ceramics, art, and hieroglyphic texts to reveal the story of this incredible city as we know it at the moment – and in terms of the ways and beliefs of those who were there.

CHAPTER FIVE

The Early Lords

Our story of Palenque now moves from exploration to ancient history. Our understanding relies on the best scholarly interpretations of what many years of archaeology have revealed, knowing full well that so much more awaits future excavators, scholars, and scientists. We also draw upon the rich history left to us in the ancient inscriptions – texts that provide a compelling account of what Palenque's kings and scribes had to say about their own world. Today, in the immediate wake of the nearly complete decipherment of Maya hieroglyphs, much of our information about Maya history, beliefs, and experience comes directly from the Maya themselves, through the writings they left behind in books, on monuments, on tablets, and in many other media.

There is a limit to what we can learn from these records, though, since their authors were concerned primarily with the deeds of kings, queens, and members of the royal courts. So their insight into the society is a narrow one; it would be like an archaeologist of the future trying to reconstruct 21st-century American culture looking only at the stone monuments of Washington D.C. and the society pages of *Town and Country* magazine. It is revealing, informative stuff, but it does not tell the whole story. This restricted view of society is commonplace in the study of ancient civilizations, but, even in light of such limitations, the evidence offered by the hieroglyphic record gives us access to a kind of rich knowledge of Palenque that early visitors to the site such as Stephens and Catherwood could only dream of.

The story of Palenque's beginnings is a difficult one to tell, for several reasons. As is often the case with sites with large, monumental architecture, most of the early archaeological evidence lies buried deep beneath massive platforms and construction fill. Another simple reason is that, despite the long history of exploration and excavation as discussed in the previous chapters, archaeologists focused their attention on only a small portion of greater Palenque. Outlying areas of the city no doubt with early buildings and settlement wait to be excavated, as do the areas beneath the great buildings that are so famous from Palenque's Late Classic heyday.

Not surprisingly, then, many questions still surround the earliest history and development of the ancient community of Palenque. When was it first settled? What circumstances led to the establishment of a community that would emerge as a great city and seat for royal authority in the 7th century AD? In this chapter we trace some of the murky evidence of Palenque's early days, broadly defined here as the few centuries before the mature city and royal court emerged during the long and pivotal reign of K'inich Janab Pakal (AD 615–683). In terms of ceramic chronology, this corresponds to the developmental phases known as Picota (Late Preclassic) and Motiepa (Early Classic).

The origins of Maya civilization have long stood as one of the big questions facing Mesoamerican archaeology, and work in the last two decades or so has transformed our view of the developments before the Classic period. If we glance far enough back into the beginnings of "complex society" in the Maya lowlands, we find that village life was well entrenched in the region during the Early Preclassic era, before about 600 BC. In the three or four centuries that followed, the Maya lowlands changed rapidly and drastically, with large and modest urban centers quickly emerging in the central Petén region – especially the El Mirador basin – by 300 BC.

The archaeology of the western Maya area presents a very different picture. The immense Late Preclassic monumental architecture famous at sites in the central Petén, and probably also found in Yucatán, does not appear in Chiapas, or in the lower Usumacinta drainage area where Palenque is situated. In this region, instead, one finds a few populous Preclassic settlements that lack any large monumental architecture, and seem to have had little role to play in the important ideological and political trends of the central region. The best example is a site called La Esperanza, located on the western bank of the Usumacinta River, near the modern town of Emiliano Zapata (see fig. 3). Although the site has only been investigated briefly, it seems to have been the largest and one of the oldest Preclassic settlements of the region. The existence of such startlingly different kinds of communities in the Maya lowlands in around 300 BC show that many of the conspicuous hallmarks of Maya civilization – such as temple pyramids, monumental art, codified iconography, and hieroglyphic writing – spread from the central area toward the west, exerting its influence at Palenque by the beginning of the Classic period, around the time the dynasty was established.

Palenque's own Preclassic community is barely visible in the archaeological record of the ruins, with only occasional finds of ceramics datable to this period. This is due partly to the nature of most excavations thus far conducted at the site, which have concentrated on the later architectural monuments. The local pottery of Preclassic date, which defines the so-called Picota phase, appears mainly in house mounds from the western part of the archaeological zone, near the Picota River that lends the ceramic phase its name. Much of this pottery, recognizable usually by its reddish-brown paste and thick-walled forms, looks extremely different from the sorts of ceramics produced even by Palenque's neighbors, leaving the strong impression that Palenque, then probably only a small community, was isolated and self-reliant during the Preclassic period. Interestingly, this very localized ceramic tradition would evolve and remain distinctive throughout the Classic period, suggesting that old habits died hard. The special material culture and artistic achievement we associate with Late Classic Palenque – so different from all its neighbors even in AD 700 – probably finds its social and economic origins in this isolated sense of community.

As we progress through the varied accounts of Palenque's fortunes and of the episodes that defined its development as a city, it is important to keep in mind that the archaeology and history are in remarkable agreement. The basic chronological outline developed over the years by the archaeologist Robert Rands on the basis of ceramic change generally accords with the major shifts in history and dynastic succession (see pages 244–48). This point is key because it helps demonstrate that the events the ancient Maya deemed worthy of record in their inscriptions may have had consequences truly reflected in the broader material culture of the Palenque. We will highlight these correspondences as they arise in Palenque's story.

The Predynastic Rulers

The written record shows us that Palenque had a history reaching far back before K'inich Janab Pakal and the other great kings of the Late Classic period. Unfortunately, we can only read about the names of various enigmatic rulers from the Early Classic period and before – virtually nothing is known of Palenque as a city or as a community before the 7th century, or of the social and political forces that led to its initial settlement in Preclassic times.

In fact, when confronted with Palenque's records of early kingship, it is difficult to say where myth ends and history begins. Our primary source for the first rulers of Palenque is the text of the Tablet of the Cross, the same remarkable monument dedicated by K'inich Kan Bahlam to commemorate the story of world creation and its direct associations with the history of Palenque (see fig. 63). The narrative of the inscription provides a bridge between the primordial events surrounding the Triad gods and their arrivals at the mythical place called Matwiil, and the first local rulers of the Classic period. There is no clear division between one era and the other, and we are surely to understand from this that continuity was the predominant idea. Much of the Tablet of the Cross inscription is devoted to a recounting of the births and accessions of the first seven rulers of the dynasty, and this has given us an outline of the key figures in Palenque's Early Classic period. Another important source, as we will see, is the Temple of the Inscriptions, where texts recount the history of Palenque up to the life and times of the great ruler K'inich Janab Pakal.

In the complex narrative of the Tablet of the Cross, where myth and history are so explicitly connected, we read of a "Holy Lord of Baakal" named something like "Snake Spine," born on 11 March 993 BC (fig. 30A). He assumed the throne on 28 March 967 BC, and the terse information provided depicts him as a king like any other in Palenque's history. Living nearly one millennium before any of the Classic lords, however, "Snake Spine" occupies a difficult liminal period in Maya historical consciousness. We have to ask: was he "real," or was he a mythical figure crafted to connect deep time and history? Schele offered the intriguing suggestion that an actual Snake Spine may have been an important "Olmec" ruler – a culture hero remembered and venerated by Palenque's kings.[1] There is no way to verify her idea, but it is a tempting interpretation. The 10th century BC was a time of enormous change throughout southern Mesoamerica, when complex chiefdoms arose at centers such as San Lorenzo, Veracruz, and smaller vibrant communities were growing throughout the lowlands and highlands. Perhaps Snake Spine ruled over one such place in the vicinity of what would later become the great Classic center we call Palenque. Whether we can ever call him "Olmec" – a cultural label that archaeologists still debate – is another matter, but there is no obvious reason to question Snake Spine's historical authenticity, no matter where or when he lived and ruled.

Another remote historical figure we call the "Ch'a" Ruler – a provisional designation based on the still incomplete reading of his personal name glyph (fig. 30B). He is named once on a tablet recently excavated from Temple XXI, where he is said to have assumed the role of Holy Lord of Palenque in 252 BC. We have no other information about him, but we will soon see that the name reappears a few centuries later in reference to yet another Palenque king. (The re-use of royal names was commonplace at Palenque.)

The kings of Late Classic Palenque clearly drew much inspiration and political prestige from early lords such the "Ch'a" Ruler and Snake Spine. In fact, by Late Classic times both of these proto-kings had in effect become nearly fused into a single archetypal ancestor. K'inich Kan Bahlam, the Late Classic ruler who dedicated the Temple of the Cross and its tablet, is shown

30 A, B *Name glyphs of two early pre-dynastic rulers, "Snake Spine," left, and the "Ch'a" Ruler, right.*

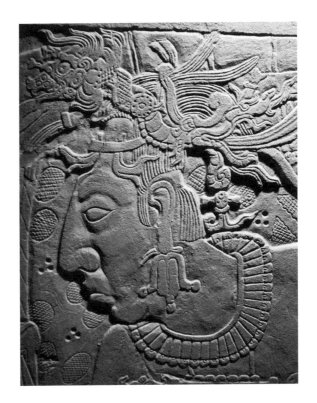

31 *Palenque rulers often embodied distant ancestral rulers. Here K'inich Janab Pakal wears in his headdress the name glyph elements of both "Snake Spine" and the "Ch'a" Ruler, fusing his identity with both heroic figures.*

in one portrait within the temple dressed "Snake Spine" (see fig. 24). Likewise in the beautiful tablet of Temple XXI, the deceased K'inich Janab Pakal assumes the explicit identity of both Snake Spine and the "Ch'a" Ruler, with their name glyphs in his simple headdress (fig. 31). Clearly by Late Classic times these two proto-kings were important players in a complex political ideology that constantly strived to establish links to the heroes of the distant past.

K'uk' Bahlam and Palenque's Dynastic Beginnings

K'uk' Bahlam ("Quetzal Jaguar") was not the most ancient of Palenque's kings, but he was considered to be the founder of the main dynasty or ruling line that continued throughout the kingdom's later history and into the Late Classic period (fig. 32). As with nearly all of the kings of the Early Classic period, we have no contemporaneous records of him: all of the history we know comes from various mentions in much later inscriptions, mainly from the temples of the Group of the Cross.

According to the Tablet of the Cross narrative, K'uk' Bahlam was born on 31 March 397, and "the white headband was tied on him" some 34 years later on 10 March 431.[2] This was a very interesting time in Maya history overall. The decade or two preceding the great Bak'tun station in the Maya calendar in 435 (9.0.0.0.0 8 Ajaw 13 Keh) saw the founding of several important ruling lines across the early political landscape of the Maya lowlands. Copán is perhaps the best known example, where the local founder K'inich Yax K'uk' Mo' took the throne in 426, just five years before K'uk' Bahlam at Palenque. While impossible to prove, it is tempting to think that the establishment of a few Maya dynasties in the years leading up to the 435 Bak'tun ending – an event of cosmic import – were in some way intentional, if not coordinated.

K'uk' Bahlam's appearance in Palenque's history corresponds remarkably well with a significant change in the local ceramic tradition. According to Rands, around AD 400 the Picota ceramic phase of the Late Preclassic and very Early Classic periods transformed into a new localized tradition called the Motiepa phase (again named after one of the streams that run through the ruins). This lasted for about a century or so, and is significant in showing the first indications of Palenque participation in a wider Maya sphere of interaction. Polychrome sherds imported from Petén are found in Motiepa, as well as obvious imitations of Early Classic Petén fine wares known from Tikal and Uaxactun. We believe that these changes in Motiepa can be interpreted in light of the foundation of the Palenque dynasty, and in the significant ideological and political changes that took place as a result. Palenque was no longer an isolated place, but in these times appears far more conscious of the large and much more powerful kingdoms to the east.

Although Palenque's archaeological record shows a substantial community of some kind was in place by the Early Classic period, the written history presents a more complicated picture of where the first kings may have resided. The founder K'uk' Bahlam goes by the honorific place title "the Holy Lord of Toktahn," and other important events through the end of the 5th century are routinely associated with this mysterious location (fig. 33).[3] "Holy Lord of Toktahn" was apparently a standard title used by early kings, in addition to the more common "Holy Lord of Baakal" honorific. But where, or what, is Toktahn? As we have seen, it may have been a very local name for a part of the archaeological zone where the Early Classic court was based – perhaps the Picota complex to the west of the familiar Late Classic center of activity. Alternatively, Toktahn could be a different and much more distant locale – a political seat occupied by a few of the early kings who later moved their court to Lakamha', the Palenque we know today. We will see that the "foundation" of Lakamha' came in 490, nearly a century after the birth of K'uk' Bahlam.

Later kings seldom mention their dynastic founder in their own political art and inscriptions, unlike the pattern we find at other important Maya kingdoms such as Tikal and Copán. Perhaps this can be attributed to his short four-year reign (the next king took office in 435). We find the only other known mention of K'uk' Bahlam on the Tablet of the Foliated Cross, where on the day of the accession of K'inich Kan Bahlam the later king "renews the edifice of K'uk' Bahlam" (*u-jelew u-pak'il K'uk' Bahlam*) – perhaps a metaphorical statement of dynastic continuity, or a literal description of a refurbishment of an ancestral shrine. Both interpretations are possible.

32 OPPOSITE *Censer stand from Group IV, possibly depicting the early ruler K'uk' Bahlam or his later namesake.*

33 RIGHT *The "Toktahn" place glyph.*

The second "Ch'a" Ruler, the successor of K'uk' Bahlam who re-used a name from long before, was also an important individual. His name is identical to that of the very early figure from way back in Palenque's semi-mythical past, recorded on the Temple XXI platform. Born in 422, he was perhaps the son of the founder, but there is no explicit record of this. He took office the day after his thirteenth birthday, on 10 August 435. Only four months after his accession came the great Bak'tun ending on 9.0.0.0.0, arguably one of the most significant ceremonial occasions in all Maya history. This too happened at the mysterious place called Toktahn. It must have been a daunting duty for a young teenage king, but he presumably did well, for he would reign for another 52 years.

The long rule of the "Ch'a" Ruler may help to account for his bearded portrait on an Early Classic stone vessel now on display at Dumbarton Oaks in Washington D.C. (fig. 34). The vase was evidently looted many decades ago, and the circumstances of its discovery are unknown. It bears the earliest known image of a Palenque ruler, and shows the seated and simply dressed king pointing to the ground, a rather curious gesture for a Maya king. The three glyphs inscribed on the vase say "it is the drinking cup of the young 'Ch'a' Ruler, the Holy Lord of Baakal." Evidently his notable status as a "youth" upon accession to office stayed with him well into adulthood.[4]

34 Onyx marble drinking cup depicting its owner, the second "Ch'a" Ruler, who acceded to the throne at the age of 13 and led Palenque for some 52 years during its early dynastic period.

35 *Name glyphs of Butz'aj Sak Chihk, left, and Ahkal Mo' Nahb I, right, possibly brothers.*

The next two lords of Palenque, named Butz'aj Sak Chihk and Ahkal Mo' Nahb I, were probably brothers (fig. 35). The ruler list on the Tablet of the Cross shows that they were born only six years apart (in 459 and 465), and from this we can perhaps infer that they were both sons of the long-lived second ruler. Butz'aj Sak Chihk assumed office when he was 27 years old, on 29 July 487 (9.2.12.6.18 3 Etz'nab 11 Xul). Remarkably, this is only one day after a full fifty-two year calendar round from his father's inauguration date. Surely this was no coincidence. He and his younger brother acted jointly on at least one occasion to leave their mark on Palenque's early history, as revealed in a tablet unearthed recently in a small, seldom visited temple near the Cross Group.

Establishing Lakamha'

In 1993, excavators working on top of Temple XVII, a modest ruined pyramid in the north sector of the Cross Group, uncovered fragments of a well-preserved and painted wall panel that like most others at Palenque originally decorated the rear wall of its interior shrine (plate 31).[5] Its beautiful carving in Late Classic style shows a militaristic scene of conquest – a rare theme in Palenque's art – with a ruler standing above a kneeling captive. Strangely, the date recorded at the beginning of the accompanying inscription is 26 August 490 (9.2.15.9.2 9 Ik' end of Yaxk'in), about two centuries *earlier* than the carving, which we know to have been made sometime in the reign of K'inich Kan Bahlam (AD 684–702). The retrospective history features Butz'aj Sak Chihk, Palenque's king in 490, and the warrior depicted in the scene may well be him. The distant history commemorated in the text is difficult to ascertain, but clues suggest that this key episode of 490 was an "establishment" or "founding" of this early king at an existing location known as Lakamha' – what we know today as Palenque. If so, it may represent some formal beginning of Lakamha' as the dynasty's ritual and political center. The event hieroglyph that accompanies the date is difficult to decipher, but we know it is a verb used in other inscriptions with the sense of "setting" or "establishing" a place.[6] Before 490, as we have just seen, the location of dynastic authority was at the mysterious "Toktahn," lending good support to the interpretation that the Temple XVII tablet gives key evidence of the actual transition of the royal seat from one place to another. The sense of the text is "Butz'aj Sak Chihk 'sets up' at Lakamha', together with Ahkal Mo' Nahb I." The mention of the two brothers strengthens the idea that they acted in tandem to re-settle the dynastic center from Toktahn – wherever that was – to the Palenque we know today.

Butz'aj Sak Chihk reigned for 14 years, and presumably after his death Ahkal Mo' Nahb I assumed rule at the age of 35, in 501. He, in turn, reigned for 23 years until his own death in 524. His tenure on the throne saw the celebration of the important calendar station of 9.4.0.0.0 – a rare K'atun ending – falling in 514, the record of which opens the lengthy historical chronicle

presented in the tablets of the Temple of the Inscriptions (these will be discussed further in Chapter 7). There we read that on the period ending Ahkal Mo' Nahb I honored the three local patron gods known as the Palenque Triad, or effigies of them (fig. 36). The tablets leave the impression that he set the stage for similar rituals performed by Palenque's rulers at each subsequent K'atun station. In a fascinating historical parallel, the same calendar station of 514 is emphasized in the chronicles of neighboring kingdoms, including Piedras Negras, Toniná, Yaxchilan, perhaps an indication that Palenque was by now part of an emergent ritual and political "network" among elites in the western Maya lowlands. Ahkal Mo' Nahb I's importance is also shown by the fact that he is the earliest king featured in the ancestral records and iconography of Temple of the Inscriptions, in both the tablets and in the design of

36 OPPOSITE *Text passage from the east panel of the Temple of the Inscriptions describing the ritual dressing of effigies of the Palenque Triad gods.*

37 RIGHT *Portrait of Ahkal Mo' Nahb I, one of the early Palenque rulers, from the sarcophagus of K'inich Janab Pakal.*

the great sarcophagus of K'inich Janab Pakal, as we will discuss in Chapter 7 (fig. 37). He seems a pivotal character in this regard, perhaps because he was, unlike his brother, a direct ancestor of the great Late Classic king.

Early Architecture and Tombs

Just to the north of the Palace lies a line of temples known as the North Group where some very significant early remains have been excavated in recent years. Archaeologist Alejandro Tovalín investigated early phases of construction in this group and revealed one of the earliest known buildings at Palenque: a modest platform beneath the line of temples, which is associated specifically with an early phase of Temple V. Only two meters in height, the platform supported a small structure with three doorways facing southward. The thin walls and small column supports suggest the building could only hold a roof of thatch, and not the large vaulted ceilings so familiar from later Palenque architecture. The archaeologists were unable to date the building precisely, but its stratigraphic placement below later construction left little doubt that it was built in Early Classic times, perhaps around AD 400. Palenque was clearly a settlement of some significance well before the "foundation" event of 490 recorded on the Temple XVII tablet.

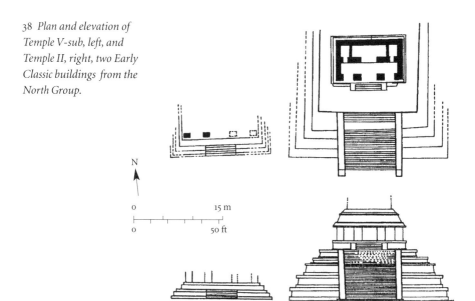

38 *Plan and elevation of Temple V-sub, left, and Temple II, right, two Early Classic buildings from the North Group.*

At some point after the completion of this early version of Temple V a far larger pyramid known as Temple II was built on its eastern side, the original remains of which can still be seen as part of the North Group (fig. 38). This is probably the earliest vaulted building now visible in the central area of Palenque, but the precise date of its construction is unknown.[7] These small clues do suggest that the North Group and its surroundings – perhaps including the ball court and early constructions still buried beneath the Palace – were places of considerable importance in Palenque's early days as a small dynastic and ritual center.

On the eastern edge of the city, just to the south of the Cross Group, lies a modest temple known as Temple XVIII-A, built against the side of the imposing hill that dominates this side of the ruins. Although unremarkable on the surface, excavations in Temple XVIII-A in 1956 revealed one of the most important tombs ever found in Palenque. The original tomb dates to the Motiepa phase, around AD 500, but evidence suggests it was modified and refurbished a century or two later.

Temple XVIII-A had two major constructions phases: the earliest was a small Early Classic platform covering the tomb and in Late Classic times a larger vaulted temple covered the platform, when the early tomb was possibly re-opened. A small stairway was built by the Maya in the southern end of an earlier phase of construction, providing access into the vaulted crypt. The stepped vault of the tomb was built to accommodate a long "psychoduct" or open tube-like structure that ran vertically to just below the temple's floor. Another far more elaborate tube was built to connect the tomb of K'inich Janab Pakal in the Temple of the Inscriptions with the outside. Clearly such small passages were built as points of access between tombs and the surface, connecting the realms of the living and the dead. They are not common in Maya architecture generally, and these two examples are the only ones known thus far at Palenque.

The tomb (officially labeled Tomb 3 of the temple) held two well-preserved skeletons of a young man and a young woman. Jewels including a jade mosaic mask and three greenstone celts identify the man to be an important nobleman and probably a ruler, although nothing in the tomb tells us about his specific identity. Rands's analysis of the ceramics within the tomb allows us to date the original deposition to the Motiepa phase (roughly around AD 500), but evidently the chamber was re-opened decades, if not centuries, later. The paintings within, while greatly damaged, appear to be of a later style, suggesting that the Maya refurbished the tomb around the time the overlaying construction was built. Upon its discovery, the plaster of the walls still bore impressions of handprints made by the ancient mason who exited the tomb via a small hole in the stone wall covering the door, which was subsequently covered.[8] The identities of the entombed people will probably remain unknown, but the date corresponds with the deaths of Butz'aj Sak Chihk or Ahkal Mo' Nahb I, both of whom are commemorated in the neighboring Temple XVII. At any rate, the presence of the burial in Temple XVIII-A is significant in revealing the ritual importance of the Cross Group even in Early Classic times.

Connections to the West

Despite the emerging historical importance of the kingdom during the Early Classic period, ceramic evidence indicates that Palenque remained strangely isolated from much of the Maya world. We nevertheless see in the art and inscriptions that Palenque participated in broader interactions between lowland Maya civilization and Mesoamerican cultures to the west, even as far as Central Mexico. Far from Palenque, in the central lowlands of Guatemala, archaeologists and historians have wrestled with intriguing evidence that Maya politics and history were heavily influenced by Teotihuacan, the vast metropolis in the Valley of Mexico, just north of modern Mexico City. The most important evidence comes from the central Maya region near Tikal, Guatemala, where early ceramics and architecture show stylistic influences from the highlands, and where one early king seems to have been identified culturally with warriors of Teotihuacan. Other Petén sites such as Uaxactun and La Sufricaya seem to have been key players in a major "arrival" of Teotihuacan influence in the region in AD 378, and there is good evidence that this had widespread repercussions for decades to come, even at a distant center such as Copán, in modern-day Honduras. The details of this cultural interaction are still being debated, but many kingdoms drew symbols of authority from Teotihuacan, even long after its own demise in the sixth century AD.

Although the evidence is still meager, Palenque too seems to have participated in this Maya preoccupation with Teotihuacan during the Early Classic period. The most compelling evidence comes from a stucco frieze excavated in the North Group which once decorated the substructure of Temple V. This remarkable image shows a human figure facing the viewer and is adorned with distinctive costume elements and stylistic traits associated with the civilization of Teotihuacan, the great city of highland Mexico. The man is probably dressed as a warrior, as indicated by the "goggles" over his eyes – a soldier's trait at Teotihuacan – and the spearthrower, or *atlatl*, grasped in his left hand (fig. 39).

Why would images of Teotihuacan warriors appear in the public art of early Palenque, and even more prominently in some other Maya centers? The history and art of Tikal and Copán, where these connections seem the strongest, indicate that Early Classic kings derived their authority in large part from the emblems and powerful militaristic ideology of the highland city. Perhaps like Rome in Europe and the Mediterranean during the Middle Ages, Teotihuacan was for a time the single most vital economic, political,

13 Detail of a general view of Palenque by Frederick Catherwood as it appeared in his 1844 lithograph. The Palace is shown at left, dominated by the towering mountain backdrop; to the right, the lofty Temple of the Inscriptions. The vertical exaggeration of the view, quite uncharacteristic of Catherwood's work, may reflect the artist's faulty memory, perhaps tempered by the debilitating fever he experienced throughout his entire stay at the ruins four years earlier.

14 The royal city of Palenque, its colors bright in the tropical sun, as it may have appeared in the early 8th century. The Temple of the Sun appears at lower left; the Palace and associated buildings, right. Nearby, the Temple of the Inscriptions and its row of neighboring structures face northward, toward the vast plain below.

15 (*Overleaf*) Aerial view of central Palenque and its backdrop of forested mountains, showing the Palace, left; the Temple of the Inscriptions, right; and the Cross Group beyond. The adjacent forest conceals hundreds of unexplored structures.

16 (*Above*) The Palace complex served as the setting for Palenque's royal court. Most of its buildings, courtyards, and the relief sculptures that adorn them date from the late seventh-century reign of Pakal, Palenque's "King of Kings" (see Chapter 6). The Palace held hundreds of yards of vaulted buildings, ranging from House E, the throne room, to a special area for private toilets, the latter so far unique among Maya ruins. In the distance, the great coastal plain of the present-day Mexican States of Tabasco and Chiapas stretches toward the Gulf of Mexico. Palenque occupies a narrow shelf of land some 122 m (400 ft) above the plain, against the backdrop of the mountains that define the state of Chiapas. This lofty mountain setting gave the inhabitants of the city not only a splendid vista, but also the all-important opportunity to exploit the diverse natural bounty of two distinct environments and the vital waters of the rivers that crossed them.

17 (*Right*) Detail of the Palace Tablet, which originally adorned the rear wall of the Palace's northern gallery, Houses A–D. The lengthy inscription records events in the life of Pakal's second son, K'inich K'an Joy Chitam, depicted in the center with his father and mother.

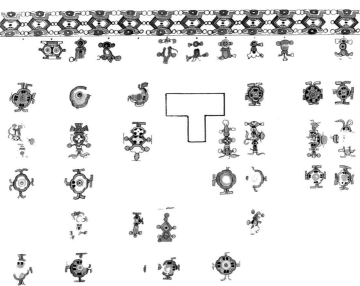

18A, 18B Palenque's "White House," House E of the Palace, top, containing Pakal's throne room and the Oval Palace Tablet (see fig. 49). This was the earliest of the major galleries built in the Palace complex by Pakal, in AD 654. Its well-preserved white exterior stood out among all of the surrounding red buildings, and was painted with numerous flower and jewel-like medallions in blue and orange, above.

19A, 19B Monuments to Palenque's revenge. House C of the Palace, above, was built by Pakal to commemorate his defeats of Calakmul's allies to the east. These crucial victories established Palenque as a regional political power, and Pakal as a great leader; a carved portrait from House C of a prisoner from the kingdom of Santa Elena, one of Calakmul's allies, left.

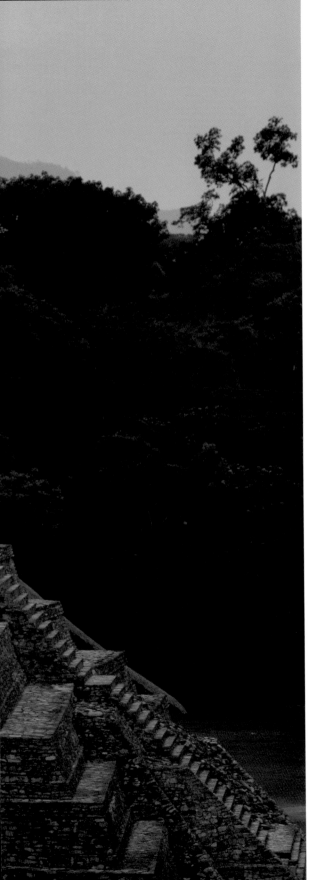

20 The Temple of the Inscriptions, shown here near the moment of sunset, served as the funerary monument to K'inich Janab Pakal, whose remains, bedecked in jade, were found inside an elaborate sarcophagus within a specially constructed crypt deep inside the pyramid (see fig. 55). The iconography of the crypt and its elaborately carved lid suggest that Pakal, like the setting sun, would enter the Underworld at death, only to emerge triumphant like the rising sun to join the pantheon of revered ancestors and gods.

21 The Group of the Cross, against the backdrop of El Mirador hill; from left to right, the Temple of the Cross, the Temple of the Foliated Cross, and the Temple of the Sun. Temple XIV can be seen behind one of the trees. The temples were built together in

D 692 by Pakal's son, K'inich Kan Bahlam, each dedicated to one of the patron gods of
ie dynasty (GI, GII, GIII), known as the Palenque Triad. The inscribed tablets within
ich building link the mythology of these gods to the reign of the newly enthroned king.

22 The plaza of the Cross Group faced on the west by the Temple of the Sun, left, and the partially restored Temple XIV, center. On the right rises the grand stair leading to the Temple of the Cross. The low square platform in the center of the plaza with its four sets of stairs symbolizes the four-sided universe of Maya cosmology.

23 (*Above*) The Temple of the Cross was the principal structure of the Cross Group, and replicated a celestial "house" of the god GI.

24 (*Right*) The Temple of the Sun, the smallest and best preserved of the Cross Group shrines, representing the cave-like interior of the earth and dedicated to the god GIII, a solar deity associated with warfare. The elaborate decoration on the outside and interior emphasize themes of warfare and the Underworld. The inner sanctuary tablet, dominated by a shield and crossed spears, depicts the ruler K'inich Kan Bahlam as a warrior facing the image of his father, Pakal (see fig. 66).

39 *Stucco decoration from the lower terrace of Temple V showing a warrior in the style of Teotihuacan.*

and religious center in its day, possibly attracting pilgrims and leaders from all of Mesoamerica. Palenque was a far more modest center than Tikal in the Early Classic period, but it is possible that one or more early local kings similarly expressed close ties to the Mexican highlands. The Temple V stucco and the foreign dress of the warrior on the much later Temple XVII tablet may indicate that Palenque, like other Maya kingdoms of the 4th and 5th centuries AD, also felt this strong lure of Teotihuacan, and participated in this strong evocation of foreign power and symbolism as it strived to establish its own historical position and significance.[9]

Middle Kings and a Queen

The murky history of early Palenque continues with several kings who reigned during the 6th century. The period saw significant transformation and growth in and around the community, but very little is known of the archaeology of this period, known as the Cascada phase in the ceramic chronology. The historical record, however, does show indications that Palenque and its dynasty was beginning to emerge as significant players in regional politics, negotiating and positioning itself within the wider geopolitical tensions commonplace during the transition from the Early to Late Classic periods.

K'an Joy Chitam assumed the throne in 529 and ruled until his death in 565 (fig. 40A). It is tempting to assume that he was the son of Ahkal Mo' Nahb I, but given that the preceding king was only 15 when K'an Joy Chitam was born, this seems unlikely. Unfortunately, the family connections among rulers and nobles of this era went unrecorded in the written accounts, all of which come from later retrospective inscriptions. Indirect evidence indicates that K'an Joy Chitam had an important role in the early planning and development of the Group of the Cross. He is named prominently in the texts of the group's three main temples built in the Late Classic period, and still later in Temple XIX's narrative as a celebrant of a period ending in 561 (9.6.7.0.0). His reign of over 35 years no doubt left a mark on Palenque's architectural history, and there is good reason to suppose that future excavations in the Cross Group and other areas will reveal some of K'an Joy Chitam's constructions.

King Ahkal Mo' Nahb II[10] took office 85 days after the death of K'an Joy Chitam in 565, but reigned for only four short years. He is mentioned as the grandson and namesake of Ahkal Mo' Nahb I, and was probably the elder brother of the next king named Kan Bahlam (the two were born only a year apart), who in turn succeeded him in 572. Kan Bahlam (fig. 40B) went on to reign for 11 years, during which time he oversaw another major K'atun ending of 9.7.0.0.0, commemorated in the Temple of the Inscriptions tablets.

40 *Portraits of the early Palenque rulers from the sarcophagus of K'inich Janab Pakal.* A *K'an Joy Chitam, far left;* B *Kan Bahlam, center;* C *Ix Yohl Ik'nal, left.*

For this period of the late 6th century, which could be called the "middle years" of Palenque's dynasty, evidence remains sparse, but more historical details begin to come into focus. The dynastic history continues with an intriguing woman named Ix Yohl Ik'nal (fig. 40C), who is one of only a handful of female rulers known in Maya history. Her reign began within a year of Kan Bahlam's death in 583. Ix Yohl Ik'nal oversaw the K'atun celebrations a decade later on 9.8.0.0.0, when, like all Palenque rulers, she offered regalia to the Triad gods, perhaps dressing their effigies.

The accession of a woman to the throne must have come about through highly unusual circumstances, but the details are lost to us. Royal descent was patrilineal in ancient Maya elite society, with offices ideally passed from father to son. History and the frailty of human relationships seldom allow for a neat realization of this plan, however. Without evidence of Ix Yohl Ik'nal's relations with her predecessor Kan Bahlam, we might suppose that she was his daughter, and no male heirs were present to assume office. From what we know of other female rulers in Maya history, power could some-times also derive from their royal offspring. For example, Ix Yohl Ik'nal may have served for a decade or so as regent while her young child and successor Ajen Yohl Mat came of age. This is only speculation, however, since we do not know that she even had a child.

The Temple XX Tomb

Recent investigations near the Cross Group have revealed another significant early tomb, as well as an important archaeological puzzle. Temple XX is located at the southern end of the Cross Group, next to Temple XIX. Approaching the pyramid, it appears to be an imposing structure, but excavations since 1999 have shown that the base is actually a masonry veneer on a small hillock of bedrock. As archaeologists Alfonso Morales and Rudy Larios Villalta have shown, the structure was modified over many years, and the earliest phase seems to date from the first part of the 6th century. After this initial construction later builders demolished part of the upper temple in order to construct a vaulted tomb beneath. The crypt has not yet been entered, but photographs taken by a camera inserted within the chamber show red-line paintings of nine figures in an unusual style, jade objects, and pottery that looks as if it may date from the 6th century (plate 35). Its size and elaboration suggests that the Temple XX tomb is a royal burial, but there are no clues about the identity of its occupant. Interestingly, a preliminary assessment of the painted figures indicates that they are portraits of royal ancestors, including Ahkal Mo' Nahb and Kan Bahlam. If this is the case, then the Temple XX tomb must date from after Kan Bahlam's death in 583. Could it be the tomb of Ix Yohl Ik'nal, as Greene Robertson has tentatively suggested? The dating of the chamber will only be known for certain once the tomb has been opened and the ceramics within examined.

Temple XX remained an important building for many years, and intriguingly its final remodeling may never have been finished. When archaeologists first began investigating the pyramid, they were very confused by the lack of any masonry veneer and terracing on its front and sides: it was an ancient construction site interrupted in mid project.

Conquests and Questions

On 23 April 599, during the reign of Ix Yohl Ik'nal, Palenque suffered a key military defeat at the hands of the king of Calakmul, the powerful realm known in ancient times as *Kan*, located far to the east in the center of the Maya world. Little is known about the circumstances surrounding this event, other than it was to remain a sore point in Palenque's own political consciousness many years later. The record of the defeat is a highlight of the text on the inscribed steps of House C in the Northeast Court of the Palace, carved many years later during the reign of K'inich Janab Pakal (fig. 41, plate 19A). As we will see in the next chapter, Pakal mentioned this earlier defeat in order to add rhetorical weight to his own military victories against Calakmul's allies. Apparently Pakal held a long-lasting grudge against his powerful rival, rooted in events that took place before his birth.

The House C inscription may mention the "throwing down" (*yajel*) of the Palenque Triad gods on the day of the conquest, and the appearance of the "Great Jaguar," known elsewhere as the militaristic totem of the Calakmul kings. One of the principal actors in this conquest drama was a lord named Lakam Chaak, ruler of a small kingdom we know today as Santa Elena and evidently an ally of Calakmul in these years.

The mention of this military loss is the first strong indication we have of Palenque's emerging importance within the larger arena of Classic Maya

41 *Hieroglyphic passage on the steps of Palace House C records Palenque's defeat by Calakmul in 599. K'inich Janab Pakal, who had acceded to power in the aftermath of the defeat, had the inscription made much later, possibly to underscore his own victories over his troublesome neighbor to the east.*

42 OPPOSITE *Conquest text of the AD 611 conquest of Palenque by Calakmul, from the Temple of the Inscriptions.*

geo-politics.[11] It is revealing that, at least from the perspective of a Palenque scribe, the king of Calakmul considered Palenque important enough to be vanquished with the help of two other prominent Maya kings. It is difficult to assess the importance of Palenque and its dynasty in the early years of the Classic period, given the scarce nature of its archaeological record. Unfortunately the simple language that the scribes customarily used in the inscriptions ("Lakamha' is conquered") tells us precious little about the character of the war – was it a surprise raid into the center of Palenque, or a defeat on a battlefield near the city? We will never know the answers, since the physical evidence of warfare is very hard to discern in the archaeological remains. We do know, however, that Ix Yohl Ik'nal probably reigned for several more years before her death in 604. As noted above, there is an intriguing possibility that Temple XX holds her funerary chamber.

Life at court remained just as lively in the decade or so that followed the war. As in many other military defeats in Maya history, Palenque seems to have retained its own community and even political identity, although perhaps now as a tributary of Calakmul. In the wake of this turbulent event a new king named Ajen Yohl Mat assumed the throne in 605, shortly after the death of Ix Yohl Ik'nal the previous year. He reigned for just over seven years before his death in 612, but his rule was eventful, suggesting that Ajen Yohl Mat was something of rabble-rouser in his day. Near the end of his reign Palenque had apparently gained enough independence to warrant yet another invasion by Calakmul's forces, on 7 April 611. The exact historical record from the Temple of the Inscriptions says "Lakamha' was conquered, it was overseen by Uk'aychan, Holy Lord of *Kan*" (fig. 42). In the years since the first conquest 12 years earlier, Calakmul itself had enthroned a new king (possibly named Uk'aychan), and it may well have been that the new ruler had to exert his power over distant Palenque in order to preserve a hierarchical status quo. Uk'aychan was committed to large-scale territorial expansion in the western Maya lowlands, and as Simon Martin has eluci-dated through his work on Calakmul's inscriptions, he may have been

reaching westward in order to control lucrative trade routes and resources in the Palenque region. Evidently he was successful: Calakmul grew into a great regional power – far greater than Palenque – while little is heard about Palenque for a generation. Palenque's history in the first years of the 7th century shows signs of dynastic instability and regional strife.

As Nikolai Grube has noted, Ajen Yohl Mat makes an intriguing appearance in a battered inscription recovered from Santa Elena, located some 70 km (44 miles) due east of Palenque.[12] The tablet is badly damaged, but enough is left to see that it records some connection between Ajen Yohl Mat and the ruler of Santa Elena. As we have seen, Santa Elena was a key player in the political machinations of the western Maya region, and is mentioned in the inscriptions of not only Palenque, but also of Piedras Negras, Yaxchilan, and La Corona, in present-day Guatemala. Santa Elena was a major enemy of Palenque, serving as a close ally of Calakmul in the wars of 599 and in 611. The appearance of Ajen Yohl Mat's name in the Santa Elena tablet is therefore intriguing – does it record his subservience? Or perhaps a brief period when the tables were turned, and Palenque ruled over Santa Elena? The eroded glyphs on the tablet cannot tell the story.

A Change of Status

A key source for the early and middle kings of Palenque's history is the long text carved on the three hieroglyphic tablets in the Temple of the Inscriptions. As we will see in Chapter 7, this temple was the funerary shrine of K'inich Janab Pakal, Palenque's greatest king. His rise to glory is told in the tablets, which begin by recounting many of the early kings and the dates of their "seatings" or enthronements.

43 *Two offices cited in Palenque's history. Before AD 605 all Palenque rulers assumed the status of* huun, *named for the royal headband; after 605 all were seated as* ajaw *(king).*

In this retrospective narrative we find a curious but revealing pattern. Typically the phrase used to describe a Maya royal accession might read something like "he sat in the rulership," and indeed several examples appear in the Inscriptions narrative: Ajen Yohl Mat "sat in the rulership" in 605; his successor Muwaan Mat "sat in the rulership" in 612; K'inich Janab Pakal himself then "sat in the rulership" in 615. But if we look further back at the records of earlier rulers cited in the Inscriptions tablets, we find a difference in one key detail. All of the rulers preceding Ajen Yohl Mat sit in a different status or position written simply as the word *huun* (fig. 43). This means "paper" or "book," but in many contexts *huun* is also "headband," referring to the paper-scarf worn by rulers upon their accession. It is not understood how this *huun* status differs from "rulership" (*ajawlel*), but the narrative consciously points to a key change if not advancement in the nature of Palenque's throne, coming sometime between Ix Yohl Ik'nal's accession (as *huun*) and when Ajen Yohl Mat succeeded her in 605 in the new role as *ajawlel*.

It is likely that the shift was connected with disruptive events during the reign of Ix Yohl Ik'nal, the most obvious being Calakmul's victory over Palenque in 599. Calakmul's dominance did not seem to last long, for we know another war was waged against Palenque in 611. Ajen Yohl Mat had already been active in the regional politics to the east, possibly an indication that he or Ix Yohl Ik'nal had successfully rebelled against Calakmul sometime before 611. This suggests that "rulership" came to Palenque with Ajen Yohl Mat at the very time Palenque was thrust into the larger regional power struggles that were rapidly changing the face of Maya geopolitics at the outset of the Late Classic period.

44 OPPOSITE *Portrait of Janab Pakal, one of the early Palenque rulers, from the sarcophagus of K'inich Janab Pakal.*

Further Loss, then Greatness

Two important members of Palenque's royal court died in the immediate wake of Calakmul's second victory in 611, suggesting that their demise was directly related to the political disruptions of the time. According to the inscription on the sarcophagus lid in the Temple of the Inscriptions, a mysterious figure named Janab Pakal "entered the path" (i.e., died) in March 612. He carried the title "Holy Lord of Baakal," suggesting that he was a previously unrecognized ruler of Palenque (fig. 44). Strangely, however, we also read that Ajen Yohl Mat was still alive on Janab Pakal's death (he, in turn, passed away later in the summer of 612). What was the relationship between these two lords? The evidence perhaps indicates that both men were co-rulers of Palenque (maybe at two separate courts) and were perhaps even brothers, but the details remain utterly obscure. It seems that a co-rulership arrangement may have existed later in Palenque's history during the reign of K'inich Ahkal Mo' Nahb, as we will see in Chapter 9.

With the death of Ajen Yohl Mat a troubled and short-lived ruler named Muwaan Mat came to the throne in October 612 (Muwaan Mat is just a partial reading of his name; some elements remain undeciphered). In a fascinating evocation of the mythical origins of the Palenque dynasty, Muwaan Mat took his name from the deified Triad Progenitor, a god-king who is said to have sired the Triad gods shortly after the creation of the current era (see Chapter 8 for a more detailed discussion). The kingdom's troubled times in the years leading up to Muwaan Mat's accession may help explain such a blatant parallelism, where creation mythology is consciously likened to the beginning of a new political order. The existence of Muwaan Mat is a new discovery in Palenque's history, for until recently it was widely thought that Muwaan Mat was an alternative name for Ix Sak K'uk', the mother of the great king K'inich Janab Pakal.

Muwaan Mat ruled for only two years. We might not have known about his existence at all were it not for his having ruled at the K'atun ending 9.9.0.0.0, as recorded in the Temple of the Inscriptions tablets. This important calendar station and its rituals are describe in remarkably dire terms. Earlier K'atun dates recorded in this temple consistently mention how the kings dressed and adorned the effigies of the Palenque Triad deities, in what was surely a key ritual symbolizing royal power, community renewal, and vitality. However, the passage devoted to Muwaan Mat's reign is very different:

> *satay k'uh, satay ajaw…*
> *ma' y-ak'aw u-tut-il…*
> The gods became lost, the lords became lost…
> He (Muwaan Mat) did not give the offerings…[13]

The Calakamul conquest had taken a huge toll: not only had Lakamha' been conquered, but also the resulting loss of power led to a break in the essential duty of Palenque's kings to care for and make the proper sacrifices to their patron gods. The kings and the gods both were indeed "lost."

Like so many of Palenque's early lords, Muwaan Mat is a character steeped in obscurity. His name recalls the mythical foundations of Palenque and the supernatural place called Matwiil, but these strange and very symbolic references only add to his mystery. Why are the gods not properly venerated and dressed under his watch? Did the king of Calakmul install him as a mere "puppet" ruler? Or had the effigies of the Triad gods been removed from Palenque in these fateful years, leaving Muwaan Mat with no choice but to fall short of his royal duty as their caretaker? We may never know the details of this fascinating time period around the K'atun ending, but Calakmul's defeat of Palenque's clearly had lasting effects on the city.

It was Palenque's historical nadir. But Palenque's fortunes would be transformed and revived by the arrival of a truly heroic figure – a man who had probably witnessed the tumultuous days of the Calakmul conquest as a child, and would leave a lasting and powerful mark on Maya archaeology and our own modern perceptions of the Maya past. This great man is the subject of the next chapter, where we will read of a legacy that predominantly shaped Palenque's later history.

CHAPTER SIX

The King of Kings

On Nine Ajaw, the Eighth of Chaksihoom
The Eleventh K'atun ended.
K'inich Janab Pakal oversaw it, He of the Five Palace Houses,
The Holy Lord of Baakal.

OPENING PASSAGE OF THE TABLET OF THE 96 GLYPHS

The 19th-century historian Thomas Carlyle is famous for saying that "the history of the world is but the biography of great men," in the sense that the course of history is ultimately shaped by certain charismatic and powerful individuals. Most modern scholars dismiss the simplicity of Carlyle's "great men theory," recognizing that events and forces in history come about primarily through societal trends, technological developments, and economic realities. There is some truth in each argument: great men and women have indeed left profound marks on the world. When considering the ancient Maya the aim is to discern the greater trends of cultural development, but sometimes it is apparent that the evolution of individual kingdoms and communities was radically shaped by the efforts one or two individuals. Palenque offers perhaps the best illustration of this, since much of what came about in Late Classic times was due to the extraordinary vision and later remembrance of one man: K'inich Janab Pakal (plate 28).

He is perhaps the best known of all kings in Classic Maya history. His name, based partly on the word for "war shield" (*pakal*), evokes that of a slightly earlier Palenque figure who was probably a direct ancestor and possibly the grandfather of the great king who would inherit his name.[1] The honorific *K'inich*, a reference to the sun god, is all that distinguishes the later king's name from that of the earlier figure. K'inich Janab Pakal was the first Palenque king to use this special solar title, which came to be used by all of his descendants in Classic history.

This simple naming pattern seen in the span of Palenque's dynastic history emphasizes the pivotal place of K'inich Janab Pakal. Looking at the list of kings (pages 244–47), one can see that the names of the kings who succeeded Pakal clearly mirror those of their predecessors discussed in the preceding chapter. The pattern places Pakal squarely in the middle of a historical and familial storyline, and, remarkably, it would seem to be an intentional "structuring" of history by the ancient Maya. This implies, however, that the ancient historians of Palenque conceived of an endpoint to their dynasty, reflecting its beginning in K'uk' Bahlam. This is an intriguing idea that we will revisit in the final chapter.

Pakal's reign was the longest of all the local rulers, and its timing in Maya history, near the start of what we call the Late Classic period, could not have been more fortuitous. It was during this era, around the beginning of the 7th century, that numerous kingdoms across the Maya landscape, including Palenque and its neighbors and historical rivals Toniná, Piedras Negras, and Yaxchilan, grew in power and influence. Several "great men" who assumed the throne at these and other kingdoms around this time – Itzamnaaj Bahlam of Yaxchilan, and K'inich Chapaht Balam of Toniná – would rule for decades, wage battles with one another, and cement the political and religious identities of their respective communities. K'inich Janab Pakal would prove the greatest of them all.

The Child King

K'inich Janab Pakal was born in 603 during the warm and damp days of late summer. Palenque was still experiencing a tumultuous political period in the wake of Calakmul's recent victory during the reign of the short-lived king Muwaan Mat. The limited archaeology of Palenque offers no material indications of a profound change in the political and social life of the community, but a few interesting clues about Pakal's own family background point to difficult days around the time of his birth and young childhood.

His father, K'an Hix Mo' ("Yellow Jaguar Macaw"), was a mysterious figure who does not seem to have occupied the throne of Palenque, and may therefore have been a noble of foreign origin. The cloudy history might even suggest that K'inich Janab Pakal was born elsewhere and came to Palenque as a child – we simply do not know. His mother was Ix Sak K'uk' ("Lady White Quetzal") and her origins are also obscure (fig. 45). What we do know about them comes mostly from the remarkable sarcophagus of the Temple of the Inscriptions – K'inich Janab Pakal's funerary temple – where his parents and several other ancestors are depicted as fruiting trees.

The historical records tell us that K'inich Janab Pakal assumed the throne in 615, when he was only 12 years old. It was just a few years after the second of Calakmul's conquests of Palenque in 611, and it is in the context of these wars and defeats that we can best understand the extraordinary circumstances surrounding the boy's crowning. First, it is remarkable that both of Pakal's parents were alive to see his accession, and would indeed live for many years.[2] Elsewhere in Maya history, as far as we know, inheritance of a throne or major office occurred after the death of a parent. Yet Pakal comes

45 *Pakal's parents Ix Sak K'uk', left, and K'an Hix Mo', right, shown as fruiting ancestral trees emerging from fissures in the earth on the side of his sarcophagus.*

to rule Palenque as something of an "outsider" without the direct pedigree we would normally expect, and we can therefore only surmise that his installment was in some way connected to the profound political disturbances of the time. Were Pakal and his parents representing some auxiliary branch of Palenque's extended royal family, brought into rule after the Calakmul defeats wiped out the main line of inheritance? Or, alternatively, was Calakmul still ruling Palenque in 615, installing the child Pakal as a puppet ruler? We may never know the specific circumstances, and there are no contemporary accounts (the earliest known inscription from Pakal's reign comes much later, in 647). Yet the unusual family background of the inheritor, coupled with his youth at the time of his accession, suggests a deliberate breaking of the existing ruling line in Palenque.

K'inich Janab Pakal's mother lived until 640, and his father died in 643. K'an Hix Mo' is not mentioned again, but Ix Sak K'uk' seems to have been an unusually powerful woman in Maya history, and judging by the history and art of Pakal's reign she may have been instrumental in Pakal's execution of political power and authority, at least in the early years of his reign. On the Oval Tablet from the Palace (see figs 49A and B), placed directly above the royal throne, we see a young Pakal on the day of his accession receiving the war headdress from Ix Sak K'uk'. The adult-sized portrait of Pakal no doubt corresponds more to his middle-aged likeness at the time the building was dedicated in 654, and not to his enthronement as a child. K'an Hix Mo' is nowhere to be seen on the Oval Palace Tablet, even though comparable images of accession at Palenque show both mothers and fathers. Arguably, Pakal's inheritance of office came through his mother. Even after Pakal became an adult, Ix Sak K'uk' is said to have overseen the important K'atun ending of 633 (9.10.0.0.0 1 Ajaw 8 K'ayab), a period of time named as her "stone-seating."[3] This is extremely unusual, given that Pakal had been king for 18 years, and is mentioned in a different record to be the celebrant of the very same K'atun ending. We can view these as contradictory statements, but they probably reflect the complex power relationships of the Palenque court at that time, with mother and son ruling in some capacity together.

Silent History

Remarkably, there is no record of Pakal's life or accomplishments between the time he assumed the throne in 615 and his great K'atun celebration nearly four decades later in 652 (9.11.0.0.0 12 Ajaw 8 Keh), which was a truly pivotal time in Palenque's history. What happened in these 40 silent years of rule? We suspect that the direct evidence may be in the ruins, in early collapsed temples and other structures still covered by rubble and forest. A tantalizing clue comes from one enigmatic building known as the *Templo Olvidado* located some 600 m (1,970 ft) to the west of the main group of buildings, still encroached upon by trees, but accessible by trial (fig. 46). This one structure is all that remains standing in the vast sea of mounds that stretches westward along the ridge; many of the other structures, as we have already seen, appear to be tantalizingly early, as indicated

46 The Templo Olvidado, *one of the few buildings outside of central Palenque that has been investigated in detail, is known for its well-preserved stucco glyphs (see plate 8).*

by preliminary test-pitting in the 1990s. The Olvidado is the earliest known standing building at Palenque, dated by its fragmentary stucco inscription to 647 (9.10.14.5.10 3 Ok 3 Pop). The text, like most gracing the exteriors of temples, probably records its dedication in that year, and it also cites the name of Pakal as well as his mother and father. Given this was only a short time after the death of Pakal's father, it is possible that the Olvidado is a funerary structure for the king's parents. Whatever the case, the building could not have existed in isolation, and we suspect that other structures in the area date to the same period, and perhaps to the early mystery years of K'inich Janab Pakal's rule.

Another clue about Palenque's strange silence in the early 7th century comes from monuments and inscriptions at other sites. One stela from Piedras Negras, located on the Usumacinta river in modern Guatemala, displays a war captive who is clearly named as an *Ajk'uhuun* priest of the "Holy Lord of B'aakal" – a clear reference to Palenque and probably to Pakal himself. The war in 624 is celebrated on the monument as a victory for the Piedras Negras king, who also captured a nobleman from the place known as Sak Tz'i ("White Dog"), which still remains to be identified with an archaeological site in the area.[4] Sak Tz'i, simply by its association with a Palenque captive on this sculpture, may have been an ally of K'inich Janab Pakal at this time.

In 635, when K'inich Janab Pakal was 32 years old but still absent from the historical records, we see the sudden emergence of Palenque's neighbor Tortuguero as a new political and military force in the area. Its written history seems shortlived, just about spanning 25 years, but in its important records we read of the arrival on the Tortuguero throne of one Bahlam Ajaw in 644, who soon thereafter engaged in wars with several neighbors. Significantly, Bahlam Ajaw uses the Palenque royal title "Holy Lord of Baakal," as if he were claiming the divine kingship at the same time that K'inich Janab Pakal ruled at Palenque. Both men were about the same age when Bahlam Ajaw took the throne, and we can probably infer that they were considerable rivals. We also get a sense of some bad blood between these kings from Bahlam Ajaw's claims of victory in 644 and 655 over a site named Uxte' K'uh, which had had close familial ties with Palenque's dynasty since the 6th century. Tortuguero also defeated the armies of Comalcalco in 649, shortly before K'inich Janab Pakal emerged from historical obscurity. Sadly, much of this tantalizing history of Tortuguero's connections to Palenque may be forever lost: during the 1960s the archaeological ruins at Tortuguero were all but destroyed when it was used as a stone quarry and cement factory during the construction of a nearby highway.[5]

The Great Transformation

The year 652 was truly pivotal in Palenque's history: the ritual calendar reached the ending of the eleventh K'atun, and with it Palenque's expression of power and importance began in earnest. The earliest contemporaneous monuments dedicated by K'inich Janab Pakal date from 9.11.0.0.0, and in the decade or so afterwards there was a radical transformation of Palenque's art and urban design. In these years Pakal was in middle age, but it was a true renaissance in the history of the city, and we can best see the renewed energy of the kingdom by looking at its architectural centerpiece known today as the Palace (plate 16).

What was the Palace? The name seems a natural one for such a compact assembly of courtyards, galleries, buried passageways, yet the true function of this central, elegant architectural gem remains an open question. A number of scholars have naturally assumed that Palenque's Palace and similar such architectural complexes were royal residences, but others have come to question this interpretation in recent years. The formal groupings of buildings seldom show much evidence of domestic use, and their associated art and inscriptions suggest far more specific ritual and political roles for the gallery-like "houses" within the Palace (fig. 47). Although some priests and other officials may have lived in the more modest structures of the great platform, in the smaller rooms and buildings near the southwest corner of the complex, the principal buildings are best understood as the stages for courtly display, probably used on a daily basis in various capacities, but kept largely separate from areas of sleeping and eating.[6]

Then where did Pakal and other kings and queens live? Clues from excavated sites elsewhere suggest that Maya elites were more practical in their

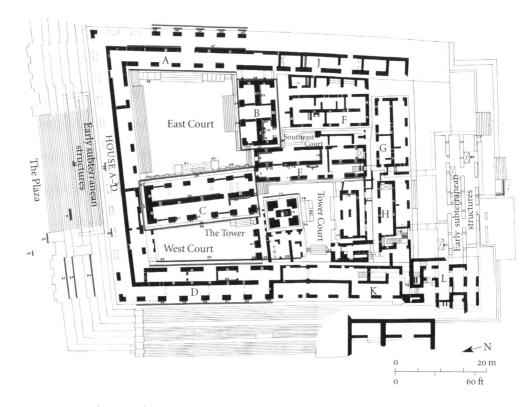

47 *Plan view of the Palace (with north to the left), showing the complex of vaulted buildings and the system of private courtyards within its walls, and the grand stairways leading up to them. House E, at right center, facing the Tower Court, served as the throne room.*

choices of domestic space, and were often in less ostentatious compounds more hidden from public view, but with ample access to water and good air. If we were to choose a likely spot at Palenque for the royal residences, it could be the tightly compacted buildings of the Otolum Group, just to the east of the Palace, across the covered aqueduct, and behind the Temple of the Cross, looking over the cascades of the Otolum stream. This would be among the best places to live at Palenque, with its views, access to fresh water, and in such close proximity to the court (see fig. 5).

Pakal's ambitious plans for the Palace began around 650 and moved forward at a very rapid pace, with significant construction phases lasting for the next decade. The transformation of this space from what was once a fairly modest architectural group to one of the most imposing in the Maya area may reflect the need Pakal felt for a truly monumental expression of his newly found political authority: his Palace was designed for the controlled reception of others, and for the display of his role as renaissance man and regional conqueror. We will examine the reasons for this profound change as we look at the symbolism of one building in the Palace in particular (House C).

The earliest known buildings of the Palace are the buried galleries known as the *subterraneos*, located at the southern end and today partially exposed from ceiling collapse. These dark, low-vaulted chambers seem labyrinthine, but it has been suggested that they were once surface structures that were covered by later and higher construction as the Palace grew and expanded. It seems far more likely, however, that the *subterraneos* are not so old, and that they were originally planned and built during the reign of K'inich Janab Pakal very much as the "underground" buildings they are today. Inner stairways provide access to the surface buildings such as House E, suggest an ambitious architectural design that integrated upper and lower storeys within the Palace. If they were indeed originally designed as dark interior halls, it is difficult to say what their function may have been. Some stucco sculpture above inner doorways in the *subterraneos* shows Underworld themes, such as the maize god being resurrected from water, and the sun passing through the body of the earth alligator on its way to sunrise (fig. 48). These lower galleries may therefore have constituted an artificial netherworld, integrated into the ritual landscape of the larger Palace.

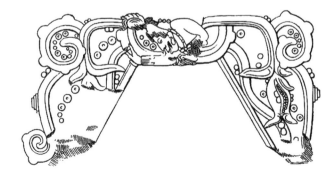

48 *Stucco decoration over interior door of the* subterraneos *depicts the maize god resurrected from primal waters.*

A handful of inscriptions recovered from the *subterraneos* are among the earliest we know from Palenque, including two hieroglyphic thrones that date to the time of the K'atun ending of 652. A series of small inscribed tablets known as the "Tableritos" – illustrated by several early explorers (see figs 9A, c) – date the construction of the *subterraneos* more precisely to June 654. After this Pakal's architects shifted their attention to the construction of House E, located above the *subterraneos* and connected to them by an access stairway. Clearly, they were all part of one plan. It seems that at about the same time the great terrace of the Palace was leveled and prepared for a series of new constructions that would be among the most powerful political and religious expressions in Pakal's reign, and of all of Palenque history.

Located in the core of the Palace, House E is the earliest of the surface constructions on the new terrace, dedicated in November 654, just five months after the *subterraneos* (plate 18A). This gallery served as K'inich Janab Pakal's main throne room after its construction and continued to be used for the same purpose by the next four Palenque kings. The building's location at the core of the Palace complex emphasizes its role as the symbolic "heart" of the city, as well as the Palenque kingdom as a whole. Three generations of descendants paid homage to K'inich Janab Pakal through their own slight modifications to the building, thereby drawing their own connections to Pakal, and establishing their own political authority.

House E's appearance was very unusual compared to other buildings within the Palace, and in Palenque in general. Its façade is nearly vertical whereas the other buildings of the Palace and at Palenque seem inclined by about another ten degrees more. Odd stone slabs carved to resemble thatch were built over the eaves of the upper façade, as if to give House E a somewhat modest look and feel. Moreover, it was the only major building at Palenque that did not have a roof comb – a feature otherwise found everywhere in the religious architecture of the city. Most unusual of all is House E's white exterior: all the other secular buildings of the complex and the vast majority of temples in the city were painted a deep ochre-like red. The color was remarkable enough to be used in the formal name of the building, the "White Skin(?) House" (*Sak nuk naah*). Painted on the exterior walls, and still remarkably preserved in some places, are various medallions and symbols in blue and orange, arranged almost like glyphs in vertical columns on either side of the central doorways. Some of the symbols seem to be elaborate quatrefoil flowers, while others seem more geometric, sometimes with eye-like motifs in their centers. The designs are reminiscent of those painted on shrouds and garments worn by both men and women in Classic Maya vase paintings, suggesting that the white color was meant to evoke a cotton covering or "dressing" for House E.

The Oval Palace Tablet adorns the back wall of House E, depicting the enthroned K'inich Janab Pakal and his mother Ix Sak K'uk' (fig. 49A). This is the earliest known example of a formulaic representation of royal accession found on several Palenque tablets. In most cases the parents of the new king (here just the mother) flank their son and present him with the "drum-major" headdress associated with sacred warfare. Such a war symbol probably dominates the political art largely because of the bellicose times in which this was carved, and because of the importance of Palenque's own militarism in the early reign of K'inich Janab Pakal. This accession portrait, as we have discussed, shows the king as an adult, and not as a 12-year-old child. This is no doubt because the portrait is more contemporaneous with the actual dedication of House E in 654, when the king was 49 years old. Lady Sak K'uk', however, had died 14 years earlier, and so the Oval Tablet cannot be seen as a scene of a real historical event: rather it is an idealized view of the mature son receiving authority from his deceased mother. In the wake of her passing, Pakal may have finally come into his own to consolidate political and economic might to transform the kingdom and give it new life. It is as if Pakal now felt comfortable in the role of king, and saw this heady time as his true coming of age.

The sculpted throne that once stood beneath the Oval Palace Tablet is battered and in many fragments and is now stored at Palenque's archaeological lab, but it was complete in 1787 when it was drawn by Armendáriz (fig. 49B). The carving on the throne included an inscription commemorating the inauguration dates of K'inich Janab Pakal and his two ruling sons. Its two front supports each depict a seated figure dressed as an aquatic deity with one hand upraised, a cosmic supporter of the earth and sky. But these are more than religious portraits: as the texts on their sides reveal, the two

49 A *The Oval Tablet from Palace House E, the throne room, left;* B *Ignacio Armendáriz's 1787 drawing, right, of the Oval Tablet with its associated throne in place before its partial removal by Antonio del Río.*

men were in fact important officials in Pakal's royal court, shown on the throne as deity impersonators who support the king himself as an embodiment of the cosmic realm. The stucco celestial band that ran along the back of the throne (again only visible in the Armendáriz rendering) emphasizes this larger spatial significance of the throne as a microcosm.

War and Political Consolidation

Palenque's renewal under Pakal came on the heels of its military victory over a site known as Santa Elena today, located on the Río San Pedro, in the plains of Tabasco to the east of Palenque. In 7 August 659, the armies of Palenque captured the ruler of Santa Elena, Nuun Ujol Chahk, and six of his lieutenants, some apparently also from Pomoná. Six days later the captured king "arrived at Palenque in front of K'inich Janab Pakal," according to the chronicles of the Temple of the Inscriptions. House C of the Palace, located just to the north of House E, was dedicated on the winter solstice of 661 (9.11.9.5.19 4 Kawak 2 Pax) specifically as a commemoration of this great defeat of Santa Elena. On the lower terrace of House C, on either side of the stairway, we can still see the graceful portraits of the six kneeling men, identified by the accompanying glyphic panels as the allies of Nuun Ujol Chahk. They also wear their hieroglyphic names in their headdresses (fig. 41).

Palenque's aggressive stance against Santa Elena can be explained through the latter's possible close ties to two other kingdoms to the east – its large neighbor Pomoná (ancient *Pakbuul*) and perhaps the more distant and powerful Calakmul (*Kan*). The beautiful inscription on the front (eastern) steps of House C (see fig. 41) offers a revealing juxtaposition of Palenque's defeat by Calakmul and the capture of Nuun Ujol Chahk of Santa Elena and his subordinates six decades later, suggesting that the two events were politically related. On the rear side of House C, in a narrow East Court that was once probably a grisly place, we find other inscriptions recording the sacrifice in 663 of several other "youths" of Santa Elena as well as a lord of Pomoná. Taken together, the message of House C seems to have been one of a successful revenge against eastern sites possibly allied with Calakmul. As the second major construction of the Palace, after the throne room of House E, House C stood as Pakal's most explicit statement of military power and regional influence. How times had changed from a generation or two before, when both the history and archaeology of Palenque suggest it was an insular and relatively unimportant place.

House A

Across the courtyard in front of House C, we see a strange alignment of carved figures set against the opposite terrace, flanking a stairway leading into House A. The wide door that faces east, toward what was probably the royal residence of the Otolum Group, provided one of the principal means of access into the Palace in ancient times. These carved figures, rendered here in a somewhat crude manner, are prisoners. According to the glyphs on two of them they were displayed in March 662. We do not know their identities, but it seems likely that they were victims of Pakal during this burst of raiding and captive taking.

House A runs along the eastern side of the Palace, overlooking the site of the Otolum stream and its covered channel. Its outer gallery and façade were built after the House C courtyard, and were finally dedicated on 22 May 668 when K'inich Janab Pakal was 66 years old. Its additions closed off the East Court of the Palace, and were probably modifications of a pre-existing building or platform. House A's exterior makes it one of the more elegant buildings at Palenque: its beautifully decorated piers greeted many of Palenque's first visitors on their approach to the ruins in the 18th and 19th centuries. The evenly spaced piers on each side all show the same refined style of stucco figural sculpture that we also see on House D, on the opposite side of the Palace (fig. 50). The theme of these repetitious sculptures seems somewhat militaristic but not overtly so. The standing figures, probably portraits of K'inich Janab Pakal, all face the central, main doorway of House A, and hold a tall axe-staff topped with the head of K'awiil, the powerful and complex god associated with lighting, ancestry, and fecundity. Two figures, male and female, are seated at his feet on each pier. It might be tempting to see them as

50 *Stucco pier, Palace House A, depicting the warrior K'inich Janab Pakal (photograph after Maudslay, 1889-1902).*

captives, especially given the subject matter of the decorations around the East Court, just inside the doorway, but it seems more likely that they are ancestral portraits. Some appear to be women, and they are seated comfortably – not kneeling in the manner typically found in prisoner imagery.

House D

Although the date of House D is lost, there is evidence that it was roughly contemporaneous with the dedication of its "mirror image," House A; both structures effectively closed off the access and visibility of Houses E and C. With their construction, the Palace took on its familiar shape and dimensions. The theme of the stucco imagery on House D's piers is remarkably different from that of House A, despite their overall stylistic affinities. Many details are difficult to read, but the scenes depicted appear to be mythological, strongly conveying an atmosphere of primordial history. They may relate to episodes of the mythic story that happened in the aquatic realm, Matwiil, the place of dynastic origin that is mentioned time and time again in the epic stories inscribed within the temples of the Cross Group.

House A–D, spanning the northern side of the Palace, has now largely collapsed, but its main construction may also date to the reign of Pakal. The massive stairway leading up to its doorways suggests that it was a significant place where public rites and presentations occurred, and possibly the main access point for visitation to the Palace. Pakal's second son, K'inich K'an Joy Chitam, clearly had much to do with its later form and design, dedicating its refurbishment in 720, but inscription fragments from the building suggest that the later king modified an original construction from his father's reign, built in 654. Interestingly, small excavations in the area by Rúz revealed portions of a buried vaulted structure that could correspond to this previous construction, or to even earlier constructions.

Whatever the case, there is no doubt that most of the courts and galleries we see today in the Palace were conceived by Pakal and his architects within just a decade, and that these buildings remained the physical and political heart of Palenque even generations after his death. It is surely no accident that two major inscriptions of the Palace, dating to after his reign, name him as "He of the Five Platform Houses," referring to his five principal architectural constructions within the Palace – Houses A, C, D, E, and possibly an earlier House A–D.[7]

Family Relations and Succession

Sometime before 635, Pakal married a woman named Ix Tz'akbu Ajaw, but apart from two portraits we know nothing of her or her background (plate 11). Like many Maya queens, she may have been a princess of another kingdom who was brought to Palenque through a diplomatic arrangement with Pakal, or Pakal's mother. She bore at least three sons who would be at the center of Palenque's political history for the next few decades: two of them would rule as kings, while a third may have died too early to become ruler himself.

Pakal's later years are surprisingly quiet. Yet as he approached old age, the question of succession apparently became an issue of great importance. Pakal, himself, had assumed the throne in a troublesome era and perhaps even as an outsider from the main ruling line. Despite his power and influence in the region, his own questionable pedigree seems to have led to some difficulties about the proper succession of rule after his own death, and about the future of his sons.

The story can be partially reconstructed from the heavily damaged stucco sculpture in Temple XVIII, which was dedicated long after Pakal's lifetime, but contains a fascinating historical statement about Pakal and the evident concerns of the royal family. The scene once had several figures sitting or standing to the sides of a central throne (fig. 51). Although most of the portraits are entirely destroyed, luckily the scene caption and the names of the participants are largely intact. The date is 26 January 679 (9.12.6.12.0 5 Ajaw 18 K'ayab), just four years before Pakal's death, and it is reasonable to suppose that the central figure seated upon a jaguar pillow was Pakal himself. To his right are three names, each corresponding to the pre-accession names of his three sons; they would later be known as K'inich Kan Bahlam, K'inich K'an Joy Chitam, and Tiwol Chan Mat. At least one other unknown figure was shown to the left of the scene. The scene caption is in two parts, but one of the main verbal statements is *tz'akbuaj*, "(they) are

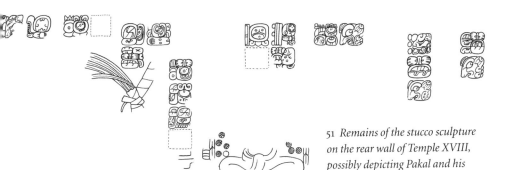

51 *Remains of the stucco sculpture on the rear wall of Temple XVIII, possibly depicting Pakal and his three sons.*

arranged in order." Another nearby statement records the spoken words: *tihmaj awohl atz'akbuij*, "you are satisfied (that) you put them in succession." The focus of these statements is *tz'akbu*, an important term in ancient Maya politics which refers to the ordering of royal succession. Here, the natural conclusion to draw is that the scene records the elderly Pakal's establishment of royal succession through his three sons, all of whom were well into adulthood or even middle age by this time. If the supposition is true, the Temple XVIII stucco is a remarkable document about the working of Maya politics, and reveals how delicate the situation for Pakal may have been, as he continued to live through the repercussions of his own unusual assumption of power over 60 years earlier.

Consolidation of the Nobility

During Pakal's early reign, as the king's court seemingly grew and expanded in power, several nobles become increasingly visible in Palenque's written record. The texts tell us little about their roles in Palenque's overall power structure, but their prominence in many records suggests that they wielded some political authority of their own. Some may also have been important subordinate rulers of smaller secondary sites near Palenque's center.

One prominent and early nobleman known as Aj Sul assumed the position of a *Yajawk'ahk'* ("Lord of Fire") – probably a military office of some sort – in 662 (9.11.10.5.14). Aj Sul had already been an important member of Pakal's court, for he was cited as a participant in the dedication of the *subterraneos* (the passages below House E) in 654, in the company of a middle-aged Pakal. At that time Aj Sul carried the title *Ajk'uhuun*, a common label among priests and nobles meaning "one who venerates" or simply "worshipper." His transformation into a Yajawk'ahk' warrior came on the heels of Palenque's victories against Santa Elena and Pomoná in 659, when presumably militaristic duties gained new prominence within the administrative duties of the palace. One gets the impression that Aj Sul was a trusted figure in Pakal's inner circle, active in steering Palenque in its new role as a regional power.

Several small archaeological sites near Palenque were probably the residences of subordinate elites who, like Aj Sul and a handful of other nobles, had direct political and maybe even family ties to Pakal's royal court. The king's claim to regional power is shown in the fragmentary tablets from Miraflores, a small and unexcavated site located some 15 kilometers (9 miles) west-northwest of Palenque along the ridge of Cerro Don Juan. Most of these tablets were taken from the site by looters in the 1950s and 1960s, but fortunately photographs were taken of some of the stones before they were looted.[8] One shows a standing figure named Chak Chan, who was a prominent junior lord or *sajal* under K'inich Janab Pakal. A second Miraflores stone names another nobleman with the same *sajal* title (fig. 52). The use of the title *sajal* indicates that Chak Chan and his fellow court member were subservient rulers of Miraflores, shown on the tablets as allies and vassals of the great king. Another subsidiary community was Xupá, located on the opposite eastern side of Palenque's domain. Today, it is a moderate and little investigated ruin, with sculpted fragments also in the Palenque mode. Xupá's location in the fertile Chancalá Valley suggests that it was used to control and administer the region's important agricultural productivity.

This wider regional perspective on the Palenque polity correlates with archaeological investigations beyond the site center. Pakal's long and transformative reign corresponds more or less with the Otolum phase in the local ceramic chronology, when we see a dramatic rise in population density and overall settlement around Palenque. Recent survey work in the surrounding region indicates that by the middle of the 7th century Palenque was becoming far less insular than it had been during the preceding Motiepa phase, with many small nucleated settlements growing up in the surrounding countryside, although they were tied closely to the central Palenque zone.

The pattern agrees strikingly well with the historical record, reiterating that the Palenque of Pakal's era was the focal point in the consolidation of a powerful regional polity spreading eastward and westward along the sierra. It is difficult to know just what specific social and political forces shaped these changes, but they established a pattern of dense human occupation on the nearby landscape that would continue and expand throughout the 8th century, and up to the very collapse of the kingdom.

The story of Pakal that we have tried to piece together here leaves many questions unanswered. What circumstances, for example, led to his install-ment as king when he was 12 years old, with parents who had not themselves been rulers of Palenque? Was the court of distant Calakmul a key player in establishing his authority, as part of its own expansive political ambitions? Pakal was hardly a very influential king before the death of his mother, but by the middle of the 7th century he began to emerge as a powerful individ-ual, and Palenque itself rapidly emerged as the dominant political, religious and cultural center of the area, bent on war and establishing its presence on a large regional stage. With its rapid rise, Pakal and Palenque no doubt caught the wary attention of its more established neighbors Toniná, Piedras Negras, and Yaxchilan, and their often strained relations would prove important over the next few generations. As we will show in later chapters, the final century of Palenque's story follows a course of political and economic conditions established and innovated by K'inich Janab Pakal, the most celebrated king in Maya history.

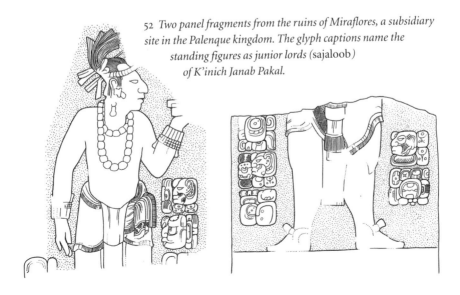

52 *Two panel fragments from the ruins of Miraflores, a subsidiary site in the Palenque kingdom. The glyph captions name the standing figures as junior lords* (sajaloob) *of K'inich Janab Pakal.*

CHAPTER SEVEN

The House of Resurrection

On the day 8 Ok, the third of the month K'anasiiy, the white headband was
fastened upon the head of K'inich Kan Bahlam, The Holy Baakal Lord.
He then offered devotion at the Nine Works House, (which is) the name
of the tomb of K'inich Janab Pakal, the Holy Baakal Lord.

CLOSING PASSAGE ON THE INSCRIBED TABLETS FROM
THE TEMPLE OF THE INSCRIPTIONS

Looming over the main plaza of Palenque is the Temple of the
Inscriptions, perhaps the most famous funerary temple of all Maya
civilization (plate 20). Its renown must have been considerable during the
Late Classic era, since it was the burial structure and temple dedicated to the
life and legacy of K'inich Janab Pakal, the greatest of all Palenque kings.
Certainly throughout the later years of Palenque's ancient history, Pakal's
presence was keenly felt through the monumentality of this "house," dwarf-
ing nearly all of the other freestanding temples in the core of the city.
And like many other large ancient Maya pyramids, the Temple of the
Inscriptions was probably conceived as a man-made mountain, constructed
to contain the house of a deceased but venerated ancestor. To this day, many
traditional Maya peoples see mountains as the dwelling places of their
ancestors, the "mothers-and-fathers," who exert a profound spiritual influence over the lives of the descendants who hold them in high esteem.[1]

The temple's role as a personal memorial to a individual king was not
always clear, but it came into focus many years later in 1952, when Ruz
Lhuillier discovered the elaborate chamber beneath the pyramid.[2] After
decades of study and debate, scientists and curious visitors can now look

upon the Temple of the Inscriptions as a vivid testament to a remarkable man, commemorating through symbol and text his influential life and his transition from divine king to a celestial ancestor. In this chapter we study the temple as a conceptual form whose strong message of immortality drew upon some of the most powerful and esoteric ideas of Classic Maya religion and its political ideology, especially with regard to elaborate concepts of death and the afterlife.

The Upper Temple and its Tablets

The Temple of the Inscriptions rests upon a high substructure built in front of a natural hill, on the south side of Palenque's principal plaza. The volume of the pyramid itself is not quite as massive as it appears to be from the front: at the back the terraces clearly rest on the bedrock face of a large hill, much like other major pyramids at Palenque such as the Temples of the Cross, Foliated Cross and Temple XX (plates 21–24). (Palenque's architects often amplified already existing sacred hills with terraces and steps, rather than construct true artificial mountains.) The upper temple of the pyramid consists of a long, well-preserved frontal gallery and a rear central chamber, where the entrance to the descending staircase that leads to the tomb was found. Three large hieroglyphic tablets dominate these rooms. They are attached to the back walls and "look out" over Palenque's main plaza and further toward the plains of Tabasco. The text panels present a single continuous inscription that is among the longest known from any Maya site (fig. 53). Partly because of this, the themes presented in the inscription are unusual, interweaving Palenque's dynastic history with highly specific descriptions of rites associated with the three patron gods of Palenque – the Palenque Triad – who are discussed in more detail in the next chapter.

The overall structure of the text revolves around the history of royal ritual covering eight K'atuns, from 514 (9.4.0.0.0) to 672 (9.12.0.0.0). Each ruler celebrated their K'atun stations through offerings to the Triad gods, decorating their effigies with adornments and ritual clothing – a Classic Maya version of the "dressing of the saints" ceremonies seen in Catholic churches to this day. Such long-term panoramic history anticipates the work of much later Maya historians who composed the famous *Books of*

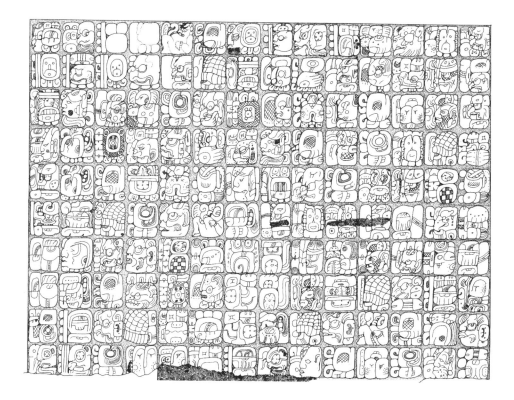

53 *The middle of the three tablets on the interior walls of the Temple of the Inscriptions. Taken together, they record 158 years of royal rites devoted to the gods, and relate them to the mythical history of Palenque with particular attention to the glory of the deceased Pakal below, in his tomb.*

Chilam Balam during the early colonial period in Yucatán, relating both past history and future prognostication using the very same 20-year units.[3] Here at Palenque, the narrative involving gods and calendar rituals is juxtaposed with the realities of politics and warfare, especially the events surrounding Palenque's conquest by Calakmul in 599. The inscription makes it very clear that the war caused a profound disruption in the routine of paying proper homage to the Triad gods. With the accession of K'inich Janab Pakal, however, we see a dramatic change in the story: the records of the K'atun rituals become more elaborate and detailed, focusing on Pakal's own offerings and ceremonies on 9.11.0.0.0 and 9.12.0.0.0, when Pakal's reign was at its apogee. Clearly we have an intentional comparison of past and "present," serving to highlight the king's restoration of political and religious order to Palenque after a period of tremendous turmoil.

There is an astonishing shift in the narrative's time-frame on the third tablet. The history here highlights the accession of the boy-king Pakal, connecting it to the inauguration of a remote deity who "became a lord" 1,247,654 years beforehand. Maya priests were greatly interested in marking similar associations between ancient gods and living kings and sometimes employed even greater spans in time to do so. Pakal's apparent "timelessness" is emphasized yet further in the Inscriptions tablet with the record of an anniversary of his accession 4,000 years in the future.

The story on the tablets also emphasizes real-world history, especially Pakal's political maneuverings with Santa Elena, a small kingdom to the east with whom Palenque had bellicose relations for years. One culminating event of the entire narrative is the "arrival" at Palenque (*huli Lakamha'*) of the Santa Elena ruler Nuun Ujol Chaak in 659 – perhaps a statement of military victory or political dominance over the Calakmul ally. The inscription concludes with a record of the death of Pakal's wife, Ix Tz'akbu Ajaw, in 672, followed by the death of Pakal himself in 683. The final passage records the accession to office of his eldest son, K'inich Kan Bahlam, who, in closing, "offers devotion to the B'olon Eht Naah, (which is) the name of the tomb of K'inich Janab Pakal."

The remarkable three-part inscription therefore serves as an elaborate dedication text for Pakal's tomb, emphasizing the deceased king's pivotal role in Palenque's history as the great restorer, overseeing Palenque's emergence as a major political force in the western Maya area. We are told that his actions as caretaker and sacrificer to the Triad deities were pivotal factors in defining his role as a great king, and the same theme of religious devotion by kings would continue and even be expanded on by Pakal's son, as we will see in the next chapter.

The outside of the Temple of the Inscriptions, much like the outer galleries of the Palace, was richly decorated in colorful painted stucco reliefs. Of the six piers of the temple (A and F) the two outermost bore large text panels, while the inner four each displayed standing figures framed by skybands (plate 4). The four people, three men and one woman, occupy four key cosmological locations in the heavens, perhaps the four solstice points near the horizon. Although damaged, two of the figures can be identified by their name-headdresses as K'an Joy Chitam (Pier B) and Kan Bahlam (Pier E). They may well be distant ancestors of Pakal, as others have suggested, but it is also possible that they are his sons, who would each rule as important Palenque kings in their own right (see Chapters 8 and 9). The woman and man on the innermost piers, flanking the central doorway, are too damaged to be identified, but they may be images of Pakal's parents, or perhaps even Pakal and his wife, Ix Tz'akbu Ajaw. All four people are shown cradling the image of a deity, "Infant K'awiil" (Unen K'awiil), better known to us as GII of the Palenque Triad. The images are barely visible in the effaced stucco, but the god is easily identifiable by its leg that transforms into a large serpent with a gaping mouth. We will learn more of this god in the next chapter: Unen K'awiil was an important symbol of royal power, re-birth, and regeneration, all of which were important for a funerary pyramid. It is likely that the outer text panels on Piers A and F would have discussed the significance of the standing figures and Unen K'awiil, but their continuous inscription – once nearly two hundred glyphs long – is nearly completely gone.

Dating the Temple

Pakal's death in 683 provides an obvious *terminus post quem* for dating the Temple of the Inscriptions as a funerary building, assuming its official dedication took place after the fact. His eldest son K'inich Kan Bahlam came to the throne in 684, and soon oversaw the final touches being made on his father's tomb and pyramid. The last passage of the inscription in the upper tablets states that K'inich Kan Bahlam was the "caretaker" for the tomb on his inauguration day. The son's "last word" in the tablets, and his conspicuous presence in the narrative presented on the temple's exterior, leads us to wonder if K'inich Kan Bahlam finally enjoyed the chance to emerge from under his father's long-lasting shadow.

The precise dating of the Temple of the Inscriptions within the early years of K'inich Kan Bahlam's reign has presented a few difficulties for archaeologists and epigraphers. Two closely placed dates of 688 and 690 have been suggested as the true dedication date of the temple, recorded on the horizontal band of glyphs that ran above all the doorways of the building.[4] These dates seem very precise within the overall understanding

54 *Four key glyphs from the stucco decoration on the Temple of the Inscriptions, collected by Juan Galindo in 1831.*

of ancient Palenque and its architecture, but more evidence might narrow the possibilities down even further. In other Palenque temples we find that the formal dedication statement was customarily written on the left-most outer pier, but on the Temple of the Inscriptions only a handful of glyphs now remain on Pier A, including the day sign "Kawak." Remarkably, the records of one early explorer might provide a telltale clue: some decades ago, Heinrich Berlin came across the 1834 report published in London by Juan Galindo, which contained illustrations of four stucco glyphs Galindo says he removed from the "Estudio" – the Temple of the Inscriptions – and took to Europe (fig. 54).⁵ Two of these glyphs are obviously portions of the opening Initial Series date, "9 Bak'tuns" and "12 K'atuns." Galindo's most telling clue is a beautiful rendition of the glyph we call "G9," the station in the cycle of nine days that routinely accompanies Initial Series dates. The remains of the horizontal inscription date above the doors points to a dedication sometime within the short span between 16 December 688 and 16 August 690. As Berlin brilliantly noted, only one date will accommodate the strands of evidence:

9.12.18.4.19   11 Kawak 17 Yaxkin   G9   6 July 690

This placement looks to be the best candidate for the opening Initial Series on Pier A, and, given the pattern seen on other Palenque temples, is probably the dedicatory date for the Temple of the Inscriptions: seven years after Pakal's death.

The Tomb and Sarcophagus

The crypt within the Temple of the Inscriptions is reached by a long stairway that descends to ground level from the temple above, turning 180 degrees halfway through its descent (fig. 55). The careful construction of the steps and the vaulted passageway suggest that the architects intended the tomb to be accessible after the chamber itself was sealed. At some point in antiquity, maybe soon after Pakal's demise, the stairway was filled with compact dirt and stones, and then covered by a huge slab in the upper temple's floor. Before the filling of the stairway, five young people were sacrificed and dismembered, and their remains left in a masonry box built outside the chamber's outer door, near various other offerings. Thirteen centuries later, the tomb's ambitious sealing process was reversed with Alberto Ruz's equally arduous excavation program.

When Ruz's team slowly dug their way down the stairway, they made note of a small stone-lined tube built along the top of the steps, and against the left-hand wall. When they eventually reached the endpoint of the steps they saw that the tube led into a triangular door in the wall which,

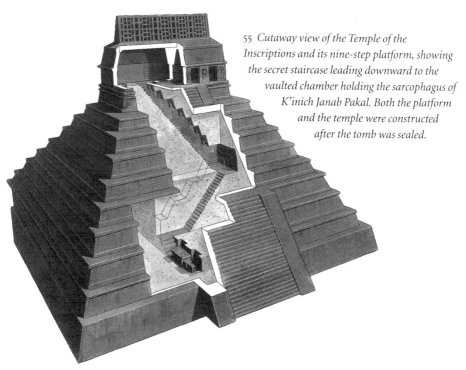

55 *Cutaway view of the Temple of the Inscriptions and its nine-step platform, showing the secret staircase leading downward to the vaulted chamber holding the sarcophagus of K'inich Janab Pakal. Both the platform and the temple were constructed after the tomb was sealed.*

when removed, revealed the stunning crypt. This unusual tube, like the one we described earlier in Temple XVIII-A (see Chapter 5), was a psychoduct meant to convey the spirit of the dead king to the world above. Within the tomb, Ruz traced the psychoduct into the sarcophagus where it was decorated with stucco, assuming the form of a snake's body. In Maya art, images of serpents are ubiquitous and they serve as animated conduits between the world of gods, ancestors, and the world of the living. Pakal's psychoduct is a remarkable replication of this idea in an architectural setting. Curiously, no feature quite like it has ever been seen outside of Palenque.

Like Howard Carter at Tutankhamun's tomb three decades earlier, Ruz finally peered into the tomb chamber in 1952, and was stunned by the expanse and beauty of the massive carved stone slab that greeted him (plates 26 and 27). Resting atop the stone were greenstone celts and mosaic masks, all that remained of an elaborate ceremonial belt placed over the center of the slab, near the king's portrait and the cruciform motif behind him.

The sarcophagus of Pakal is possibly the most famous of all Maya monuments, presenting in text and image a compelling story of Pakal's royal ancestry and of his own divine resurrection after death. Unique in its design and presentation, the sarcophagus body and lid convey a visual and textual metaphor of the king as the rising sun, possibly reborn at winter solstice. The sides of the coffin are also richly carved, bearing portraits of Pakal's ancestors emerging from the earth as animated fruit trees. Studied as a whole, the sarcophagus can be seen as a carefully composed model of the cosmos, with the sky (the lid) placed above the earth and its verdant realm (the coffin). Pakal's body was placed in the interior as a cosmic centerpiece, primed for resurrection into the world of his ancestors.

At the center of the ornate lid is the reclining human figure of K'inich Janab Pakal, surrounded by a complex assortment of cosmological imagery. A celestial band, or sky-band, frames the entire scene and indicates what takes place in the heavens. Pakal's awkwardly posed figure rests atop a bowl decorated with the *k'in*, "sun" sign, which in turn forms the forehead of a grimacing skull. From the bowl and behind Pakal's midsection rises a cross-shaped tree, draped with an animated jade necklace, upon which a great supernatural bird is perched. The lower section of the lid also displays the symmetrical jaws of a large serpent or centipede. Scattered throughout the background of the image are medallions and circlets that represent jade and preciousness, marking the scene as one of great sacredness.

Since the discovery many different interpretations have been put forward, but it is important to remember that when Ruz opened the tomb, no archaeologist believed that Maya art and inscriptions related historical information, and the identity of the human figure was a complete mystery. Nevertheless, even half a century ago it was clear to Ruz and others that the resurrection of the dead was the theme of the carving. Today, advances in the study of the glyphs and of Maya iconography have advanced to the point where we can confidently interpret the lid's image in significant detail.

As we saw in Chapter 4, upon its initial discovery, it was not at all obvious that the chamber was even a royal tomb. For a very short time Ruz considered the massive carved stone monument within to be a ceremonial "altar," with its top showing a scene displaying a scene of human sacrifice: only later that same year did Ruz lift the lid to reveal the cavity of the sarcophagus beneath. Modifying his interpretations soon thereafter, Ruz wrote:

> Seeing that it is a funerary crypt, and not a ceremonial space, the interpretation of the lid's scene should be modified. It should not be considered an expression of the idea that life is based on human sacrifice, but rather that life (symbolized by the cross motif, a tree or maize) continues after death, and that the man, upon falling into the jaws of the earth monster (symbol of death) survives as an incorporation of vegetal life. The young man represented there may be the figure of the interred individual, personifying human destiny.[6]

Following this initial interpretation, nearly all scholars followed Ruz's suggestion that the reclining figure on the lid was falling into the jaws of the earth or the Underworld, as the setting sun. The large mandibles and skeletal head beneath the *k'in* or sun motif were seen as markings of an entrance to the earth, and of the sun in its transition into death.

The interpretation of the image as Pakal's descent into the earth remains widely popular today, but, based on new readings of several motifs, it could be that the dead king is rising or emerging *out of* the earth. This new interpretation is strongly indicated by the solar bowl, which serves in the hieroglyphic script as the word *el*, meaning "exit, rise" or sometimes "burn," and is used mostly in the word for "east," *el-k'in*, "exiting sun."[7] It thus stands to reason that Pakal's placement in the solar bowl is an explicit reference to the east, indicating an upward movement for Pakal *out of the earth* with the sun as it rises. Such an interpretation gains in credibility when one considers that in Maya iconography the open skeletal maw is often shown as a place of cosmic emergence, and *not* as an entrance. Like their fleshed snake counterparts, the skeletal maw often appears as a double-headed "serpent" or centipede from which deities emerge, probably as a visual metaphor for birth and sacrifice.[8] On the sarcophagus, it is natural to see the maw working in the same way, as a transitional point of emergence from the earth and the underworld.

Pakal's strange posture also points to the idea of re-birth and resurrection. Elsewhere in Maya art we find a similar reclining position is reserved for the depiction of infants, or of deities shown as infants. Sometimes, as in the case of a reclining maize god, it is used to convey the idea of young, new corn (fig. 56). Elsewhere we also see infants reclining in bowls, evidently offered as child sacrifices. If we understand that the large vessel in which he reclines symbolizes the eastern sun, the image of Pakal as an infant maize god rising from the earth begins to make sense. The large grimacing skull beneath the bowl serves to represent an animate seed (like a skull, with its white bony exterior), further emphasizing the idea that this is a place of birth, growth, and creation.

56 *Reclining maize god as shown on a vase from Calakmul.*

The large cross that dominates the lid is an abstract tree, with three branches ending in animated blossoms shown as serpent-like heads. The flowers are decorated with rows of jade beads, and the tree trunk bears the divine face of lightning and resplendence, all indicating that it is made of precious stone. This cruciform tree is often thought to be a "world tree," but scholars are seldom clear just what they mean by this. To the Maya, and to other Mesoamerican peoples in the tropics, trees had very complex and important cosmological significance. Some suggest that the cross is a stylized ceiba tree (*Ceiba pentandra*, the kapok or silk cotton tree), the centerpiece of the schematic ideal of the Maya universe, and the animate flowers on the three branches of the tree-cross may have been based on the natural form of ceiba blossoms.[9] But the Classic Maya gave this tree-cross its own special name: the "Shiny Jeweled Tree." In the upper temple's text, the same tree is said to "sprout" on the great K'atun ending 9.11.0.0.0, which, as we have seen, was the historical turning point for Pakal's reign and for the whole kingdom of Palenque. One wonders if it was some figurative allusion to the riches of Pakal's court, as he expanded his political power and exerted his power in exacting tribute. Whatever the case, the terminology used by the Maya themselves suggests that we should turn away from the vague notion that it is simply a "world tree" as it more accurately embodies the specific notion of wealth and preciousness, resplendent as the rising sun.[10]

On the sarcophagus Pakal's identity is fused with the newborn sun as well as the youthful maize god, one of the most important figures of Maya creation mythology and religion. A striking parallel to the sarcophagus image appears on an Early Classic cache bowl probably from the Tikal region, where the head of the maize god (presumably the cob) rests within the *k'in* bowl (fig. 57). The cycle of new maize was in this way visually equated with the cycle of solar emergence from the earth – a connection that reveals a fundamental, unifying idea of natural process in Maya and Mesoamerican philosophy.

Looking at the sarcophagus lid anew, we can see that it presents a powerful scene of life-affirming re-birth, and not a scene of Pakal's death and descent into the Underworld, as has often been said. In this way the sarcophagus lid becomes a forceful statement of the divine nature of Maya rulers,

57 Maize cob in a bowl as depicted on an Early Classic cache vessel from the Tikal region.

and of the transformation they undergo as the figuratively sacrificed and re-born maize. K'inich Janab Pakal's own transformation was interwoven with the two basic and natural cycles of existence: the continuous reappearance of the sun each day and of maize each planting season.

The Sarcophagus Sides

Ten named ancestor portraits grace the exterior of the sarcophagus itself, an earthly space that continues to stress a theme of regeneration. Seven named individuals are shown emerging from the earth as fruit trees (three of the ten images are repetitions). On each narrow end of the sarcophagus are Pakal's mother and father, Ix Sak K'uk' and K'an Hix Mo'. The other ancestors singled out for reference are Ahkal Mo' Nahb, K'an Joy Chitam, Kan Bahlam, the queen Ix Yohl Ik'nal (depicted twice on opposite long sides) and Janab Pakal. Schele brilliantly showed that there is a remarkable pattern to the design of these ancestral portraits: the earliest ancestor, Ahkal Mo' Nahb, appears at the northern end of the west side, and to view the subsequent generations of ancestors the viewer (if looking from within the sealed tomb!) is forced to move back and forth from one side of the massive stone to the other. Schele also noted similar patterns and symmetries in the distribution of many of the costume elements, poses, and fruits of the arboreal ancestors.[11] Above the ancestral portraits we find the inscription that runs around the entire perimeter of the sarcophagus lid, providing some much needed explanation of the scene's meaning and significance.

The cramped quarters of the tomb chamber meant that no audience could ever see the sarcophagus and read its full imagery – the rich message was there for its own sake, to exist in the afterlife. Simon Martin has evocatively suggested that the imagery of ancestor-trees is closely tied to the

Patbu-iiy u-kuch(?)-il Ixiim	The burden of the maize (god) formed (so?):
Jo' Ka'an Jo te' Mak	(On) Five Kaban the Fifth of Mak
ochbih Ahkal Mo' Nahb	Ahkal Mo' Nahb I entered the path.
Wuk Ki' Chante' Kanasiiy	(On) Seven Kib the Fourth of K'anasiiy
ochbih K'an Joy Chitam	K'an Joy Chitam entered the path.
Bolon Manik Jote' Yaxk'in	(On) Nine Manik the Fifth of Yaxk'in
ochbih Ahkal Mo' Nahb	Ahkal Mo' Nahb II entered the path.
Wuk Ajaw Uxte' Uniiw	Six Ajaw the Third of Uniiw
u-chumtuun Kan Bahlam	Was the stone-seating of Kan Bahlam.
Buluch Muluk Chante' K'anasiiy	(On) Eleven Muluk the Fourth of K'anasiiy
ochbih Kan Bahlam K'uhul Baakal Ajaw	Kan Bahlam, the Divine Baakal Lord,
	entered the path.
Cha' Eb Ti' Chaksihoom	(On) Two Eb' the Edge of Chaksihoom
ochbih Ix Yohl Ik'nal	Lady Yohl Ik'nal entered the path.
Cha' Kimi Chanlajunte' Mol	(On) Two Kimi the Fourteenth of Mol
ochbih Ajen Yohl Mat K'uhul Baakal	Ajen Yohl Mat, the Divine Baakal Lord,
Ajaw	entered the path.
Ux Chuwen Chante' Wayhaab(?)	On Three Chuwen the Fourth of Wayhaab(?)
ochbih Janab Pakal K'uhul Baakal Ajaw	Janab Pakal, the Divine Baakal Lord,
	entered the path.
Chan Chikchan	(it is) Four Chikchan
Hun Ajaw Waxakte' K'anasiiy	One Ajaw the Eighth of K'anasiiy
u-chuumtuun Sak K'uk'	Is the stone-seating of Sak K'uk'.
Uxlajunte' Yaxsihoom	The Thirteenth of Yaxsihoom
ochbih K'an Hix Mo' K'uhul Baakal	K'an Hix Mo', the Divine Baakal Lord,
Ajaw	entered the path.
u-?-il K'an Hix Mo'	The seed(?) of K'an Hix Mo'
u-juntahn Ix Sak K'uk'	The precious one of Ix Zak K'uk'
Waxak Ajaw Uxlajunte' Sihyaj	(On) Eight Ajaw the Thirteenth of K'anjalaw
	he is born.
Wak Etz'nab Buluchte' Yaxsihoom	Six Etz'nab the Eleventh of Yaxsihoom
Chan-u-chumtuun i-ochbih	Four are the stone-seatings,
K'inich Janab Pakal	then K'inich Janab Pakal,
K'uhul Ajaw	the Divine Lord, entered the path.
u-tz'akb'u-ij u-chab'-ij-iiy	The ancestors of the ? Great Serpent arrange it,
u-mam ? ? to'? Noh(?) Chan	they oversee it.

interred body of K'inich Janab Pakal and his identity as the maize god.[12] In Martin's interpretation, the ancestors emerge from the earth that the deceased king inhabits and nourishes through his final sacrifice. Martin's analysis finds vivid support in the inscription around the lid's outer edge (fig. 58). The text of the sarcophagus runs above the figures of the ancestors, starting at the southeast corner and running counterclockwise. Not surprisingly, its theme is closely related to the imagery of floral regeneration of the dead. Opposite we present a new translation of the full text.

The repetitive-sounding text seems deceptively straightforward, but it is arranged in a highly unusual way that gives insights into Maya conceptions of ancestry and death. The dates and names can all be anchored historically within the dynasty, spanning nearly two centuries of history.[13] If we read it in light of the portraits directly below, we find a broad correlation between the phrase for death – "entering the path" – and the image of ancestors sprouting from the earth as fruit trees.

The most revealing phrase is the simple opening statement: "The burden (*kuch*) of the maize (god) formed so…". As a kind of preamble, it serves to orient the repetitive death records in a proper meaningful context. The underlying idea is that upon death the ancestors transform into the edible fruits and riches of earth – the burden of the maize god – embodied in this setting by K'inich Janab Pakal. Drawing upon a variety of Mesoamerican myths, Martin has rightly emphasized that the maize god encompassed much more than animated maize itself, but was the entity from which all fruits and sustenance originated. Maize god portraits in Maya art sometimes show him with a large bag of grain and riches, no doubt as more literal illustrations of the deity's *kuch*. With the sarcophagus, this idea is extended into the dimension of human life and death.

58 Opening passage of the hieroglyphic text that runs around the edge of the sarcophagus lid in K'inich Janab Pakal's tomb, below the Temple of the Inscriptions.

The likening of royal ancestors to fruiting trees may relate to the way the text records their deaths in such a repetitive way, as if the generations echoed the natural cycles of demise and growth. The static wording of the inscription ("so-and-so entered the path") reinforces the imagery because the process of growth is predicated on death and demise of earlier life. In this sense, the text and image of the sarcophagus present us with a reconciliation of mortality and immortality that reflects a strong Maya pattern of belief, and one that is almost universal in its history and human thought.[14]

The walls of the tomb were decorated with nine large human figures, sculpted in stucco and shown with ornate jewelry and feather regalia (plate 10). Each grasps in his or her hand a serpent staff topped by the head of K'awiil, the deity of royal power and ancestry that we have already encountered in the decoration of the upper temple. These again are Pakal's ancestors, named by their headdresses much as we see in the images on the sides of the sarcophagus itself. Among the portraits we can identify are Ahkal Mo' Nahb, Ix Yohl Ik'nal, and possibly the founder K'uk' Bahlam.[15] The images of these ancestors throughout the king's tomb were of course invisible to the nobility and populace of ancient Palenque, but there can be little question that the name of the great pyramid – The "Nine Works House" – evoked royal ancestry and dynasty, and Pakal's own intimate connection to these nine predecessors.

Bones of Contention

The skeleton of Pakal, resting for nearly 13 centuries in its crypt, still bore much of its jade finery, including wrist and ankle ornaments, a large collar composed of hundreds of beads, earspools, and a spectacular mosaic mask of his face (fig. 59, plate 25). Pakal also held two curious jade objects – a large spherical bead in his left hand, and a cube-shaped jade of similar size in his right hand. The meaning of these two jades remains elusive, and no similar examples are known in other Maya burials. In addition, two small jade figurines, including a small portrait of the deity who personified the spirit of trees and plants, accompanied the skeleton.

59 The remains of K'inich Janab Pakal as discovered inside the sarcophagus. Remains of the jade mosaic funerary mask can be seen to the right of the skull.

Red powdery cinnabar (mercury oxide) covered the bones and interior of the crypt – a practice that has parallels in many parts of the Maya world and beyond. The red color of the cinnabar held great meaning for the Maya, perhaps as a material representation or substitute for the blood of the living body. Interestingly, in Pakal's tomb and in many other burials, we see evidence that the cinnabar was applied not to the body soon after death, but rather to the surface of the bones themselves. If this was the case, it would of course tell us that the body of the king was allowed to decompose within the tomb, with a ritual "annointing" of the skeleton some time later. With its elaborate stairway, it is possible that the tomb was accessible for rituals of veneration for a considerable time after Pakal's death, although we suspect that the sealing and filling of the stairway took place in the reign of his son, K'inich Kan Bahlam.

When found, the skeleton presented archaeologists with the rare opportunity to study the bones of a Maya king, even if his precise identity was unknown in 1952. Physical anthropologists analyzed the bones in the tomb shortly after its discovery, and determined that the bones were that of a tall male who died between 40 and 50 years of age. The methods used to reach this conclusion were never made clear, and they came to be widely accepted by scholars until the historical identity and recorded lifespan of K'inich Janab Pakal was studied further in the early 1970s. As we have seen, the inscriptions tell us that Pakal was 80 years old on his death – nearly twice the age estimate provided by the physical skeletal analysis. The discrepancy is glaring, and it has been a topic of considerable hand-wringing and debate among archaeologists and historians for over three decades. Some have claimed that the scientific evidence clearly shows that Maya history was somehow manipulated, and that the records of an 80-year-old Pakal were an "exaggeration" with a propagandistic intent.[16]

More recent scientific analysis of the skeleton has gone far to resolve the issue, showing that the historical records of an elderly Pakal probably reflect historical reality. In 2003 a conference was convened to revisit the scientific study of Pakal's skeleton, and to see if written history and science could somehow be reconciled. The physical anthropologists and historians who contributed to the dialogue often expressed different opinions, but several concluded that the skeleton, despite its poor preservation, is entirely consistent with the remains of an elderly man of 80 years of age. As they note, it is extremely difficult to determine the exact age of an adult skeleton once it is about 50 years of age at death. That is, the bones of a healthy and well-cared for 80-year-old can look very much like the bones of a 50-year-old in moderate or average health.[17]

We can confidently say that K'inich Janab Pakal did die when he was 80, if only because the contemporaneous records of Maya history, anchored so firmly in the mechanisms of the Maya calendar, leave little doubt. His birth and death dates are immovable, and they come from inscriptions that were composed during his lifetime or soon thereafter. Despite what others have argued, we cannot believe that any Maya king could have manipulated the structure of contemporary history to exaggerate his own age. Pakal was notable for being 80 years old, and Maya historians at Palenque seem to have taken some pride in mentioning his advanced age whenever possible, especially using the title "the Five-score Year Lord."

The Red Queen and Adjacent Tombs

Palenque's architects evidently had to keep a watchful eye on the Temple of the Inscriptions. Structural weaknesses in the body of the pyramid called for new construction work several times during the Late Classic period, evidently meant to strengthen and support the outer terraces. The sequence of modifications is easily seen today near the wide lower steps of the temple, themselves a late addition to the original narrow staircase that once run up the entire pyramid. The remodeling may have been part of larger construction projects undertaken on a row of smaller temples to the west of the Inscriptions, on Temples XIII, XII-A, and XII (also known as the Temple of the Skull). Were they not adjacent to the Temple of the Inscriptions these buildings would be considered very impressive on their own. They were built up over the decades following Pakal's death, possibly as funerary structures for several of his relatives and descendants.

Temple XIII is the closest to Pakal's pyramid. In 1994, archaeologists Arnoldo González and Fanny López revealed the richest tomb found at Palenque since Pakal's own crypt was discovered by Ruz over four decades earlier.[18] They first exposed an elaborately constructed chamber with a front hallway and side rooms, all buried within the substructure of the temple. These may have once been rooms of an earlier building covered by the later pyramid above. Probing further behind the main wall, the excavators revealed a burial chamber with a large sarcophagus brightly colored in red, but otherwise undecorated. On either side of the coffin, lying close the wall of the chamber, were skeletons of two sacrificial victims – a boy of about 11 years of age to the west, and a woman of about 30 to the east. Once the lid of the sarcophagus was removed, the investigators looked upon a well-preserved skeleton of a middle-aged woman, covered in a massive number of jade beads, and shell decorations, and also colored with astonishing amounts of cinnabar – hence her common label, "the Red Queen" (plate 36).

Who was this important woman buried so close to Pakal's own funerary temple? One problem faced by the archaeologists who exposed the Red Queen was the surprising lack of any inscriptions in or near the tomb – no labels anywhere to indicate the woman's identity (presumably a text originally decorated the collapsed temple above the tomb). Of course, two women who were close to Pakal immediately spring to mind as possible names to link to the skeleton – his powerful mother, Ix Sak K'uk', and his prominently celebrated wife, Ix Tzkab'u Ajaw. Without textual evidence to provide a lead, scientific analysis of the DNA preserved in the woman's bones has just recently shown that she had no close genetic relationship to

Pakal, dismissing conclusively the possibility of her being Ix Sak K'uk'.[19] We are left to speculate, but with somewhat more confidence, that the Red Queen was Pakal's wife, who died a decade before her husband in 672.

Another important tomb was discovered in Temple XII (the Temple of the Skull) around the same time as the Red Queen was revealed. Smaller in size, it too contained a wealth of jade and other riches, including an heirloom jewel presented in 697 by the king of Pomoná, a neighboring kingdom to the east, near the Usumacinta River. The lack of inscriptions in Temple XII prevent us from knowing who was buried here, but it may well have been a Late Classic king of Palenque. There may still be other undiscovered tombs awaiting excavation under Temples XII and XII-A.[20]

K'inich Janab Pakal ruled Palenque for nearly 70 years, and if the message of his funerary pyramid could be reduced to one word it might be "timelessness." His long reign was one element that made him such an important and influential king, but we sense that a powerful persona must have been part of the equation as well. His charisma not only brought Palenque to the forefront of the ancient Maya world, but it also led to the creation of works that live on in the historical and cultural consciousness of the present day. In many ways, the rest of Palenque's story is little more than a playing out of Pakal's legacy, and a continuation of the political and ideological ideas he set in action. As we will now see, his sons and grandsons did much to shape Palenque's history, but in doing so they constantly hearkened back to the glories of their long-lived ancestor.

CHAPTER EIGHT

Gods and Rulers

*Palenque, broken chapels in the green
basement of a mount…*

ALLEN GINSBERG, *SIESTA IN XIBALBA*, 1956

Nestled against the base of the pointed hill known as El Mirador, on the eastern end of the city, the three beautiful temples of the so-called Cross Group were the most sacred buildings of Late Classic Palenque (plates 21–24). Dedicated on the same day in 692, they were built to honor and house the three great patron gods of the city, the Palenque Triad. The timing of their construction is telling: K'inich Janab Pakal had died a decade earlier, after which his eldest son K'inich Kan Bahlam had surely then faced the daunting task of securing the continuation of Palenque's political and economic fortunes. He quickly embraced ambitious projects in what must have been a strange "post-Pakal" world, turning much of his attention to the construction of the Cross Group temples soon after completing his father's funerary shrine in the Temple of the Inscriptions. Today, the well-preserved Cross Group offers a goldmine for the study of ancient Maya religious belief, with its integrated triadic design, rich symbolism, and lengthy hieroglyphic texts. They are arguably the most revealing temples from the entire ancient Maya world.

The atmospheric setting of the Cross Group complex, surrounded by mountains and streams, was no doubt intentional. The entire layout was an elegant expression of a sacred landscape, part natural and part man-made, where kings, nobles, and priests performed many of their most sacred duties and venerations. It seems to have been used for an extended period of time, and was continuously built upon since the days of K'inich Janab Pakal, if not earlier. Other features of the natural terrain added to the religious signifi-cance of this area: just to the south of the three temples a large spring issues directly from the nearby mountainside and becomes the Otolum River, the beautiful channeled stream that still courses through the heart of the site, falling as wide cascades below the ruins (fig. 60). The ancient inhabitants called this vital stream and its spring Lakamha' ("wide waters"); the name was extended to refer to Palenque's ceremonial center.

The Cross Group, named after its principal member, the Temple of the Cross, stood for decades as Palenque's ritual centerpiece. It was an architec-tural vision that conveyed a number of fundamental ideas about Maya religion, at least as formulated by Palenque's royalty and priesthood. The careful three-part plan and the remarkable inscribed tablets found within each temple communicate a multitude of complex ideas that are just

60 LEFT *The Otolum River with walled banks on its passage through the ruins.*

61 OPPOSITE *Plaster portrait head of K'inich Kan Bahlam, possibly from the architectural decorations of the Cross Group.*

beginning to be understood by scholars. Among the themes we find are the Triad's creation of the world order in mythic time, the significance of each god as a symbol of cosmic space and movement, and especially the ways in which these essential deities were seen as forebears of the Palenque kings themselves. Above all the temples were compelling statements about the ideology underlying Maya kingship, all centered on Pakal's son and successor, K'inich Kan Bahlam.

A New Generation

As the eldest of Pakal's three sons, K'inich Kan Bahlam (fig. 61) had for most of his adult life held the title of heir designate, *Baahch'ok* or "Principal Youth." Finally assuming the throne when he was 48 years old, the designation hardly seemed fitting. On 6 January 684, he was enthroned within House E of the Palace, in front of the old carved portrait of his father's own accession in the company of his grandmother.[1] Very few still living in the community at the time could have remembered the distant crowning of K'inich Janab Pakal nearly seven decades earlier, and the festivities and ceremonies surrounding the installation of the new king must have been a special occasion indeed.

K'inich Kan Bahlam quickly set to work on various projects, and had an ambitious vision of leaving his own mark on the city. One priority was the final construction phases and elaboration on his father's funerary structure, the Temple of the Inscriptions. As we saw in the previous chapter, this was probably dedicated on or near the winter solstice of 688: the four years after Pakal's death gave ample time to construct the pyramid over the tomb. It is possible that the Inscriptions pyramid had already been built before Pakal's death, but we know for certain that Kan Bahlam oversaw the carving of the interior tablets and the outer decorations on the temple's exterior, where his name was displayed.

In the midst of this project the new king also directed attention to the brewing political and military situations that had deteriorated during the final years of his father's long reign. In September 687, Palenque's armies defeated Toniná, the major kingdom located in the mountains to the south in what is now the Ocosingo Valley.[2] Toniná's king was captured and probably killed, and a new ruler named K'inich Baaknal Chaak took office in 688. This was the first in a series of wars and entanglements between these two great western cities. We also know that K'inich Kan Bahlam was at this time looking to spread Palenque's power eastward, at least as far as the important but little-known site of Morál-Reforma. On a monument from the site known as Stela 4, Simon Martin has discovered the remarkable record of one local lord's shifting alliances.[3] "Hawk Skull," as we might tentatively call him, had assumed office as a local king of Morál-Reforma in 661. Just a year later the written history on the stela tells us of his "second crowning" before the king of Calakmul, indicating Hawk Skull's subordination to the great city that was apparently still bent on exerting influence in the Tabasco plains. However, in 690 the very same inscription tells us that Hawk Skull had a "third crowning," this time as a vassal of K'inich Kan Bahlam of Palenque. We can discern from this that K'inich Kan Bahlam, evidently strengthened by his defeat of Toniná's king in 687, was able to extend his political domain much further eastward, past the kingdom of Pomoná and toward the territories of Palenque's long-time enemy, Calakmul.

As these political developments unfolded and the Temple of the Inscriptions neared completion, K'inich Kan Bahlam set his architects on a new and ambitious project to build the three temples of the Cross Group. He chose a sacred area of Palenque located on a terrace just to the east of the Otolum stream, to the north of at least two already existing funerary buildings, Temples XVIII-A and XX. Earlier temples probably stood here, today still buried beneath the new plaza that was leveled for the foundation of the Cross Group. As we will now see, these temples are three jewels of Maya architecture, and today they still stand as among the most powerful expressions of ancient American religion.

The Palenque Triad

To begin to understand the significance of the Cross Group temples, we first have to explain a few essential facts and theories about the set of gods known as the Palenque Triad (fig. 62). The Triad were the focus of much of the religious expression in ancient Palenque, serving collectively, it seems, as the local patrons of the royal dynasty (as individual deities, however, the members of the Triad find expression in many other Maya kingdoms). Their existence was first revealed by the great Mayanist Heinrich Berlin in 1963, who, not knowing how to read their names, gave them the somewhat awkward designations God I (GI), God II (GII) and God III (GIII).[4] We still commonly refer to these deities by their abbreviated labels (as they will be cited in this book), even though we now have a better idea of what the ancient Maya named them, and what they meant as important cosmological entities. The three gods were hierarchically arranged from most-to-least prominent, and each had special meanings and significances within Palenque's own vision of ancient Maya cosmology. What follows is a summary of what we know about the individual Triad gods, which is expanded on later when we closely examine the symbols and meanings of their temples:

GI. His ancient name remains obscure, but we do know that GI was the chief member of the Triad, the first to be born at the mythical realm of Matwiil on 21 October 2360 BC. His shrine was the Temple of the Cross, the highest and most dominant of the three buildings. GI was an aquatic deity with strong solar associations, symbolizing some sort of "ocean sun" associated with the east and with its rising movement out of the primordial sea. He is an old deity known from early Maya religion, but his birth as a Triad member seems to emphasize his resurrection into a new and localized religious order at Palenque.[5] Near the time of Maya creation, GI is said to have "descended from the sky" and been housed within a northern temple known as

62 *Names of the three Palenque Triad gods: GI, GII (Unen K'awiil), and GIII.*

"Six ? Heaven." Later this would become the explicit conceptual model for the Temple of the Cross.

GII. Named Unen K'awiil, "Infant K'awiil," GII was housed in the Temple of the Foliated Cross, the middle-sized shrine of the Cross Group.[6] He was the youngest of the three members of the Triad, born on 8 November 2360 BC, even though he is always named and depicted as the middle member of the three gods. GII is always shown as the infant manifestation of the ubiquitous god K'awiil, who was the deity of lightning and, more abstractly, a manifestation of royal power and agricultural growth. Agriculture and sustenance seem to be the principal themes of his temple. One of his titles, still poorly understood, was "Young Lord of the Five Heavenly Houses(?)."

GIII. The third member was a specific aspect of K'inich Ajaw, the sun god, born 14 days before Unen K'awiil on 25 October 2360 BC. His shrine is the Temple of the Sun, the smallest but best preserved of the three, as he is the most junior member of the Triad. GIII remains an enigma in many ways, but as we will soon see from the symbolism of his temple, there is good reason to think that he was the warrior sun, which is sometimes depicted in Maya art, and tied closely to the Underworld.

Other triadic groups of deities appear in records at other Maya kingdoms, such as Tikal and Naranjo, but the individual members vary from place to place.[7] One might imagine that each major Maya kingdom had their own particular arrangement of a GI, GII, and GIII, and that we simply do not see the evidence as clearly as at Palenque: perhaps, but it seems to us that the triadic gods held an especially important place in Palenque's history and religion. This can be best seen in quickly revisiting the Temple of the Inscriptions, where the three tablets recount the histories of the K'atun rituals celebrated from Palenque's early days. The protagonists throughout that lengthy narrative are not so much the kings, but rather GI, GII, and GIII, who receive proper offerings and are "dressed" by the rulers at each turn of the K'atun. It was the rulers' duty to give them ornaments and ritual clothing, possibly in acts of ceremonial dressing of clay or wooden effigies.

This caretaking aspect of veneration was keenly important to the Maya, signaled by the way the Triad gods are called the "cherished ones" of the king throughout the Cross Group texts. According to such poetic language, the gods were to the king as children were to their mothers, and they were dressed and fed accordingly. The dressing rituals described in the Palenque texts are startlingly reminiscent of rituals in modern Mesoamerican communities, where great effort is spent to dress the images of Catholic saints in native ceremonial *huipiles* and necklaces of gold coins.[8] No full-form effigies of the Palenque Triad gods have survived, but it is reasonable to suppose that elaborate ceramic or wooden statues once stood in the inner shrines of the Cross Group temples, as well as in earlier ritual buildings devoted to the three deities.[9]

As we saw in the last chapter, earlier written sources indicate that when Palenque's own political fortunes were not good, as just before Pakal's birth at the end of the 6th century, it is the Triad who suffers – they are "thrown down" and not given proper care and attention. K'inich Janab Pakal's own history was written as a political and religious renaissance, with the Triad rituals reinstated in their proper way. It is likely that when K'inich Kan Bahlam began his ambitious plans to build the three temples to the Triad, he was quite conscious of Palenque's own defeats and backslides in the previous century. He was determined to make houses for the Triad that were more opulent and impressive than any ever seen before. For at Palenque, more than we see at any other site, the Triad gods served as a metaphor for the trials and triumphs of the kingdom as a whole.

Symbolism of the Cross Group Temples

As shown in our earlier analysis of the symbolism within Pakal's tomb, the symbols of ancient Maya religion can often appear infinitely complex to the modern eye. There is a conscious and almost intentional "otherworldliness" to Maya religious art, and our understanding is hampered by the limited sources available with which to work. There were, we know, scores of gods and mythical characters, many of whom we can visually recognize, and story elements that we see repeated in occasional vase paintings or temple walls. However, often we have little idea of who the gods really are or what significance was given to the myths in which they participated. We lack any written canon of texts for untangling Classic Maya religion, which would allow close access to the intricacies of religious practice and esoteric knowledge. Probably no such overarching "Bible" existed, given the variations that can be discerned in the ways gods and myths were interwoven with local political history. The famous *Popol Vuh* epic of later K'iche Maya history might appear to be the answer for interpreting much ancient Maya iconography, but in fact there are only occasional or distant strands to connect the great document and the cosmology and mythology recorded at places such as Copán, Tikal, and Palenque.[10]

In fact, the only lengthy written narrative of Classic Maya mythology comes from the set of the three tablets set in the temples of Palenque's Cross Group. Not only are the three temples themselves still standing for the most part, but the carved decorations in stucco and stone offer modern viewers a rich and compelling vision of Maya history, cosmology and the relations of gods to the divine kings of Classic Palenque.[11]

Before we look at the three temples in detail, it is key to orient them with regard to their immediate natural surroundings. As we have mentioned briefly, Palenque's topography is dominated in its eastern side by the tall and pointed hill known today as El Mirador, "the Lookout." The modern label may indicate something of its original importance, as at its very top there rests a large ruined structure, from which anyone would have been able to look over the myriad buildings of Palenque's center, and out over the coastal plains to the north. In ancient times this sacred mountain was called *Yemal K'uk' Lakam Witz*, "big hill of the descending quetzal," and at its base Palenque kings, including K'inich Kan Bahlam, chose to build many of their most important religious buildings. On the southern end of this elongated terrace, behind Temple XIX, the spring of the Otolum stream emerges out of the mountainside. The Otolum, or what the ancient Maya called Lakamha', is the channeled watercourse that runs northward through Palenque's center even today, falling down the cascades toward the plain below. The building atop the Temple of the Cross pyramid was intentionally oriented so as to face directly toward the Otolum spring.[12]

All three temples of the Cross Group were dedicated on the same day, 10 January 692, when, according to inscriptions gracing the temples, the three patron gods of the Palenque dynasty were "housed" in their respective shrines. The dedication was timed to coincide with the upcoming arrival of the great Period Ending in the Maya calendar, 9.13.0.0.0 – that is, the completion of the thirteenth K'atun. This was an event of cosmic proportions, taking place on 18 March of that year. K'atun endings occurred roughly every 20 years, and their celebration involved what the glyphs describe as the "seating of the stone." This was the first in a series of 20 stones that were used in some way to mark the passage of time, and in later years the word *tuun* would come to mean simply "year." The 13th K'atun ending was extremely special in its own right, given the sacred nature of the number 13 in Maya numerology. In fact, one can perhaps imagine the anticipation felt by priests and rulers in the Palenque court as the great day approached – one whose import had not been experienced for generations. The ruler K'inich Kan Bahlam, long living in the shadow of his great father, no doubt wanted to leave his mark on the kingdom through the elaborate dedication of new temples devoted to the three patron gods of the kingdom.

A modest square platform in the very center of the Cross Group plaza symbolizes the importance of the sacred calendar in the greater design and conception of the temples (plate 22). This small construction is the focal point of the Cross Group, and in some ways it might rightly be considered the most important building of the entire complex. The square surface is less than a meter high, and has steps on its four sides. The platform is a small example of what archaeologists call a "radial pyramid" – a raised surface without a temple or structure on its top, and is designed to replicate the four-sided structure of the world. Large examples of such platforms appear at Tikal and Chichén Itzá, and at many ruins there is strong evidence that they were closely connected to K'atun endings and other calendar stations. Simpler radial platforms were perhaps once foundations for the very tall wooden poles employed in ritual dances such as the "volador" ceremony, and there is some evidence from the inscribed tablets to suggest this was the case here in the Cross Group. What we can say with confidence is that this platform was the locus of rituals taking place on 9.13.0.0.0. Its presence in the Cross Group tells us that the three temples were designed and dedicated very much with the calendar station in mind, if not for the explicit purpose of properly housing the gods in anticipation of the event.

Each temple was richly decorated in plaster and only small sections survive, but this was especially visible on the Temple of the Sun. Most of the discernible symbolism comes from inside, where in the large vaulted galleries of each temple we find a small miniature "house" or sanctuary, also with its own rich décor. Inside these inner shrines were the large carved tablets that have attracted the attention of Palenque's earliest explorers. Each tablet is very similar in layout and design, with a central icon and standing figures at each side.

The temples of the Cross Group together represent a tri-partite conception of world space and of royal power. A god of the Triad presides over each of these fundamental categories of cosmology and existence, although none are explicitly represented in the tablets. Rather, we find in each composition a central icon that embodies many of the meanings and symbols associated with each deity. Beginning with the Temple of the Cross and following the rigid hierarchical structure of the three temples, we move progressively downward in a clockwise fashion, pivoting around the K'atun platform at the center. The Temple of the Cross, as we will see, is the sky temple associated with solar re-birth and ancestral authority of rulership. The Temple of the Foliated Cross represents a middle space where maize agriculture and water predominate, symbolizing the procreative powers of the king. The small Temple of the Sun is, in turn, an explicit depiction of a cave within the earth, housing the solar deity associated with warfare and military authority. In the brilliant design of the three temples, K'inich Kan Bahlam set forth a vivid and remarkable statement about basic cosmology (sky, water, cave) and how these regions each symbolized vital aspects of his own political authority (ancestors, agriculture, warfare).[13] These were the three overarching processes and activities that defined cosmological order and royal duty for Palenque kings. The juxtaposition would seem to suggest that, just as the sun would rise in the sky and maize would grow from water, so too warfare would drive the fate of kings and people. Palenque's history is probably a good testament to the power of such a statement.

In each tablet we see a remarkable double portrait of K'inich Kan Bahlam, once as a child of six in AD 641, and later as a new king of 48 in 684. As child and as adult he venerates the central symbols of each tablet, associating his own fate and royal duty to their respective themes. The meaning of these images can only be understood in light of the time at which they were created, in the first years of K'inich Kan Bahlam's reign. The new ruler, already in middle age, must have felt the great weight of his father's incomparable legacy, and he set out to convey his own long-lasting role as protector of the gods. He reached back to his first childhood rites of sacrifice and initiation in order to establish that he, too, had decades of experience leading up to his new role as leader of the kingdom. Closely studying each of the temples allows these very complex statements of royal politics and their religious underpinnings to be explored.

The Temple of the Cross

The front of the Temple of the Cross has fallen away for the most part, but like all other Palenque structures it was once lavishly decorated with stucco. Remains of the outer façade on the north and western faces show scant vestiges of a large cosmological alligator (*ahiin*), seen crouching and facing the viewer, with its thin arms bent at the side of the imposing head. This alligator was a complex symbol that often served as a symbol for the sky (plate 23).

On the front slope of the Temple of the Cross, Stephens found a life-size statue – a rare example of Palenque sculpture in the round, very much in the style of carving at neighboring Toniná, which Palenque had defeated in war just a few years earlier. The freestanding monument commemorated the K'inich Kan Bahlam ritual connection to the 9.13.0.0.0 Period Ending, indicated solely by the "8 Ajaw" glyph upon which he stands.

A number of different excavations of the basal platform of the Temples of the Cross and the Foliated Cross revealed a remarkable number of large and elaborately decorated ceramic stands that supported bowls used for the burning of incense. All show human or deity faces with complex headdresses and iconographic symbolism (plate 9). Fragments of these have been found in earlier excavations at Palenque as well, but the Cross Group revealed a remarkably dense concentration. Once lined up along the terraces of the three temples, mostly facing to the west, the censers reveal that the platforms and terraces of Maya pyramids could often be accessible and important ceremonial locales in their own right. The censer stands were constructed by ceramic appliqué around a tall central support column. Many depict the face of GI or the jaguar god of the Underworld, or else human faces that surely portrayed deified ancestors. Their symbolism is largely cosmological.

Throughout the long history of exploration at Palenque, the temples of the Cross Group attracted the attention of many researchers who excavated the floors and probed the temple's chambers. Excavations by del Río, Ruz, Sáenz and others revealed a number of cache deposits in the temple floors, evidently placed as offerings to the deities and to the temples themselves. These usually consisted of surprisingly modest ceramic bowls, holding a few preserved ritual implements of jade or obsidian.[14]

According to the inscriptions that adorned the upper Temple of the Cross, the inner shrine had its own proper name (as is also the case in the other temples). The name is not completely deciphered, but "six" and "sky" are two of the main elements. A "six sky place" is also prominently mentioned in the mythic narrative of the main tablet as the place where creation took place at the beginning of the current era. The celestial nature of the space is conveyed very clearly by the symbols that decorated the upper roof of the shrine, where the remains of plaster decoration still show sky-band borders. Sky-bands also appear in the main tablet, probably to emphasize the notion of GI's celestial resurrection from the sea.[15]

The main tablet of the Temple of the Cross (fig. 63, plate 3), now housed in the Museo Nacional de Antropología in Mexico City, is one of a set clearly designed together as monuments to the three gods and to K'inich Kan Bahlam's direct association with them. As on the other tablets, we see a three-part image: a central icon which varies from temple to temple, flanked by two standing humans in profile to the right and left. The human figures are the same pair in each temple: a short richly attired male and a taller more simply dressed lord. Each faces the central icon, holding ritual objects and offerings. On the Cross Tablet, the central image is of course the

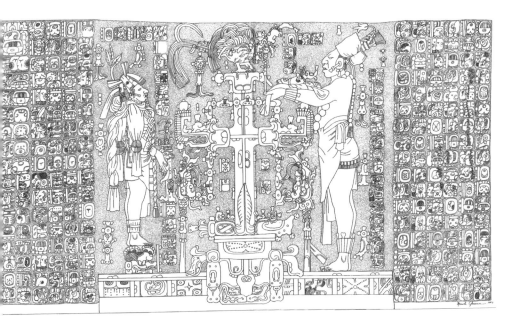

63 *The Tablet of the Cross, perhaps the most publicized sculpture from Palenque. Its appearance in print in 1822 led to the first productive efforts to decipher the Maya hieroglyphic script (see fig. 12, fig. 17, and plate 3).*

great cross itself – a representation of a sacred world tree atop of which perches an elaborate supernatural bird. The tree is adorned with jewels and three large flower blossoms emerge at its top and sides.

The larger of the two standing figures is K'inich Kan Bahlam as he looked on the day of his inauguration as king in 684. This day is recorded in the caption next to his portrait on all of the three tablets. Interestingly, his taking office occurred on 10 January of that year – exactly eight solar years before the dedication of the three temples and the "housing" of the three gods. In his outstretched arms he holds the open bundle containing the effigy of the so-called "jester god" – probably an animate spirit of sacred maize. The opposite figure is a childhood portrait of K'inich Kan Bahlam on the day of his initiation rites on 17 June 641, when the future king was only six years old. As on the other two tablets of the Cross Group, in his child portrait he is dressed in an odd costume of ribbons and twisted strands of cloth, clearly associated with a specific but still obscure ritual event.[16]

The inscription of the Tablet of the Cross is extremely long and of primary importance for understanding Palenque's mythology and history. As the principal of the three tablets, it provides much of the mythological background of the origins of GI and other members of the Triad. The opening phrase related to the birth of an aspect of the all-important maize god, who serves as the creator deity for the Triad gods. GI later descends from heaven to occupy a mythical temple bearing the same name as the temple's inner shrine. The inscription ultimately goes on to record the birth and accession dates of numerous early kings of Palenque, beginning with the semi-mythical "Snake Spine" and the more historical K'uk' Bahlam. The detailed records on this tablet form the basis for understanding most of the early dynastic history of the kingdom. The repetitive list of births and crownings cites nine kings in all, ending with the Early Classic ruler Kan Bahlam, the ancestor and namesake of the reigning king. His role in the narrative is clearly to set the stage for the coming of his like-in-kind descendant, providing the new ruler with a long and powerful pedigree.[17]

Analyzing the tablets' overall message, we see that the principal theme of the temple is solar rebirth in the heavens. At the center of the tablet, rising above the celestial band at the base, is the cross-like motif that depicts what the Maya called the "Shiny Jeweled Tree." It is the same symbol that dominates the design of Pakal's sarcophagus lid, where the significance is largely the same. This sacred tree was associated with the eastern sky, emerging into heaven out of the sacred offering bowl shown near the base of the composition. This bowl, with its *k'in* or sun symbol, is the symbolic womb of the cosmic alligator that represents the surface of the earth or the nocturnal starry sky. The skull beneath the bowl is the animate seed that gives rise to sacred trees and also to maize. The jade jewel tree is an important symbol of GI, who perhaps embodies the sun in its transitional pre-dawn state. As protagonist of the Temple of the Cross, GI also served to animate the larger theme of ancestral resurrection through the sun's eastern ascent.

64 OPPOSITE *The Temple of the Foliated Cross showing the internal system of vaults, doorways, and the interior sanctuary at rear center, all exposed by the collapse of the front of the building.*

The Temple of the Foliated Cross

The Temple of the Foliated Cross (fig. 64) rests against the slope of the tall and conspicuous Mirador hills. The temple's façade, like that of its taller neighbor, collapsed onto its front terraces, leaving a glaring peek within the open vault of its front chamber. Inside its rear room we also find an inner "house" shrine richly decorated and with an associated tablet. Although not restored and consolidated to the extent of its neighbors, the substructure of the Temple of the Foliated Cross was excavated by Miguel Angel Fernández in 1954, when numerous ornate incense burner stands were revealed.

The imagery of the Foliated Cross is quite different from that of the Cross. Nowhere do we find celestial symbolism: rather, the emphasis seems to be on water, agriculture, and the primordial sea. Its outer façade or

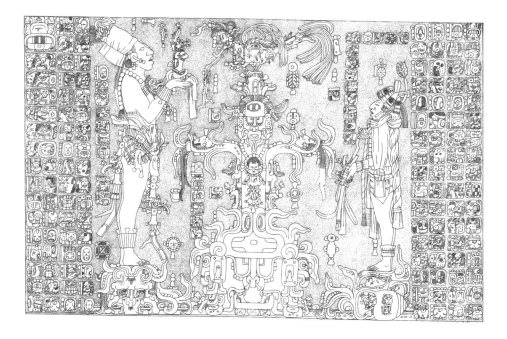

65 *The Tablet of the Foliated Cross, depicting the king K'inich Kan Bahlam as both a youth and an old man facing a fantastic maize plant surmounted by a gigantic mythical bird.*

roof-comb once bore large shells with the hieroglyphic label of "Matwiil", a place continually mentioned in Palenque's mythological texts in association with the birth of the Triad gods and also of the dynasty itself. In the inner shrine, the stucco décor is replete with K'an crosses and bands possibly representing sprouting maize.

The main tablet once again shows K'inich Kan Bahlam, both young and old, flanking a central cruciform motif (fig. 65). Now, however, the middle image is the animated and jeweled maize plant, rising from a basal head that reads as the hieroglyph *K'an Nahb*, the "precious sea." Appropriately, a water band runs along the base of the scene, replacing the celestial band found on the Temple of the Cross. In the plant we see heads of the maize god replacing the cobs, indicating that the icon corresponds to an important symbol that the ancient Maya called the *K'an Nahb Ixiimte'*, the "precious sea maize plant." This was the tree of sustenance and growth that, as Simon Martin has suggested, was far more than a simple maize plant – it encapsulated many

25 *(Above)* The funerary mask of K'inich Janab Pakal, newly reconstructed from scores of individual jade mosaic pieces. The mask was placed directly over the deceased king's face, where it was found by Alberto Ruz.

26, 27, 28 *(Overleaf, clockwise from top left)* The crypt within the Temple of the Inscriptions; the sarcophagus lid depicting Pakal's re-birth as the maize god and the eastern sun; and K'inich Janab Pakal as a young man, left, and as king, right. These life-size stucco portraits were found beneath his sarcophagus in the Temple of the Inscriptions.

29 *(Right)* The beautiful Tablet of the 96 Glyphs, dedicated by K'inich K'uk' Bahlam in AD 783. One of the last inscriptions known from Palenque, it celebrates this king's 20-year anniversary on the throne, and his role as the successor of his great-grandfather, K'inich Janab Pakal. The incised hieroglyphs carefully evoke a calligraphic style (see also plate 7).

30 *(Below)* Detail of the Temple XXI platform relief, with its curious scene of a richly dressed rodent-like figure presenting a ritual bundle to a young K'inich Ahkal Mo' Nahb, probably some years before his own enthronement.

31 *(Opposite, below)* The Temple XVII tablet, depicting the warrior king K'inich Kan Bahlam and a kneeling captive, perhaps an ally of his Toniná rival. The king's identity is likened to that of his Early Classic ancestor Ahkal Mo' Nahb, who established Palenque's site as a political center.

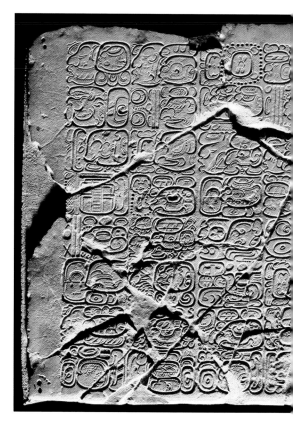

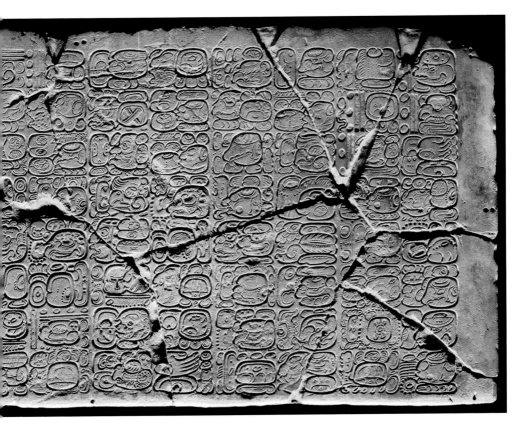

32, 33, 34 Detail of the Temple XIX painted stucco panel depicting Upakal K'inich Janab Pakal, possibly the younger brother of K'inich Ahkal Mo' Nahb, opposite, above; the south face of Temple XIX's interior platform, depicting the crowning ceremony of K'inich Ahkal Mo' Nahb in the company of three noblemen as the new king depicts himself as a reincarnation of the god GI, opposite, below; and a detail of Temple XIX's limestone panel, above, depicting K'inich Ahkal Mo' Nahb in an elaborate feathered dance costume showing the fineness of the carving and the effective treatment of portraiture (see plate 12).

35 *(Left)* Detail of the wall painting decorating the royal tomb of Temple XX. The dress and form of the heavily stylized figures resemble those of ancestral portraits in Pakal's later tomb. This photograph was taken before the tomb's opening, by lowering a camera through a small hole in the ceiling.

36 *(Below)* Archaeologist Arnoldo González Cruz and the stone sarcophagus in the tomb of the "Red Queen" in Temple XIII. The skeleton of the interred royal woman, heavily bejeweled with jade, was covered in red cinnabar. Her identity remains a mystery – no inscription identifies her – but the tomb's age and proximity to the Temple of the Inscriptions suggest she was Pakal's wife, Ix Tz'akbu Ajaw.

interrelated ideas of food, richness, and the forces of life itself. The theme conveyed by this central icon can be summarized as the power of agricultural growth and procreation from precious water. Unen K'awiil (GII) is the appropriate overseer of this theme, combining in his small form the ideas of fertility and rainmaking through lightning.

On the main tablet the adult king stands atop the animated symbol of the sacred mountain of sustenance, Yaxhal Witznal, out of which billows the leaves of maize plants. The younger king-to-be, at the right, stands atop the snail shell labeled as the "precious shell of Matwiil" – a watery place of rebirth and germination. The juxtaposition places the new king in his proper role as actor in the cosmic process of maize's growth, dependant on the substances of water (the shell) and the earth (the mountain).

The Temple of the Sun

On the western side of the Cross Group lies the smallest of the three temples, the well-preserved Temple of the Sun (plate 24). Its deity, GIII, was the second born of the three, and he seems to be a solar god associated with the themes of warfare: this much is obvious from the inner tablet, where the varying central icon now becomes the ceremonial shield and two crossed spears, supported on the backs of two hunched underworld deities. The young K'inich Kan Bahlam offers a small statue of the animated spirit of knives and flint, with a circular shield, up to the image. Together this represents the combined words *tok' pakal,* "flint and shield," signifying the duty of sacred warfare.

The Temple of the Sun's shrine was conceived and named as a mountain interior. The decorations of its inner shrine include stacks of animate *witz* (mountain) heads – standard markings of a cave – that form the border of the flanking outer panels, where K'inich Kan Bahlam is shown holding a long spear. The scene of the tablet (fig. 66) is likewise probably meant to be seen as the interior of the underworld, for we see along its base repeating symbols for "earth" (*kab*), replacing the sky-band of the Cross tablet and the water band of the Foliated Cross. Such symbols directly convey the ancient name of the shrine as recorded in nearby inscriptions: *K'inich Paskab,* perhaps best understood to mean "the radiant dawning."

66 *K'inich Kan Bahlam as a warrior, from the sanctuary panel of the Temple of the Sun Tablet.*

As Mathews has pointed out, the image of K'inich Kan Bahlam as a warrior is rooted in historical reality. Using the Armendáriz drawing of 1787 (before it was smashed to pieces), Mathews has shown that the glyphs accompanying his portrait record the date of the Toniná war of 687. The sudden appearance of real world politics among the abstract symbolism of the Cross Group temples is jarring, perhaps, but it demonstrates that political power and authority are at the root of the Cross Group's overall message.[18]

The Tablet of the Sun emphasizes sacred warfare of the earth, explicitly symbolized as the crossed spears and shield on its tablet, marking this as a temple of warfare. In the conception of this smaller temple, K'inich Kan Bahlam was placing his recent historical exploits in a cosmological framework, emphasizing in its imagery his role as conqueror of Toniná. It was this singular event of his early reign that may have given him the confidence and ambition to design and construct the Cross Group temples with such force of vision.

We see how the three temples together symbolize three basic spaces of the cosmos: sky, the surface of water, and the underworld. Not coincidentally, the heights of the three temples perfectly replicate this symbolism – the Cross is the highest, and the Temple of the Sun is the lowest, with the Foliated Cross occupying the intermediate role. All of these spaces were stations in a ritual cycle of ceremonies presumably performed by the king on the great K'atun ending 9.13.0.0.0, and perhaps by others as well on subsequent occasions.

The Mythology of Creation

As we have seen, each temple highlights the supernatural birth or arrival of one of the three gods at a watery place called Matwiil. This mythical setting of re-birth was the origin place for the Palenque gods and, ultimately, for the Palenque dynasty itself, and its importance here probably reflects a widespread Mesoamerican idea that communities have their origins in lakes, springs, or caves.[19] This makes us wonder if the emphasis on Matwiil has some connection again to the temples' clear orientation toward the Otolum spring, which was in all likelihood the most significant sacred spring on Palenque's landscape.

The Palenque Triad were the "creation" of another deity who was an aspect of the all-important maize god. This character, while still not completely understood, is called the Triad Progenitor, and he served as the initial "ruler" in Palenque's wider historical narrative, where myth and politics were inseparable. Before his identity as the maize god was firmly established, Lounsbury and Schele considered him to be Palenque's "mother goddess" (fig. 67). His birth in 3121 BC appears in the opening passage of the Tablet of the Cross, and he assumed the throne in 2325 BC, well after the arrival of the Triad. His overseeing of the creation and establishment of the Triad deities served as a model for kingship at Palenque, and established a mythical charter for how rulers interact with the gods they are entrusted to care for and protect.[20]

But the larger story of Palenque's mythology reaches even further back in time. According to religious texts from other buildings, the god GI is

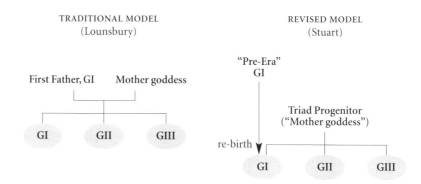

TRADITIONAL MODEL
(Lounsbury)

REVISED MODEL
(Stuart)

"Pre-Era"
GI

First Father, GI   Mother goddess

Triad Progenitor
("Mother goddess")

GI   GII   GIII

re-birth

GI   GII   GIII

67 *Genealogy of the gods.*

a major player in an earlier narrative. In the remarkable panels recently discovered in Temple XIX by archaeologist Alfonso Morales and his team, we
read that GI was seated as a king in 3309 BC – well before the birth of the
Triad Progenitor. But king of what? In that inscription GI is not called
a Palenque ruler, and the vagueness of the language probably indicates that
he was king in some broader sense, "in the heavens," as the Temple XIX
text states. GI was crowned by another deity named Yax Naah Itzamnaaj,
a creator god who was an aspect of Itzamnaaj, arguably the most supreme
of all Maya gods.

In addition according to the recently discovered inscription from
Temple XIX, which we will examine further in the following chapter, GI
participated in, if not actually conducted, the sacrifice of a great alligator
representing a primordial earth monster. We read of similar myths in the
creation accounts of later Mesoamerican cultures, and no doubt these are
glimpses of some very ancient story elements.[21] In the Palenque narrative,
we read that the sacrifice results in the flowing of three streams of blood,
and perhaps also in the drilling of a ritual fire. Again, blood sacrifice and
fire-making are two intimately related ceremonies in ancient Mesoamerica,
essential to the creation and sustaining of the cosmos.

After the birth of the Triad Progenitor in 3121 BC, the stage was almost set
for the arrival of the Triad deities. But first we read of a key calendar date on
13 August 3114 – the end of the 13th Bak'tun, or 13.0.0.0.0 4 Ajaw 8 Kumk'u.
This day was cited throughout all of the ancient Maya area as the starting

point for the current Creation era, when according to some sources, the gods of the world were set in their proper order. At Palenque and elsewhere, it is also described as the date when "the hearth was changed," strongly indicating the making of a "new fire," much in the way the Aztecs conceived of different creations and their renewal. On the Tablet of the Cross, no actor oversees this event, but in another narrative we read that Itzamnaaj himself was an important player in the setting up of three sacred stones in the heavens. It is as though the three Temples of the Cross Group echo the triangular arrangement of such a hearth, with the small radial pyramid – a place for burning – at its very center.[22]

Returning to the epic story of the Cross tablet, we read of another major event that occurred over one year after the 13 Bak'tun creation day. This was the "descent from the sky" of GI, the god who had been crowned as king at the beginning of our story. It was on this day, too, that a mythical temple named (in part) the "Six Sky House" was dedicated for him "in the north" (fig. 68). Not coincidentally, this is the very same name given to the inner shrine of the Temple of the Cross, the northernmost of the Cross Group's buildings, and naturally the celestial symbolism of the temple's decoration is meant to evoke this mythical place where GI descended.

68 *Passage from the Tablet of the Cross describing the mythical dedication in 3113 BC of the "House of the North." The Temple of the Cross replicated this cosmic structure.*

Finally, looking at the larger narrative of the three temples, we come to the seminal births or re-births of three gods as formal members of the Palenque Triad, separated by only a matter of days in 2360 BC. The earliest "arrival at Matwiil" by GI, a god who we have seen as the main protagonist of the mythology up to this point, is clearly to be understood as his "re-birth" as a member of the Triad.[23] The inscriptions also refer to the births of all three gods as their "arrivals at Matwiil," the mythical place that is in many ways at the center of Palenque's political and religious identity. The metaphorical language used to describe their births as journeys to some new physical place is very different from the way the Classic Maya described historical births of real people, and suggest the creation or foundation of a new order or being. Four days after GI's birth, we read of GIII's arrival, followed 14 days later by that of GII. We do not know why their birth-order disagrees with the order in which they are always named, and in the order we refer to them today.

The maize god who gave rise to the Triad gods, although we resist calling him a true father, was in many ways a model ruler for the later kings of Palenque history. He became "ruler of Matwiil" in 2325 BC (2.0.0.10.2 9 Ik' Seating of Sak), and according to one source he was "the first becoming a lord."[24] Later kings, especially K'inich Kan Bahlam's nephew, took great pains to clarify their own connection to this seminal figure in Palenque's mythology. By proclaiming their descent from this creator god, the kings established their own charter for rulership, and proclaimed their duty to sustain and nourish the gods through their own rituals of self-sacrifice. We will explore this theme a bit further in the next chapter, when we see how one ruler added a new twist to the ideology of equating gods and rulers.

The epic story related by the Tablet of the Cross continues by moving forward over 13 centuries to record the birth and accession of an enigmatic figure possibly named "Snakes Spine" (see fig. 30A) (his Maya name remains somewhat elusive to decipherment). The year of his seating was 967 BC, when he was 26 years old. With his mention the epic story shifts to a more historical time frame, and indeed the entire right portion of the tablet's text goes on to record the Early Classic history of Palenque's dynasty. Snake Spine may well have been historical in some sense – we will probably never know – yet at the very least we can see how Palenque's rulers saw him as a proto-typical king, worthy of emulation and commemoration. On the outer panel of the Temple of the Cross's inner sanctuary K'inich Kan Bahlam himself wears an antique styled costume, and in his headdress wears the symbolic name of Snake Spine.[25] In keeping with the temple's theme of GI's own re-birth, he personally manifests the image and identity of this ancient, semi-mythical figure.

The interwoven stories of cosmic origins and local mythic leave a somewhat confusing picture, but in Maya thought these spatial distinctions were often unimportant. Palenque, and especially the account of its political foundation, was seen as an event of cosmological proportions: it is no wonder that scholars have sometimes been confused as to whether we are reading accounts of a broadly conceived Maya creation mythology, or accounts of Palenque's creation mythology. In all likelihood the tablets interlaced elements of both visions.

K'inich Kan Bahlam died in 702, over a decade after he dedicated the three remarkable temples of the Cross Group. The last years of his life remain poorly understood, though evidence suggests that conflicts with Toniná continued even after Palenque's celebrated defeat of its neighbor in 687. Just five years later, in 692 – and just after the great K'atun ending celebrated in the Cross Group – at least two Palenque lords appear prominently in Toniná's militaristic sculptures, shown as bound and humiliated captives (fig. 69). This war took place soon after Toniná's powerful new king K'inich Baaknal Chaak assumed the throne, perhaps with vengeance at the forefront of his mind. Belligerent relations between Palenque and Toniná would continue for decades to come, reaching a head during the reign of Kan Bahlam's younger brother.

69 *Image of a Palenque captive, K'awiil Mo', on a step from Toniná.*

K'inich K'an Joy Chitam

When K'inich Kan Bahlam became king in 684, his younger brother took over as the *baahch'ok*, the "main youth" and presumed heir to the throne. K'inich K'an Joy Chitam was already 40 years old, born in 644 during Pakal's obscure early years as king. Even as a young man and junior sibling, he had nevertheless held many important ritual duties. One beautiful sculpture depicts K'inich K'an Joy Chitam when he was 25 years old, performing a ritual dance in the guise of Chaak the rain god, as his seated parents look on (plate 11). Many years later he assumed the throne himself, soon after the death of his elder brother in 702, when he was 57 years old. K'inich K'an Joy Chitam reigned for at least 18 years before his own death probably in 722.

His accession as king is shown on the Palace Tablet (fig. 70, plate 17), the large panel that decorated the center of the back wall of his gallery of the Palace (House A–D). Here he is shown, as in other Palenque sculptures, assuming key emblems of his new office – the military headdress and a war bundle – from his parents, Pakal and Ix Tzakb'u Ajaw. According to the text caption, the new king saw himself as a reincarnation of one Uxyophu'n, probably a Preclassic Maya hero-king who ruled far away and several centuries earlier, cited in the histories of other Maya kingdoms.

Palenque's political and economic standing experienced a curious series of highs and lows during K'inich K'an Joy Chitam's reign. He was, like his older brother, a remarkably active king in terms of overseeing building programs within the city. But less than a decade into his reign Palenque also suffered a major military setback when, in 711, troublesome Toniná gained the upper hand, defeating Palenque's armies and taking the Palenque king prisoner. The Toniná ruler K'inich Baaknal Chaak was still adopting his aggressive strategy against his northern rival.

Ironically, one of a handful of K'inich K'an Joy Chitam's known portraits actually comes from Toniná, where on a small sandstone panel he is depicted bound and defeated, lying in an awkward pose on the ground, yet still wearing the jade headband of a king (fig. 71). Tellingly, his name caption is written directly upon his thigh, apparently a conveyance of disrespect we

71 OPPOSITE K'an Joy Chitam, early 8th-century ruler of Palenque, appears here as a bound captive of the ruler of nearby Toniná, lying on the ground in a posture of humiliation. Named in the panel of glyphs on his thigh, the defeated ruler still wears his royal jade headband and necklace.

70 *Scene on the uppermost part of the Palace Tablet showing K'inich K'an Joy Chitam, center, flanked by his deceased parents, K'inich Janab Pakal, left, tendering his son the headdress of royalty, and Ix Tz'akbu Ajaw, right, offering him the symbols of divine ancestry.*

see in many portraits of Maya war captives. We can probably conclude that the unfortunate king, by now 66 years of age, was displayed in humiliation in Toniná's court not long after his defeat.

In a very odd and unexpected twist, K'inich K'an Joy Chitam, according to several texts, remained Palenque's king for some years *after* his capture in Toniná in 711, and an active one at that, at least until about 722. For many years scholars assumed he was sacrificed at Toniná, but we now believe he was returned to Palenque.

Among his important duties was a significant modification to House A–D of the Palace, the large northern gallery that is now collapsed, and built atop much earlier constructions probably dating to the reign of his father. The construction of the northern side of the Palace was a remodeling of the Palace's main entrance: it is here that the broad stairway would have greeted visitors to Palenque's site center, rising up to the doorways above (fig. 72). In the back wall of the house K'inich K'an Joy Chitam dedicated the large sculpted panel known today simply as the Palace Tablet.[26] Its lengthy inscription is one of the most beautiful at Palenque, and recorded much of the elderly king's life history. The story it tells sidesteps any mention of Palenque's subjugation at the hands of Toniná. The tablet closes with a commemoration of the dedication of the Palace's House A–D in 720, shortly before the end of K'inich K'an Joy Chitam's tumultuous reign. The name of the building is the "headband binding house," posing the strong suggestion that it was designed as a place for crowning and political display. K'inich K'an Joy Chitam had been king for 18 years when the panel was carved, so we

doubt that the "binding" rites were connected with royal accessions, as in House E of the Palace, but rather, we believe that House A–D served as a place for installation of subordinate political offices overseen by the king. Such offices were expanding its members exponentially in most kingdoms of the Late Classic, as elite families grew and political networks became more complex. As one of the most conspicuous places in Palenque, with its open doors looking northward out over the plains of Tabasco, House A–D's role as a venue of installation would have been a bold political statement of Palenque's regional influence after its domination by Toniná. Of all the galleries of the Palace and other major Palenque structures, House A–D was among the most theatrical in its design and focus on political performance.

With the death of K'inich K'an Joy Chitam, sometime before 722, Palenque again had to pass through a difficult political transition. The generation of Pakal's sons had finally succumbed, and no son of K'inich Kan Bahlam or K'inich K'an Joy Chitam appears to have ever been designated as heir, at least according to the records left to us. The situation of brother-to-brother inheritance was highly unusual, but not without occasional precedent in Palenque's dynastic history. For reasons we may never know, rule would now pass on to the nephew of the previous two sibling kings, the son of a third brother named Tiwol Chan Mat. The nephew was named K'inich Ahkal Mo' Nahb, and he would prove to be one of the most significant players in the approaching demise of Palenque.

72 *The main grand stairway on the north side of the Palace, as remodeled by K'inich K'an Joy Chitam around 702 (see fig. 47). This, one of three stairways providing access to the complex above, leads directly to the now partially destroyed House A–D.*

219

CHAPTER NINE

A City Fades Away

*Then the white headbands were fastened upon the heads of the Four Lords, of
the Nine Descenders(?), (and upon?) Six Death, Janab Pakal…*

CLOSING PASSAGE FROM THE LAST KNOWN INSCRIPTION
FROM PALENQUE, 799

Palenque's last century of history presents a striking contrast in fortune.
With the arrival of the next generation of kings – the grandsons of Pakal
– Palenque seemed well on its way to renewal and a new-found vibrancy,
after several years of conflict and even possible brief subjugation to Toniná.
Once its political identity was strengthened and apparently stabilized,
Palenque even began to flex its military muscle again in the region. Yet after
a span of just a few decades, something happened to change all of this,
and the very fabric of Palenque's community somehow faltered and came
undone. By 850 if not before, well into the Balunté period, the city was
largely abandoned and the rainforest began to rapidly reclaim the Palace,
the temples, and the residences of the people. It would remain in this overgrown state for another nine centuries, until the arrival of the first explorers
in the late 18th century. In this chapter we will look at what could have happened at Palenque to cause this stunning reversal and collapse, and in doing
so speculate as much as archaeology will allow on why Palenque, and other
kingdoms of the Classic Maya, came to such an abrupt end.[1]

The beginning of the end centers on two generations of kings who
strived to uphold the legacy of their illustrious ancestor, K'inich Janab
Pakal. This preoccupation with the past came at a time when Palenque tried
to reassert its own identity and independence in the years after Toniná's

domination during the later years of K'inich K'an Joy Chitam's reign. In many respects they may have succeeded, if we can judge by the remarkable monuments built and designed through the middle years of the 8th century.

The succession of rule may have been a sensitive matter after the death of K'inich K'an Joy Chitam, sometime around 722. We have no records of an heir ever being produced by the two sons of Pakal who ruled, and it remains difficult to understand why the throne passed from brother to brother. No details of family relations in the courts of K'inich Kan Bahlam or K'inich K'an Joy Chitam have survived. Whatever the odd circumstances, the throne thereafter went to their 41-year-old nephew, K'inich Ahkal Mo' Nahb, in 722 (9.14.10.4.2 9 Ik' 5 K'ayab). As we will see, much of his political art was concerned with establishing legitimacy through his close kinship with K'inich Janab Pakal, and historical figures from even further back. Pivotal to these messages was the role of his father, Pakal's "lost" third son, named Tiwol Chan Mat.

Tiwol Chan Mat was never a king, but he provided the vital link between two powerful generations of Palenque royalty (fig. 73).[2] He would also be completely lost to history were it not for the written accounts of him recovered from Temple XVIII, a small building built against the hillside within the Group of the Cross. This modest structure originally bore a beautiful stucco panel and inscription on its back wall, nearly all of which had fallen off by the time Blom first began to record it in the 1920s.[3] Little of the figural scene in plaster survived, save for a few indications of a man seated on a throne, as well as the name captions of a few other people who evidently faced him (see fig. 51). Most of the decoration took the form of a large inscription composed of over 130 glyphs in modeled stucco, all which fell from the wall like tiles and into a jumbled pile on the floor, where they were eventually excavated. The inscription, as far as we can tell in its jumbled state, tells the life-story of Tiwol Chan Mat, highlighting his death and burial in 680, and the establishment of his son as ruler over four decades later. K'inich Ahkal Mo' Nahb built his version of Temple XVIII sometime after 722, evidently to feature his father's own historical significance as a son of Pakal, and thereby legitimating his own rightful claim to rulership.

Tiwol Chan Mat's tomb is in all likelihood a small but elaborate crypt found beneath the floor of Temple XVIII, known as Tomb 1. It held

73 RIGHT *Detail of the Tablet of the Slaves showing Tiwol Chan Mat.*

74 OPPOSITE *The Tablet of the Slaves found in Group IV.*

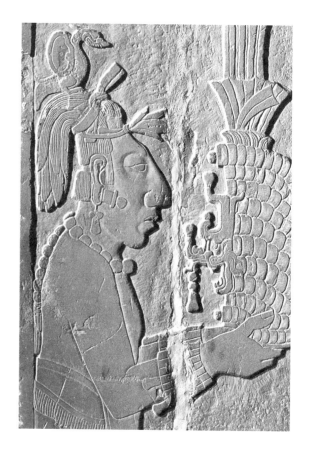

a significant amount of jade, but the skeleton had completely disintegrated.[4] The placement of Temple XVIII and its tomb within the larger Group of the Cross, where a number of other small elite burials were incorporated into the temples of the Triad, lends further support to the idea that the interpretation was important for ancestor veneration, at least in connection with members of the royal family.

The first decade or so of K'inich Ahkal Mo' Nahb's rule is silent in terms of the records, but this may be attributable to the continued political fallout of Toniná's earlier domination of Palenque, or it could be due to the new king's need to consolidate power after a difficult succession. Whatever the case, beginning around 730 we see a renewed emphasis on warfare in the Palenque region, much of it instigated by K'inich Ahkal Mo' Nahb and his military officers against neighboring communities. The Tablet of the Slaves, with its remarkable portraits of K'inich Ahkal Mo' Nahb and his parents, records a number of these earlier battles and conquests, and emphasized the

active participation of an important warrior named Chak Sutz' ("Red Bat"), who for a time was one of the most important and powerful men in Palenque (fig. 74).[5]

Chak Sutz' was a *sajal*, a title used for junior lords or military captains. He resided in the elaborate compound of buildings known today as Group IV, a very old and important lineage compound located near Palenque's center alongside the road that winds its way into the archaeological zone. Excavations in Group IV by Robert and Barbara Rands revealed some of the earliest and best defined ceramic stratigraphy for the site.[6] Chak Sutz' was important enough to warrant his own small throne room – probably a reception space for important visitors – where the exquisite Tablet of the Slaves was placed on the rear wall, echoing the arrangement of the much larger Palace Tablet in House A–D of the Palace, as well as the Oval Palace Tablet in House E. The relief tablet was found in 1950, very close to the ground surface during road construction. Its central portrait is not of Chak

75 *The "Tribute Fragment" discovered in Temple XVI, so-called for the huge and enigmatic cloth bundle being manipulated by three men, one of whom is named as "Ahkal Mo' Nahb."*

Sutz', but rather depicts K'inich Ahkal Mo' Nahb on his accession, flanked by remarkably life-like portraits of his mother and father. Once more it is an example of the very formulaic presentation scene we have already noted on the Oval Palace Tablet and the Palace Tablet. In the inscription we read of Palenque's aggressive attacks on sites that lie to the west, including a place called K'ina', a possible subsidiary of Piedras Negras. Chak Sutz' is the primary actor in this narrative of warfare, yet the imagery solidly establishes K'inich Ahkal Mo' Nahb as the true protagonist. In his throne room in Group IV, the *sajal*'s own power and authority was literally backed by the king.[7]

Another intriguing carving from this early period in K'inich Ahkal Mo' Nahb's reign bears the date 731 (9.14.19.10.17 4 Kaban 10 Zip), and it is perhaps the most unusual figural sculpture from Palenque (fig. 75). Excavated by archaeologist González in Structure XVI – part of the modest complex of buildings behind the Temple of the Cross – the fragment depicts three men standing above a kneeling figure with an immense cloth bundle on his back. A stairway or set of small terraces appear in the background, indicating an unusual architectural setting for the scene. The central dominant figure is named as Ahkal Mo' Nahb (no K'inich title here), and he appears to grasp or even lift the bundle with his outstretched arms. Two lieutenants assist him and the scene looks to depict a delivery or perhaps even the packaging of a tribute bundle, perhaps one delivered in the context of these complex political and military events in K'inich Ahkal Mo' Nahb's early years on the throne.[8]

Temples XIX and XXI

The evidence of K'inich Ahkal Mo' Nahb's deep concern about his royal pedigree came into sharp focus with the recent excavations at two previously unheralded buildings, known simply as Temples XIX and XXI. Nestled to the south of the Cross Group is the larger of these two closely related edifices, Temple XIX, excavated by a joint Mexican-American team of archaeologists in the late 1990s. Its smaller partner was completely dug in 2002 by the INAH project, and together the results have led to major changes in our understanding of Palenque's history and mythology. The newly discovered texts and sculptures illustrate in compelling fashion the ways these closely knit themes of living kings and distant gods closely intersected in ancient Maya thought, and specifically how K'inich Ahkal Mo' Nahb and his priests became masters at connecting the past glory of Palenque with his own assumption of power.

Temple XIX is a very strange structure by Palenque's standards. It is a long, vaulted edifice with two parallel galleries, but there was only a single, small doorway on its northern side, facing directly toward the Temple of the Cross (see map of Cross Group, fig. 7). All other temples at Palenque have very open frontal access, typically with three or more prominent doors. The interior of Temple XIX is also unusual because it has a series of square piers or support columns dividing the two long galleries within (plate 32). One gets the sense from this odd arrangement that the temple is somehow "inside out," with the open accesses within the building, and only a single door on its exterior. The novel architectural design was disastrous, however, for within a fairly short time after its construction the massive roof the temple, poorly supported by the open interior columns, collapsed in on itself. Temple XIX was the first ruin of Palenque, never to be rebuilt. Temple XXI, set slightly to the north and west of Temple XIX and also facing the Temple of the Cross, is smaller and far more practical and elegant in its design. It too had only a single doorway, linking it visually with its massive neighbor.[9]

The most striking feature of Temples XIX and XXI is the single masonry platforms found within each, evidently used as pedestals or benches. They are not thrones like those found elsewhere at Palenque, and their true

76 *The monolithic front, or south face, of the platform in Temple XIX, which is the longest of its three exposed and carved sides and depicts the enthroned ruler K'inich Ahkal Mo' Nahb flanked by six high-ranking members of the royal court at the moment he leans forward to receive the royal headband of rulership, 3 January 722.*

function still remains a mystery. Both platforms, built near the corners of the interior rooms, were decorated with elegantly carved and inscribed panels depicting royal rituals, with multiple participants. They are among the finest of all Maya carvings, clearly designed in tandem and carved by the same small group of master sculptors. The one in Temple XIX is larger and carved on two sides, whereas the version in Temple XXI was topped by a horizontal slab bearing a hieroglyphic text.

The south face of the Temple XIX platform, apparently the first of the pair, depicts K'inich Ahkal Mo' Nahb at the moment when he was crowned king (fig. 76, plate 33). He leans forward to accept the sacred headband of rulership, held before him by a priest or official named Janab Ajaw. This important man may also have been a grandson of Pakal, and thus a cousin of the new king, but for some reason not in direct line to the throne.[10] Other lords of the Palenque court look on, including the man directly behind the king who may have been a priest associated with Temple XIX itself. The other lords are all named, but they remain largely unknown in the kingdom's history.

The headdresses of K'inich Ahkal Mo' Nahb and Janab Ajaw are unusual in their design, and convey a powerful message. The king wears a small heron grasping a fish in its beak, above a jeweled medallion. These are the distinctive emblems associated with the deity GI, the chief member of the Palenque Triad. Janab Ajaw, for his part, wears the headdress depicting the avian aspect of the powerful Creator god Itzamnaaj.[11] According to their glyphic name captions, the two men are specifically named *as* these gods, their identities fused with them.

The explanation for the supernatural role-playing – it is much more than this, of course – comes from the text accompanying this scene. As mentioned briefly in the last chapter, the lengthy narrative opens with the statement that in 3309 BC, "GI was seated as king, by the authority of Yax Naah Itzamnaaj, in the heavens." The story moves forward to the familiar births of the Triad gods at Matwiil, and goes on to highlight the accession of the Triad Progenitor as a "Palenque king" in 2325 BC. The inscription then closes with a record of K'inich Ahkal Mo' Nahb's accession in AD 722, corresponding to the crowning scene on the tablet. The distant inaugurations of GI and K'inich Ahkal Mo' Nahb thus frame the epic story of the creation of the Triad. In the carved scene, the king's historical accession is depicted explicitly as a reenactment of the GI's own seating, an event that appears to have established the charter of rulership as well as the supernatural authority of GI, Palenque's main patron god.

The link between myth and history is not simply visual, however. A close analysis of the dates of these remote events shows special numerological connections, and suggests that the Maya sought to highlight connections between them through basic calendric and astronomical mechanisms. For example, the day of GI's crowning took place on "9 Ik'" in the 260-day calendar. So too did GI's supernatural re-birth, as did the enthronement of K'inich Ahkal Mo' Nahb. The calendar priests of Palenque must have carefully chosen the date of the king's accession in order to evoke a cosmological link between all of these events in order to establish K'inich Ahkal Mo' Nahb's claim to be a reincarnation of GI himself.[12]

With this message, it is no surprise that Temple XIX was erected so close to the Cross Group temples. Temples XIX and XXI both face directly toward the Temple of the Cross, the house of GI. K'inich Ahkal Mo' Nahb evidently wanted to leave his mark on this most sacred territory within Palenque by designing a novel temple that was a shrine to GI and celebrated his own intimate connection to the principal member of the Triad. The tall and beautifully carved tablet on the inner pier takes the message even further, showing him dressed in a remarkably elaborate dance costume in the form of a giant cormorant head, the symbol of Matwiil (perhaps "Place of Cormorants"), the watery place of origin that was the realm of GI and the other Triad members (plates 12 and 34).

Temple XIX did not last long: it was left as a ruin, and the ancient Maya apparently neglected to repair or restore the inglorious pile of rubble. Some people did however excavate fragments of the temple's pier tablet and move them several meters to the interior platform, where they were ritually deposited in front of the scene of the king's inauguration. Ceramics found in association with this deposit were of Balunté phase, indicating the time before it had been abandoned. What does this abandonment of a major temple say about the community and the royal court at this time? Perhaps the structure caved in at the same time as the kingdom's larger demise several decades later – we cannot be sure of its exact timing – K'inich Ahkal Mo' Nahb was on the throne for many years, and at least two more kings were to reign after him, building at least modestly on the earlier works of the Palace, for example.

One puzzling question stood out from the initial analysis of Temple XIX. The building was evidently dedicated to GI, yet its inscriptions also mentioned the dedication of another building or buildings in honor of GII and GIII. But where would these be? The answer came very quickly with González's 2001 excavations in nearby Temple XXI. This freestanding structure is smaller than Temple XIX, but

77 *The Temple XXI platform face, evidently carved by the same hands as its counterpart in Temple XIX, shows K'inich Janab Pakal, center, offering an elaborately decorated bloodletter to his grandson, K'inich Ahkal Mo' Nahb.*

noticeably similar in its unusual floor-plan and design. It also had an unusual single door on its front – only Temple XIX shows the same pattern. When González excavated the structure, he was intrigued to find fragments of tablets from other buildings, including large pieces of the panel that once graced the inside of neighboring Temple XVII. These were taken from their original contexts and deposited in Temple XXI by squatters who occupied Palenque's buildings after the abandonment of the city. Most significant of all, González discovered a small masonry platform over to the side of Temple XXI's inner room, faced with another beautifully carved panel (fig. 77). The size of the curious platform, the style of its sculpted face, and content of the inscription carved upon it make it abundantly clear that Temple XXI was designed in conjunction with Temple XIX, though dedicated two years later. This was, without doubt, one of the "missing" shrines mentioned in Temple XIX's narrative.

The Temple XXI carving is one more masterpiece, clearly carved by the same team of artisans, but in some ways different from its Temple XIX companion. At the center of the composition is a portrait of the enthroned K'inich Janab Pakal, who holds in his right hand a feathered bloodletter, handing it to another man identified as K'inich Ahkal Mo' Nahb. The grandson, dressed in a leafy cape, faces away and engages with a fantastical rodent-like animal dressed in a priestly garb (plate 30), who grasps in his paw a curious bundled "bouquet"; it is difficult to say what this object is. On the opposite side of the panel, on Pakal's left, we find an identical arrangement of a large rodent with a man identified by the glyphic caption as someone named Upakal K'inich, probably the king's younger brother.

Both men are shown with their grandfather, who had by the time of its carving been dead nearly a century.

It is difficult to interpret the strange scene of multiple generations and large costumed animals, but one comes away from it thinking that Pakal is the protagonist, not some distant historical figure. The illustrious grandfather passes the sacred instrument of bloodletting to his elder grandson, and in so doing, one easily imagines, he conveys one of the fundamental duties of kingship to his descendants. The message is not too different therefore from the courtly scene of Temple XIX, with the newly installed king surrounded by his officials. In making Pakal the center of attention, K'inich Ahkal Mo' Nahb emphasizes his own pedigree as occupant of the throne – a role that that we must remember may have been contestable, at least in the early years of his reign.

K'inich Ahkal Mo' Nahb ruled Palenque until 741 (9.15.10.0.0 4 Ajaw 13 Yax), if not slightly later. In these years he oversaw renovations within the Palace, including a painting of the interior of the throne room in House E, and perhaps also the construction of the nearby Tower.[13] There is the intriguing possibility that he is buried in a temple near to the main plaza, such as Temple XI or the Temple of the Count, both of which have fragmentary inscriptions mentioning his name.

Upakal K'inich came to office sometime after 741, when his name became Upakal K'inich Janab Pakal – a clear evocation of his grandfather. His role in Palenque's history was completely unknown until he was identified through the careful historical research of Guillermo Bernal, who noticed his name in fragmentary records, including portions of a broken tablet recovered from the Palace. The discovery of Temple XXI confirmed Upakal K'inich's existence, as well as his close and seemingly equal status to K'inich Ahkal Mo' Nahb during the latter's own reign. We do not see any mention of the precise family tie between the men, but we believe that they were brothers who shared much of the authority of kingship even before K'inich Ahkal Mo' Nahb's death. Oddly, both men held the royal title "Holy Lord of Palenque" at the same time, suggesting an unusual power arrangement – something we have seen hints of among other powerful brothers in Palenque's history.

Another K'inich Kan Bahlam?

The mid-8th century is a murky time in Palenque's history, with few inscriptions known from the decades after Temples XIX and XXI were dedicated. Between 741 and 764 we see no new buildings or tablets, at least in the archaeological record as it exists today. One might be tempted to see Palenque being unusually "quiet" and inactive for this decade or two, but we must remember that the growing numbers of elites at the time may have shifted their architectural efforts to other portions of the city, and that some day further excavations may reveal what was happening at this time.

The K'atun ending of 9.16.0.0.0, in 751, is unknown at Palenque – a conspicuous omission, no doubt. We do find it prominently celebrated at the neighboring kingdom of Pomoná, however, where according to a stela unearthed there several years ago a ruler by the name of K'inich Hix Mo' Bahlam "bound the stone" on the completion of the K'atun. A priest who was in charge of ritual paper and headbands (a *Ti'sakhuun*) aided him in this rite, as did, surprisingly, an individual named "K'inich Kan Bahlam, the Holy Lord of Baakal." The name is identical to that of the earlier famous Palenque king, and there seems good reason to accept this, at least for now, as a new ruler named K'inich Kan Bahlam, or Kan Bahlam III.

The Pomoná text tells us that the Palenque king was an active participant in the calendar rite at Pomoná: had he been conquered and captured? If not, why would a Palenque king travel to a historical rival to perform the ceremony? Was the Palenque king somehow "exiled" to Pomoná, at least temporarily? We cannot know without further sources. The 20 years or so after the reign of K'inich Ahkal Mo' Nahb present a significant gap in Palenque's records: future excavations may provide the key evidence we need about the leading up to the period of the final members of the dynasty.

K'inich K'uk' Bahlam

The last certain king of Palenque was Pakal's great-grandson, K'inich K'uk' Bahlam ("The Great Sun Quetzal Jaguar"). The name is identical to that of the dynastic founder who lived four centuries earlier. The later K'uk' Bahlam was the son of K'inich Ahkal Mo' Nahb and a woman whose name, although still resistant to decipherment, may have been "Lady Eagle Seed." His reign began in 8 March 764 and continued for at least 20 years, after which time Palenque's lengthy history falls nearly silent for good. A stone censer stand excavated in Group IV (see fig. 32) bears the image of a king named in his headdress as K'inich K'uk' Bahlam, but this might well be the distant ancestor recorded in the Cross Group tablets as the dynastic founder.[14]

K'inich K'uk' Bahlam commissioned some small-scale construction projects within the Palace, including modifications to his father's great Tower, at the base of which he placed the Tablet of the 96 Glyphs with its beautiful incised inscription, perhaps inset into the tread of a small stairway (plate 129).[15] This small ornate tablet, discovered in 1936, celebrates his first k'atun anniversary as king, placing it in a narrative of previous monarchs who followed in the legacy of Pakal. The story begins, in fact, with a retrospective mention of K'inich Janab Pakal's dedication of House E, located just a few feet behind the Tower, and continues with mentions of the accessions of two subsequent generations of kings, K'inich K'an Joy Chitam and K'inich Ahkal Mo' Nahb. Remarkably, the text closes with the statement that K'inich Janab Pakal, at this time dead for a century, "governed over" his great grandson's anniversary, as if blessing the occasion. Pakal's oversight of the event might even be taken literally, since the placement of the tablet in the House E's courtyard ensured that it would be in close proximity to his ancestor's throne, and Pakal's portrait on the Oval Palace Tablet.

K'inich K'uk' Bahlam is the last king who can be identified with certainty, but this is not to say he was the very last: it is possible, if not likely, that our sample is incomplete, and evidence of later rulers will emerge. Probably the latest inscription we have is the fragmented tablet of Structure XVI, with its long historical list of priests who were installed by many of Palenque's kings. We do not know its dedication date, but it seems to be late in style and includes the name of K'inich K'uk' Bahlam near its end.[16]

78 *The so-called Murciélagos Vase, named for the group where it was discovered, bears a Long Count date equated to 17 November 799, and records the name of one "Six Death Janab Pakal," possibly the last king of Palenque.*

A Vase's Story

It is perhaps telling that the last historical record we have from Palenque comes not from a temple's tablet, but from a small ornately inscribed bowl (fig. 78). This important object was discovered near the ground's surface in front of the door of the residential compound known as the Murciélagos Group (originally called Group III).[17] The elegantly shaped ceramic vessel is made from a distinctive fine grey paste that comes from the Tabasco plains, to the north of Palenque, which was widely imported during the Balunté ceramic phase. It is highly unusual to find an inscription on any fine grey ware from any Maya site, suggesting that this vessel was a highly prized object, evidently owned by an elite family at the very end of the 8th century. The long count date written on the vessel (9.18.9.4.4 7 K'an 17 Muwan) falls on 17 November 799, and was evidently the inauguration day of a man with a partially familiar name, "Six Death Janab Pakal." The "Six Death" portion is a personal calendar name (6 Kimi), which, although rare among the Maya, was generally common in most other Mesoamerican cultures. The nobleman, who we cannot place in the family history of Palenque, also took on the illustrious name of Janab Pakal, once more evoking the glories of Palenque's past. Portions of the text are still hard to decipher, but it is possible that he was the last known king of Palenque.[18]

The vessel and other representative ceramics of the late Balunté phase seem especially pronounced in the elite residential complexes excavated

thus far on the hill slopes to the northeast of the site center (the Murciélagos Group and Groups B and C) (fig. 79). The situation indicates that, for a time, Palenque's nobility continued to occupy the prime area of the city, even when the royal history itself remains strangely quiet in the final decades of the 8th century. No large-scale constructions seem to date from this time, save for perhaps some modifications within the Palace.

Foreign Powers

As Robert Rands has long noted, the appearance of fine grey ceramics in the early facet of Balunté, during the last gasp of elite culture at Palenque, indicates strong influences from the distant Tabasco plains to the north, where considerable populations seem to have been concentrating toward the end of the Late Classic period. It was during this time as well that Comalcalco, an important Maya kingdom located in Tabasco to the northwest, grew and expanded its own influence. Most of its inscriptions cluster around the close of the 8th century and the beginning of the 9th, when Palenque's own court was on the verge of complete collapse. Significantly, one late inscription from Comalcalco, no doubt from this same period, refers to a "Holy Lord of Baakal."[19] Could this be an obscure late Palenque king? Or perhaps it refers to the usurpation of the Baakal name by a Comalcalco lord? It is difficult to say, but it seems likely that Comalcalco is pivotal in the archaeology and

79 OPPOSITE *A building within Group C, a late elite residential complex to the north of the site center, adjacent to the Otolum stream.*

80 RIGHT *The fragmentary Panel 1 from Chancalá, depicting the feet of a local lord who ruled near the time of Palenque's collapse.*

history of the Terminal Classic period in Tabasco, and that it may have had a hand in the ultimate demise of Palenque as a political and ritual center. Hopefully, future work at Comalcalco will reveal some answers.

It was in this same period that we also see a growing prominence among some of Palenque's more immediate neighbors. In the Chancalá Valley to the south and east, fragments of sculpted tablets from the Terminal Classic period point to vibrant, if short-lived, emergence of smaller polities at the end of the Late Classic period (fig. 80). Similarly, the kingdom of Pomoná, to the east, seems to have lived longer, at least as indicated by a monument from a nearby site called Panhale, dating to 830. A poorly known but important site near Tila, Chiapas, to the southwest, also has very late monuments, possibly indicating an upsurge of activity after Palenque's demise. The remains from many of these and other neighboring communities, while sometimes imprecise, look to be later than anything now known from Palenque, and may indicate a new rise of peripheral centers and neighboring kingdoms that had previously been under sway or influence of the Baakal kings.

The Fall of Palenque

These patterns among the recorded dates at Palenque and its neighbors beg the simple question: why did Palenque collapse when it did? The issue becomes even more important to consider when we understand that

Toniná, Palenque's old nemesis to the south, continued as a major ritual center for many more generations, well into the 10th century at least. Why did the story of these two neighboring rival cities differ so much? All major Maya kingdoms had their own differing story of collapse and change during this tumultuous period in Mesoamerican history. To understand Palenque's situation better, it might help to look at the broader forces that could have caused the collapse of nearly all of the elite Maya in the southern lowlands over the course of the 9th century.

Many experts prefer to play down the idea of a Classic Maya "collapse," stressing that instead a number of kingdoms continued to hold on to populations and even thrived into the Postclassic period (Toniná seems to be one of them).[20] But the cases of polity survival after about 850 are hardly the norm. When viewed in its wider context, the rapid abandonment of Classic Maya cities was a devastatingly real and widespread pattern. In simple terms of demography, most important Maya kingdoms of the southern lowlands saw a drastic departure or destruction of their core populations. Below is a list of some major kingdoms with their last known historical dates, arranged in chronological order:

Piedras Negras 795, Palenque 799;
Copán 805, Yaxchilan 808, Quiriguá 810, Tikal 869;
Toniná 909

The variation in the timing of the abandonment of different kingdoms indicates something about the complexity of the Maya collapse, yet it is still striking that after centuries of development and growth these and other centers were abandoned in only a century or so – a remarkably short span of time. The answer must lie in trying to understand what ills in Maya society set the stage for one of the most remarkable transformations in human history.

Archaeologists still discuss and debate the causes of the collapse phenomenon, lending different weight to factors such as endemic warfare, climate change, disease, and population growth, all of which we know were present in the Maya area in the 7th and 8th centuries.[21] So how do we find a cause among so many variables? Most scholars rightly stress that no one overriding factor was the cause, and we can see that different communities probably came under somewhat different combinations of stresses at this time. Despite the variations, though, one driving factor always seems to loom large in the background: rapid population growth.

Settlement archaeology throughout the Maya area has done a very good job of documenting the rapid growth of Maya populations during the Late Classic period. Palenque is no different, but it is in the late Balunté period (770–850) that we see clear indications of a phenomenal growth in population density around Palenque's ritual center. The recent settlement surveys conducted by Rodrigo Liendo Estuardo amply demonstrate a near doubling of the population density in the century leading up to the collapse.[22] No community could adapt well to such a simple and profound stress on resource management and livelihood. Looking at the overall map (see fig. 4), we can imagine that in these final years, around 800, Palenque was a difficult place to live, with housing complexes densely covering the hillside, crowding the precious streams, and spilling down into the low areas of the city. The spring water may have been flowing with enough regularity, but for many downstream it would not have been very healthy to drink. The map also shows us that the desirable flat terraces along the ridge had reached their carrying capacity: room was at a premium.

Near the end, too, not everyone had access to this core, well-watered area of Palenque. These conspicuous remains of households and other architectural forms, so visible today when one walks through the forests surrounding the main ruins, were no doubt mostly claimed by the elites. It is important to consider that just as the general population grew over time, so did the small segment of society that claimed political and religious privilege. The courts of Palenque grew nearly exponentially during the Late Classic period, as the sons and daughters of kings, princes, and priests aged and produced their own offspring. In time this produced its own troubles and stresses on the politics and social cohesion of the community. It is no accident, therefore, that a rapid increase in warfare and conflict among elites appears in the historical record in the century or so before the overall collapse.

As in other Maya communities, the social consequences of overpopulation had a direct impact on Palenque's political world, affecting the very foundations of Maya kingship, with its ideology based on concepts of renewal and close interactions with the gods who oversaw the equilibrium of the cosmos. In a world out of balance, the rules of authority were severely undercut. The political and economic pressures exerted under such conditions must have been formidable, and they were ultimately fatal for the community at large.

Another very different factor may help us to understand Palenque's demise, at least when it comes to explaining the end of the dynastic line. The list of kings we know from the historical records includes 16 rulers, ending as we have just seen with K'inich K'uk' Bahlam. Many royal names were recycled throughout the Classic period, so that, save for the usual addition of the honorific solar title K'inich, we often find two examples of the same name, one early and one late: K'uk' Bahlam, K'an Joy Chitam, Janab Pakal, and so forth. If we list all of the royal names we find a remarkable pattern to such repetitions: the name of the founding king is also the name of the last; the name of another early lord, Ahkal Mo' Nahb, is also the name of Pakal's grandson; the names of two Early Classic kings were reused by Pakal's two ruling grandsons, and so on (pages 244–47). In others words, the reuse of names by later kings is not random, but conforms to a reversed re-ordering. The symmetry is not perfect – some names do not repeat – but the pattern is consistent, with five separate names serving as mirror images of one another. In the center of this pattern of reflection, literally pivotal figures, are the lone woman who ruled Palenque, Ix Yohl Ik'nal, and her successor Muwaan Mat, who himself made use of the name of the creator maize god who begat the Palenque Triad. His own successor was, of course, the renaissance king K'inich Janab Pakal, who was the first to reuse an ancestral name.

The overall king list suggests a closed system. With K'inich K'uk' Bahlam's installment on the throne, would the Maya of Palenque have understood that he was, as a mirror of the founder, "the last" king? We hesitate to think that Maya dynasties were predestined to end by themselves, given that the Maya collapse was a real phenomenon that came about through a combination of environmental, economic, and political factors.

A number of people – we may never know how many – continued to live at Palenque and other centers for some years after the elites had gone and their monuments ceased to be erected, but even these small populations also eventually left, abandoning the temples, palaces, and modest households which became overgrown by the rain forest. Excavations of the Palace and of the Group C complex have uncovered a few distinctive potsherds of so-called Fine Orange wares dating to after 850 (the poorly attested Huipalé phase). They represent a very different kind of pottery for Palenque, with a widespread distribution in southern Mesoamerica and show many non-Maya characteristics in their decoration. The users of this pottery were evidently the last residents of Palenque. They occupied many of the prominent structures with easy water access, but in no great numbers. Some may have been squatters, or perhaps others were true holdouts with long-standing family roots at Palenque. In either case, one must wonder what they thought as they witnessed the decay of the once-glorious city that surrounded them. The final abandonment probably happened before 1000, after which the jungle quickly reclaimed the terraces and hillsides of the city, soon covering the Palace, the temples, and the residential complexes under a dense green canopy.

The demographic collapse was complete, and no steady population of Maya appears to have lived in the region of the ruins until the 16th century. At this time, in the wake of the conquest, the largely unexplored forests surrounding Palenque were incorporated within the newly founded Captaincy General of Guatemala. As we saw in Chapter 2, the Spanish founded Santo Domingo de Palenque in 1567, an outpost mission intended to pacify and convert the Ch'ol and Lacandón groups of Maya inhabiting the surrounding forest. These Maya, many of whom were relocated to Palenque throughout the colonial era, had no cultural memory or explanation of the vast ruins lying nearby. They simply called the strange buildings and the vaulted aqueduct the *otolum*, "Houses of Earth," a name that today lives on as the name of the stream that passes by the Palace and the ruined pyramids' main temples. The earliest explorers also called the ruins "Otolum," equating the name of the site with that of the once-sacred stream, just like the ancient inhabitants of Lakamha'. Of all that Palenque once was, now lost in history, it was this ancient and elemental connection between city and its landscape that somehow survived.

Palenque Today & Tomorrow

Those of us who attended the First Mesa Redonda at Palenque in December 1973 share many memories of the town, the ruins, and the region, and most of all the hospitality of the Morales family at La Cañada, then on the north edge of town. Santo Domingo de Palenque, now home to some 20,000 people, has expanded farther north since then to meet the growth of Pakalna, the settlement centered on the railroad station to the north, beyond the airport. The whole area now teems with tourists on their way to and from the ruins. The number of visitors to ancient Palenque is now more than 300,000 – over 40 times the estimated population of the city at the height of its prosperity in around AD 750! Appropriately, more than half of these visitors are Mexican nationals, including descendants of the very Maya who built ancient Lakamha'.

At the last count there were 20 hotels in and around Palenque town and the number is growing – a startling contrast to the state of things a century or so ago, when Benito Lacroix, who worked with Alfred Maudslay in 1891, opened the first hostelry in town. The 8-km (5-mile) road to the ruins, now punctuated by first-class restaurants, lodgings, and campgrounds, soon passes through a massive stone gate into the 23.3 sq. km (9 sq. mile) Parque Nacional Palenque. First, on the right, one sees the new Museo Alberto Ruz Lhuillier, one of the finest among the nation's many great museums. With adjacent stores and restaurants, it lies near the spot where the old trail – the very path trod by every early visitor from José Antonio Calderón to Frans Blom and beyond – turns abruptly uphill, following the bank of the Otolum and its cascades. Meanwhile, the paved road passes the trailhead and climbs quickly toward the central core of old Palenque. In its final S-curve the road is well within the ruins. Dozens of ancient mounds and broken buildings lie concealed in the dense vegetation nearby, some just a few feet from the pavement's edge, like Group IV, where archaeologists discovered the now-famous Tablet of the Slaves. The parking lot at the top is lined with vivid vendor stalls, and one immediately notices Lacandón and other Maya people in distinctive regional dress. They are here to sell crafts or are tourists themselves. Beyond the INAH ticket office and turnstile, visitors follow the wide foot trail that soon opens into a spacious plaza fronting the western façade of the Palace. To the right, near the base of the monumental staircase of the Temple of the Inscriptions, lies the tomb of Alberto Ruz Lhuillier, a miniature temple built of Palenque stone in the classic style. For us, this fitting resting place serves as a tangible reminder of the two centuries of unremitting archaeological effort by Ruz and many other colleagues, past and present.

What little we know of Palenque – and one will never know it completely – is gleaned almost entirely from a relatively few surviving elite tombs, complemented by the surviving fragmentary hieroglyphic record of official history and mythology graven in stone. Such remains provide us with a dazzling panorama of the old days in Palenque's royal court. Portraits of richly garbed rulers and royal relatives strike poses of haughty power against gaudy backdrops of carved and painted stone and stucco; successful war captains preside over the humiliation and sacrifice of captives in the secret courtyards of the Palace; and monstrous figures of Palenque's supernatural world, or their royal impersonators, direct political and religious events that pace the sacred cadence of time's relentless passage. Though clearly self-serving (as the written word tends to be), the talkative hieroglyphic texts tell us much about Palenque, not only in terms of individuals connected with the royal court, and at the same time reveal rare glimpses into the rich but shadowy world of ancient Palencano myth and the supernatural heroes who roamed there.

Despite the powerful appeal of Palenque's tombs, temples, and glyphic texts, and the knowledge they have given us of the ancient city, this is only part of the picture. For the whole story we must pay equal attention to the largely unknown parts of the city that lie beyond the Palace, the Temple of the Inscriptions, and other private spaces trod only by the ornate sandals of the aristocracy. It was in these parts of the city that thousands of anonymous

Palencanos dwelt and died over the course of at least a thousand years. Lacking further details about the commoners of Palenque, we cannot know with certainty who first settled among the "big waters," nor can we fully understand how and why Palenque, the city, worked so well for so long, and why, in the end, it failed. Most of the answers to these, as well as other key questions, yet unformed, lie concealed among the thousands of structures buried in the solitude of the forest.

Our colleagues are already beginning to address these fundamental questions about space, time, and culture in ancient Palenque. As we mentioned in Chapter 4, the detailed mapping of every mound, terrace, and other signs of ancient construction that define the archaeological zone is complete – save for the extreme western part of the ruins, where a land dispute prevented access. That area will, we hope, be surveyed in detail before long. As for the fundamental question of the timeline of Palenque's history, we have already noted several times the extraordinary contribution of Robert Rands and his colleagues working with the sequence of ceramic styles and their distribution over Palenque and its locality. In addition to these fundamental efforts, archaeology at Palenque is alive and well. Following in the tradition of the likes of Alberto Ruz, Heinrich Berlin, and César Sáenz, is the important ongoing fieldwork of Arnoldo González, Guillermo Bernal Romero, and Martha Cuevas García in various parts of central Palenque, as well as the crucial survey of settlement patterns in the city's outskirts and surrounding rural areas by Rodrigo Liendo Stuardo.

Thus does our future knowledge of the human story of what happened in ancient Palenque depend on a variety of approaches that ranges from "dirt archaeology" to epigraphy, and includes everything from studies of ancient pollen deposits to art history and the knowledge of modern Maya culture. Truly, the proper interpretation of this incredible city of the ancient Maya will only come from the continuing interplay and intercommunication among many scholars with different interests, outlooks, and approaches.

This diversity of related disciplines is exemplified in the excellent detailed summary of recent research at Palenque recently published under the editorship of Damien Markent, who began working at the site more than a decade ago.[1]

81 *Maya schoolchildren of Tenejapa in front of the Temple of the Sun.*

During our most recent visit to Palenque together, we observed an impressive event. As we rested under a shade tree in the manicured plaza of the Group of the Cross, a crowd of school children suddenly appeared, rounding the base of the pyramid of the Temple of the Cross. The boys wore conventional blue school shirts and trousers. The girls, however, were dressed in the brilliant red and black huipiles, traditional style of the Maya highlands. Several town elders in belted black tunics and beribboned hats accompanied them. The students filled the open space at a run, and, laughing, were followed by their teacher and the officials. But as they entered it, their pace slowed and they became quiet, partly because the adults raised their hands in command, and partly, we were sure, because they were truly awed by the space. For a moment we talked with some of them who paused under our shade tree. They had come by bus, they told us, all the way from Tenejapa in the mountains of Chiapas, not far from San Cristóbal de las Casas. They had been traveling, we realized, since the early hours of the morning, over winding mountain roads – roughly the identical route followed by Antonio del Río more than 200 years before – just to see the city built by their ancestors (fig. 81). We chatted for a short time in Spanish and broken Maya. Then they all assembled in two rows in front of the Temple of the Sun, girls in front, boys behind, and posed, unsmiling, for their photographer. For us, the memory of those Maya youths of today, so carefully arranged in one of ancient America's most hallowed settings, reminds us that, for the Maya, and indeed for all of us who know it, Palenque lives.

Summary Histories of the Rulers of Palenque

All dates are converted into Gregorian form using the standard 584285 correlation constant (GMT). Alternate names refer to the main designations for Palenque rulers found in earlier publications.

PRE-DYNASTIC RULERS

"Snake Spine"
Alternate name: U-K'ix-Chan

Birth:	11 March 993 BC (?)	5.6.11.3.4	7 Kan 2 Kumk'u
Accession:	28 March 967 BC (?)	5.7.17.10.17	11 Kaban seating of Pop

Source: Named on the Tablet of the Cross, seemingly as a historical ruler. His reign would correspond with the height of Olmec civilization during the early Middle Formative period.

"Ch'a" Ruler I
Alternate name: "Casper"

Dedication of shrine:	17 July AD 252	7.5.3.10.17	10 Kaban 5 Muwaan

Source: Temple XXI platform

DYNASTIC RULERS

K'uk' Bahlam
Alternate names: K'uk' Balam I, Bahlum K'uk'

Birth:	31 March 397	8.18.0.13.6	5 Kimi 14 K'ayab
Accession:	10 March 431	8.19.15.3.4	1 K'an 2 K'ayab
Death:	unknown		

Source: The first dynastic ruler named in the historical king list of the Tablet of the Cross.

"Ch'a" Ruler II
Alternate name: "Casper"

Birth:	9 August 422	8.18.6.8.8	11 Lamat 6 Xul
Accession:	10 August 435	8.19.19.11.17	2 Kaban 10 Xul
Period ending:	11 December 435	9.0.0.0.0	8 Ajaw 13 Keh
Installation of priest(?):	10 February 445	9.0.9.5.9	3 Muluk 7 Muwan (?)
Installation of priest(?):	20 November 460	9.1.5.5.11	6 Chuwen 19 Sak
Death:	unknown		

Sources: Named in the king list of the Tablet of the Cross, as well as on the Structure XVI Tablet (or K'an Tok Panel). His portrait may be on an onyx vase in the Dumbarton Oaks Collection in Washington, D.C.

Butz'aj Sak Chihk
Alternate name: Manik

Birth:	15 November 459	9.1.4.5.0	12 Ajaw 13 Sak
Conquest:	7 March 487	9.2.11.17.15	3 Men 13 K'ayab
Accession:	29 July 487	9.2.12.6.18	3 Etz'nab 11 Xul
Foundation(?) event(?):	26 August 490	9.2.15.9.2	9 Ik' end of Yaxk'in
Death:	unknown		

Sources: Named in the king list of the Tablet of the Cross, and in the opening passage of the Temple XVII tablet.

Ahkal Mo' Nahb I

Alternate names: **Lord Chaac, Chaacal I**

Birth:	6 July 465	9.1.10.0.0	5 Ajaw 3 Tzek
Accession:	5 June 501	9.3.6.7.17	5 Kaban seating of Sotz'
Installation of priest(?): 26 September 508		9.3.13.15.7	10 Manik' 15 Ch'en
Period ending:	18 October 514	9.4.0.0.0	13 Ajaw 18 Yax
Death:	1 December 524	9.4.10.4.17	5 Kaban 5 Mak

Sources: Named in the king list of the Tablet of the Cross; accession cited on the Temple XVII tablet; Period Ending mentioned on the east tablet of the Temple of the Inscriptions; Death recorded on the sarcophagus of Pakal, from the Temple of the Inscriptions, where his portrait is also found.

K'an Joy Chitam

Alternate name: **K'an Xul I**

Birth:	4 May 490	9.2.15.3.8	12 Lamat 6 Woh
Childhood ritual:	20 November 496	9.3.1.15.0	12 Ajaw 8 Keh
Accession:	25 February 529	9.4.14.10.4	5 K'an 12 K'ayab
Period ending:	13 February 561	9.6.7.0.0	7 Ajaw 8 K'ayab
Death:	8 February 565	9.6.11.0.16	7 Kib 4 K'ayab

Sources: Tablet of the Cross; Tablet of the Sun; Temple XIX platform; Inscriptions sarcophagus.

Ahkal Mo' Nahb II (Yitk'aba'il Umam Ahkal Mo' Nahb)

Alternate names: **Chaacal II, Akul Ah Nab II**

Birth:	5 September 523	9.4.9.0.4	7 Kan 17 Mol
Accession:	4 May 565	9.6.11.5.1	1 Imix 4 Zip
Death:	23 July 570	9.6.16.10.7	9 Manik 5 Yaxk'in

Sources: Tablet of the Cross; east tablet of the Temple of the Inscriptions; Inscriptions sarcophagus.

Kan Bahlam

Alternate names: **Chan Bahlum I, Kan-Balam I**

Birth:	20 September 524	9.4.10.1.5	11 Chikchan 13 Ch'en
Accession:	8 April 572	9.6.18.5.12	10 Eb Seating of Woh
Period ending:	3 December 573	9.7.0.0.0	7 Ajaw 3 K'ank'in
Period ending:	11 November 578	9.7.5.0.0	13 Ajaw 18 Keh
Death:	3 February 583	9.7.9.5.5	11 Chikchan 3 Wayeb

Sources: Tablet of the Cross; east tablet of the Temple of the Inscriptions; Inscriptions sarcophagus.

Ix Yohl Ik'nal

Alternate names: **Lady Kan, Lady Kanal Ikal**

Birth:	unknown		
Accession:	23 December 583	9.7.10.3.8	9 Lamat 1 Muwaan
Installation of priest(?): 11 September 595		9.8.2.1.8	12 Lamat 1 Yax
Period ending:	12 May 613	9.8.0.0.0	5 Ajaw 3 Ch'en
Death:	7 November 604	9.8.11.6.12	2 Eb end of Keh

Sources: East panel of the Temple of the Inscriptions; Inscriptions sarcophagus.

Ajen Yohl Mat

Alternate names: **Aahc-Kan, Ac-Kan, Ah K'an**

Birth:	unknown		
Accession:	4 January 605	9.8.11.9.10	8 Ok 18 Muwaan
Period ending:	18 June 606	9.8.13.0.0	5 Ajaw 18 Tzek
Death:	11 August 612	9.8.19.4.0	2 Kimi 14 Mol

Sources: East panel of the Temple of the Inscriptions; Inscriptions sarcophagus.

Janab Pakal
Alternate name: **Pacal I**
Birth: unknown
Accession: unknown
Death: 9 March 612   9.8.18.14.11   3 Chuwen 4 Wayeb
Sources: Inscriptions sarcophagus; Group IV censer stand.

Muwaan Mat
Alternate name: "Lady Beastie"
Birth: unknown
Accession: 22 October 612   9.8.19.7.18   9 Etz'nab 6 Keh
Period ending: 12 May 613   9.9.0.0.0   3 Ajaw 3 Sotz'
Death: unknown
Source: East tablet of the Temple of the Inscriptions.

K'inich Janab Pakal
Alternate names: **Lord Shield, Pacal, Pakal, Janaab Pakal, Kinich Janab Pakal II**
Birth: 26 March 603   9.8.9.13.0   8 Ajaw 13 Pop
Accession: 29 July 615   9.9.2.4.8   5 Lamat 1 Mol
Installation of priest(?): 9 November 625   9.9.12.12.4   4 K'an 7 Mak
Period ending: 27 January 633   9.10.0.0.0   1 Ajaw 8 K'ayab
Period ending: 6 December 642   9.10.10.0.0   13 Ajaw 18 K'ank'in
Period ending: 14 October 652   9.11.0.0.0   12 Ajaw 8 Keh
Dedication,
north Palace(?):   3 May 654   9.11.1.10.12   12 Eb 10 Sotz'
Dedication,
subterraneos: 12 June 654   9.11.1.12.6   7 Kimi 4 Xul
Dedication, House E: 4 November 654   9.11.2.1.11   9 Chuwen 9 Mak
Conquest: 16 August 659   9.11.6.16.17   13 Kaban 10 Ch'en
Dedication, House C: 25 December 661   9.11.9.5.19   4 Kawak 2 Pax
Dedication, House A: 22 May 668   9.11.15.14.19   4 Kawak 7 Tzek
Period ending: 1 July 672   9.12.0.0.0   10 Ajaw 8 Yaxk'in
Period ending: 10 May 682   9.12.10.0.0   9 Ajaw 18 Sotz'
Death: 31 August 683   9.12.11.5.18   6 Etznab 11 Yax
Sources: Temple of the Inscriptions tablets; Inscriptions sarcophagus; many texts from the Palace.

K'inich Kan Bahlam
Alternate names: **Snake Jaguar, Chan Bahlum**
Birth: 23 May 635   9.10.2.6.6   2 Kimi 19 Sotz'
Childhood ritual: 17 June 641   9.10.8.9.3   9 Akbal 6 Xul
Accession: 10 January 684   9.12.11.12.10   8 Ok 3 K'ayab
Dedication,
Cross Group: 10 January 692   9.12.19.14.12   5 Eb 5 K'ayab
Period ending: 18 March 692   9.13.0.0.0   8 Ajaw 8 Woh
Period ending: 26 January 702   9.13.10.0.0   7 Ajaw 3 Kumk'u
Death: 20 February 702   9.13.10.1.5   6 Chikchan 3 Pop
Sources: Cross Group temples; Temple XVII.

K'inich K'an Joy Chitam
Alternate names: **Lord Hok, K'an Xul, K'an Xul II**

Birth:	5 November 644	9.10.11.17.0	11 Ajaw 8 Mak
Accession:	3 June 702	9.13.10.6.8	5 Lamat 6 Xul
Capture:	30 August 711	9.13.19.13.3	13 Ak'bal 16 Yax
Installation of priest(?): 13 November 718		9.14.7.0.15	6 Men 13 K'ank'in
Dedication,			
House A–D:	14 August 720	9.14.8.14.15	9 Men 3 Yax
Death:	unknown		

Sources: Palace Tablet; Tablet of the 96 Glyphs; K'an Tok panel (Temple XVI); Toniná Monument 122.

K'inich Ahkal Mo' Nahb
Alternate names: **Chaacal III, Ah Kul Ah Nab III**

Birth:	16 September 678	9.12.6.5.8	3 Lamat 6 Sak
Accession:	3 January 722	9.14.10.4.2	9 Ik' 5 K'ayab
Period ending:	22 August 731	9.15.0.0.0	4 Ajaw 13 Yax
Dedication,			
Temple XIX:	14 January 734	9.15.2.7.16	9 Kib 19 K'ayab
Dedication,			
Temple XXI:	13 June 736	9.15.4.15.17	6 Kaban 5 Yaxk'in
Period ending:	26 July 736	9.15.5.0.0	10 Ajaw 8 Ch'en
Death:	unknown		

Sources: Temple XVIII stuccoes and jamb; Temple XIX; Temple XXI; Tablet of the 96 Glyphs.

Upakal K'inich Janab Pakal
Alternate name(s): none

Birth:	unknown		
Period ending(?):	18 June 709	9.13.17.9.0	3 Ajaw 3 Yaxk'in
Accession:	unknown		
Installation of priest(?): 29 January 742(?)		9.15.10.10.13	8 Ben 16 Kumk'u
Death:	unknown		

Sources: Temple XIX stucco pier; Temple XXI platform.

K'inich Kan Bahlam II
Alternate name(s): none

Birth:	unknown		
Accession:	unknown		
Period ending(?):	9 May 751	9.16.0.0.0	2 Ajaw 13 Tzek
Death:	unknown		

Source: Pomoná, Stela 7.

K'inich K'uk' Bahlam
Alternate names: **Lord K'uk', Bahlum K'uk'**

Birth:	unknown		
Accession:	8 March 764	9.16.13.0.7	9 Manik 15 Woh
Installation of priest(?): 20 December 767		9.16.16.15.9	13 Muluk 2 K'ayab
Period ending:	17 November 783	9.17.13.0.0	13 Ajaw 13 Muwaan
Anniversary:	24 November 783	9.17.13.0.7	7 Manik seating of Muwaan
Death:	unknown		

Sources: Tablet of the 96 Glyphs; K'an Tok panel (Temple XVI).

The Palenque Dynasty

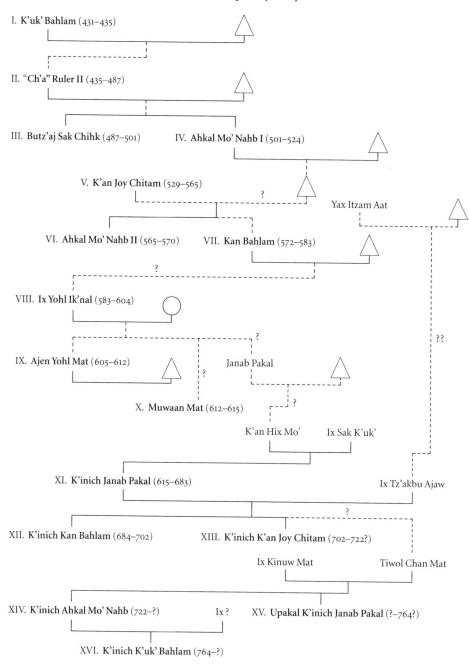

I. K'uk' Bahlam (431–435)

II. "Ch'a" Ruler II (435–487)

III. Butz'aj Sak Chihk (487–501)   IV. Ahkal Mo' Nahb I (501–524)

V. K'an Joy Chitam (529–565)   ?

Yax Itzam Aat

VI. Ahkal Mo' Nahb II (565–570)   VII. Kan Bahlam (572–583)

?

VIII. Ix Yohl Ik'nal (583–604)

IX. Ajen Yohl Mat (605–612)   Janab Pakal   ?

?

X. Muwaan Mat (612–615)   ?

??

K'an Hix Mo'   Ix Sak K'uk'

XI. K'inich Janab Pakal (615–683)   Ix Tz'akbu Ajaw

XII. K'inich Kan Bahlam (684–702)   XIII. K'inich K'an Joy Chitam (702–722?)   ?

Ix Kinuw Mat   Tiwol Chan Mat

XIV. K'inich Ahkal Mo' Nahb (722–?)   Ix ?   XV. Upakal K'inich Janab Pakal (?–764?)

XVI. K'inich K'uk' Bahlam (764–?)

Notes

CHAPTER ONE *Palenque and its World*

1 Stephens, 1841, 2: 356.

2 Paul Kirchhoff, 1943, was the first to formally define the concept of "Mesoamerica," which has changed little since his time. Some (i.e., Wauchope, ed., 1965 and Stuart, 1968, etc.) have used the term "Middle America" to convey the same general concept.

3 Such terms as "formative" and "classic," or even "decadent" and "florescent," which have been used in the past to designate periods in Mesoamerican or Maya archaeology, carry "loaded" implications of cultural development. The current designations "Preclassic," "Classic," and "Postclassic," are really no better, for they have a subtle influence on how we think about the human past in Mesoamerica. Until a new system is devised, however, these must serve.

4 Miller and Martin, 2004.

5 *Diccionario de Autoridades*, vol. 3.

6 Morales, 1974.

7 Barnhart, 2001, v-vii.

8 Ibid., Map 5.1.

9 The description, translated by the authors, comes from Calderón's manuscript report of 1784: "un Palacio que por su constructura, y magnitud no pudo ser menos." (Ballesteros-Gaibrois, 1993: 131).

10 Barnhart, 2001: 9.

11 See Robertson, 1983–1993, for the definitive documentation of Palenque sculpture.

12 Gendrop, 1974.

13 These structures are often referred to as "roof combs."

14 Merle Greene Robertson on guide lines for the sculptors.

15 Van Stone, 2005.

16 Coe in Miller and Martin, 2004.

17 Miller and Martin, 2004: 199–200.

18 Barnhart on population density, 2001.

19 Liendo Stuardo, 2001.

CHAPTER TWO *An Ancient City Discovered*

1 Original letter in the collection of the Center for Maya Research, Barnardsville, North Carolina, gift of Ian Graham (see Appendix I). Originally part of the Kingsborough correspondence, the manuscript passed into the collection of Sir Thomas Phillipps.

2 Paillés and Nieto, 1993, provides an excellent summary of the 18th-century political setting of Palenque.

3 English translation by Baily, 1823: 18, based on Juarros, 1808–18 (Juarros's work also appeared in 1857). See also Saville, 1928: 124.

4 As Juarros, 1808–18, recognizes, the modern discovery of Palenque generally coincided with that of Pompeii, Italy, buried by volcanic ash in AD 79 – one of the few truly "lost cities" of history.

5 See Brasseur de Bourbourg, 1866: 3–4; Hardy, 1985: 23, citing Lacroix González, 1976: 11, Paillés and Nieto, 1993; and Navarrete, 2000.

6 Charles III (1759–88), the "enlightened despot," is remembered by historians today as the greatest of the Bourbon rulers of Spain. With regard to his attitude toward Spain's American lands, R. Tripp Evans notes: "Following the War of the Spanish Succession, the newly established Bourbon monarchy had displayed a keen interest in its overseas empire. Because this interest primarily concerned the generation of greater colonial revenue, Charles III actively encouraged his viceroys to explore the mineralogy, geology, and geography of New Spain" (Evans, 2004: 16, 17 and see Cabello Carro, 1992: 33).

7 For a review of this and other official documents related to the early expeditions, see Castañeda Paganini, 1946; Cabello Carro, 1992; and Ballesteros-Gaibrois, 1993. For a useful timetable of the period of Palenque's discovery and publication from 1746 to 1837 see Navarrete, 2000: 48–51.

8 A map of the trail as it was in 1922 is given by Blom, 1982: 17 and Ferrer, 1993: 83–85, gives an excellent history of this trail.

9 Ballesteros-Gaibrois, 1993: 159–62.

10 Ibid., 161

11 Muñoz had doubtless read Gregorio García's *Origen de los Indios de el nuevo mundo* (Madrid, 1729 [1607]), which mentions "Edificios antiguos, a donde ai figures de Hombres de gran estatua, I armadas, I gravado todo en piedra near Ocosingo, certainly the ruins of Toniná, not far from Palenque".

12 For the complete text of Muñoz's recommendations, see Ballesteros-Gaibrois, 1993: 169–72.

13 Del Río and Cabrera, 1822; Ballesteros-Gaibrois, 1993: 215–16.

14 Griffin, 1974: 10, was the first to recognize this thought-provoking aspect of the episode.

15 Ballesteros-Gaibrois, 1993: 216 (translation by the authors); and see del Río and Cabrera, 1822: 2.

16 For listings and illustrations of the objects removed from Palenque by del Río, see Cabello Carro, 1989 and Riese, 1993.

17 Ballesteros-Gaibrois, 1993: 226 (translation by the authors), see also del Río and Cabrera, 1822: 16.

18 Del Río's narrative refers to the set of 30 figures that Armendáriz drew in 1787 (see Ballesteros-Gaibrois, 1993 and Olmos Pieri, 1993). The first publication of all 30 Armendáriz drawings along with the del Río account is that of Castañeda Paganini, 1946.

19 Ignacio Armendáriz may be the least known name in the history of research at Palenque. Del Río's report fails even to mention him, and the few times the artist's name has appeared in the literature he is referred to as either "Ignacio Armendáriz" or "Ricardo Almendáriz" (Castañeda Paganini, 1946: 15; Berlin, 1970: 111; Stuart, G., 1992: 5; Cabello Carro, 1992: 26; and Ballesteros-Gaibrois, 1993). In using the former name, we follow the evidence of an actual signature, a copy of which was supplied by Peter Mathews (personal communication), who presented it at the University of Texas Maya Meetings in March 2006.

20 Aramoni Calderón, 1991: 418.

21 Kingsborough, 1830: 5.

22 The final versions of the 127 sheets containing the drawings that Castañeda produced on the three Dupaix expeditions, including the 27 devoted to Palenque, are part of the collection of the Biblioteca del Laboratorio de Arte at the University of Seville. All are reproduced by Alcina Franch, 1969: 2.

23 For a summary of Palenque amid the politics of the early 19th century, see Navarrete, 2000: 37–45.

24 Of the two known complete contemporary copies of Armendáriz's "Estampas de Palenque," one is in the Biblioteca del Palacio Real in Madrid (see Ballesteros-Gaibrois, 1993 and Olmos Pieri, 1993). The other is part of the Jay I. Kislak Collection in the Library of Congress, Washington, D.C. A cursory comparison of the two reveals that the Kislak copy holds more details in both figures and hieroglyphs than the Palacio Real version. Such details include elements of dress in the Tablet of the Temple of the Cross and the fish held in the mouth of the bird in the headdress of the figure shown on the west sanctuary jamb of the same building as shown in fig. 52. For other discussions of the confusion among the earliest illustrations of Palenque, see Kluckholn, 1935; Castañeda Paganini, 1946; Cabello Carro, 1992; Ballesteros-Gaibrois, 1993; and Olmos Pieri, 1993.

25 Humboldt, 1810: plate 11.

26 Howard Cline, 1947: 299, suggests that the enigmatic "McQuy" may be a disguised reference to James MacQueen, owner of the lithography firm that produced the plates for the 1822 Berthoud publication of del Río and Cabrera. MacQueen was apparently traveling in the West Indies during the Guatemalan revolution (also see Evans, 2004: 34, no. 45).

27 Cabrera apparently found this and a partner medallion somewhere, perhaps Palenque (see Ballesteros-Gaibrois, 1960: 37). Cabrera may have given the companion piece to fellow antiquarian Ramón Ordoñez de Aguiar in Ciudad Real. The illustration of this curious and irrelevent medallion crops up like the proverbial "bad penny" throughout the known corpus of Castañeda's work illustrating the Dupaix expeditions (see Kingsborough, 1830, vol. IV; Dupaix, 1834; and Alcina Franch, 1969, 2: plate 87).

28 The review appeared in no. 303 of the *Literary Gazette*, 9 November 1822. See Brunhouse, 1973: 15 for a more complete treatment of this matter.

29 Saville, 1928: 125–26.

30 Warden, 1827: pls XIV–XVIII.

31 Volumes I to VII of the *Antiquities of Mexico*, published during Lord Kingsborough's life, first appeared in 1829 and 1830. The last two volumes did not appear until 1848, 14 years after Lord Kingsborough's death.

32 The first appeared in Kingsborough's Volumes V and VI, issued in 1830. Volume IV, issued the same year, held almost all of José Luciano Castañeda's 125 drawings, including 33 of Palenque.

33 The first sets of Kingsborough's work to reach the United States may have arrived as late as 1839, for in April of that year, historian William H. Prescott wrote, "I am daily expecting from Europe…the magnificent works of Lord Kingsborough. There is not a copy, I believe, in the United States" (von Hagen, 1947: 77, no. 4). Prescott evidently obtained a set, for in September 1848 he wrote a letter, now part of the collection of the Center for Maya Research, Barnardsville, North Carolina, agreeing to lend the massive volumes to the archaeologist (and diplomat-to-be) Ephraim George Squier.

34 Griffin, 1974: 11 and see Saville, 1928: 136, 137.

35 The Edward Ayer Collection at the Newberry Library, Chicago, contains many yet-unpublished drawings that Waldeck made during his stay in Palenque, including views of local Palencanos, as well as others made elsewhere. Also see Baudez, 1993: plates 23, 28, 44, etc., for excellent samples of Waldeck's paintings of Palenque.

36 Rafinesque, 1836: 148.

37 The *Saturday Evening Post*, Philadelphia, 13 January 1827.

38 This same group of ten hieroglyphs frequently illustrated works of the period between 1829 and 1841, sometimes in their original columnar form, sometimes as two rows, and sometimes sideways (see Rafinesque, 1832; Priest, 1833, 1841, etc.; and Stuart, 1989: fig. 5).

39 Graham, 1963: 12. Glyphs taken from Palenque by Galindo are now in the possession of the Society of Antiquaries, London.

40 Rafinesque, 1832, 1: 1; 1: 2.

41 Dupaix, 1834 and Villaseñor Espinosa, 1978.

42 For some reason, both the 1830 and 1834 editions of Dupaix failed to include the drawing of Pier F of Palace House D – an image that Armendáriz drew in 1787, and that Castañeda later copied (see Alcina Franch, 1969, 2, Lam. 16).

43 The main distinction of Delafield's work is its 5.5-m (18-foot) folding frontispiece on thin tissue – a virtual facsimile of the Aztec Codex Boturini.

CHAPTER THREE *Visitors Spread the Word*

1 Excerpt from *And We Shall Sleep and Heed It Not* (Anonymous, 1845).

2 Von Hagen, 1947: 70–73.

3 Von Hagen, 1947: 70, 71, no. 4.

4 Von Hagen, 1947: 72, 73, no. 5.

5 Von Hagen, 1947: 79, 80.

6 Stephens, 1970, ed. Von Hagen. The original contract between Stephens and Catherwood is part of the Stephens papers in the Bancroft Library, University of California, Berkeley. The full text of the document is given by von Hagen (in Stephens, 1970: xlii).

7 Pendergast, 1967: 6, 29–32.

8 Graffiti in the Palace: Stephens, 1841: 1 and von Hagen, 1947: 158.

9 Stephens, 1841, 1: 137, describes Catherwood's methods of making his field drawings. The *camera lucida* he used to compose his views consisted of a prism mounted on a vertical rod clamped to the drawing table or board so as to project an image of the subject onto a blank sheet of paper. For a picture of Catherwood's initial despair in trying to render the complex Copán monuments accurately, see von Hagen, 1947: 114–15.

10 Griffin, 1974: 12.

11 Stephens, 1841, 1: 342–43.

12 Stephens, 1841, 2: 356–57. See also von Hagen, 1847: 166–67, where he evocatively re-creates the scene.

13 Von Hagen, 1947: 188.

14 Von Hagen, 1947: 197, 198.

15 Von Hagen, 1947: 197ff.

16 *The New World*, New York, 4 July 1841.

17 MacKay, 1852: preface.

18 See Evans, 2004: 86, 87, for the Barnum story. There are at least three editions and an unknown number of printings of the Iximaya pamphlet (see "Velazquez," 1850, etc.).

19 Wauchope, 1962, stands as the classic commentary on the history of popular beliefs on the origins of Native Americans.

20 Williams, 1991, provides an excellent and detailed history of all manner of individuals, ranging from charlatans and cranks to free-thinkers and mystics, who devoted themselves to the origins of the ancient Americans.

21 Davis, 1842, etc.

22 Von Hagen, 1947: 259.

23 *The Mountain Democrat*, Placerville, California, vol. 26, no. 24 (14 June 1879), p. 1, col. 4, middle.

24 Anonymous personal communication, *c.* 1975, to one of the authors.

25 Following their return from Palenque in 1840, and the publication of Stephens's two volumes on Central America in 1841, he and Catherwood made a second journey, picking up at Uxmal and continuing through Yucatán. For the results of this trip, see Stephens, 1843.

26 Morelet [1857] 1871: 98, 107.

27 Forresta and Wood, 1995: 11. See also Mace, 1990 and Kenneth E. Nelson on the history of the daguerreotype (www.daguerre.org/resource.php).

28 Catherwood took the necessary equipment for making daguerreotypes on his and Stephens's second expedition to the Maya area in 1841. The results of his work were subsequently lost.

29 Charnay and Viollet-le-Duc, 1863: pls 19–22, Davis, 1981.

30 Waldeck's drawings and paintings are mostly distributed between the Edward Ayer Collection at the Newberry Library, Chicago, and the Bibliothèque nationale, Paris (see Baudez, 1993).

31 Larrainzar, 1875–78: I, 162–65.

32 Charnay, 1863.

33 Brunhouse, 1975: 7, Hermann, 1992: 22–[33].

34 Stephens, 1841, 2: 346.

35 For details of the story of the journey on the right-hand slab, see von Hagen, 1947: 177.

36 Rau, 1879: 3, 4, cites Barnard's "American Journal of Education," January 1868, for the first publication of Matile's identification of the Smithsonian carving. In 1878, Philipp J. J. Valentini independently arrived at the same conclusion in the *Proceedings of the American Antiquarian Society*, no. 71.

37 Rau, 1879: 3.

38 Holden, 1881 and 1881a.

39 Charnay renamed the Maya ruins of Menché "Lorillard City" in honor of Pierre Lorillard IV. The name didn't last, and the ruins are now known as Yaxchilan. Parenthetically, Lorillard is also credited as the inventor of the tuxedo.

40 Ruz, 1973: 22, 24.

41 The *Washington Post*, 18 June 1883.

42 Maudslay and Maudslay, 1899: 224ff.

43 Barnhart, 2001: 3.

44 See Graham, 2002: 222–23, for details of the remarkable Annie Hunter and her contributions to the field.

45 Holmes, 1897: 206 and Thompson, 1895.
46 The wealthy American bibliophile and philanthropist Joseph Florimond, duc de Loubat (he was granted the title by Pope Leo XIII for his generosity to the Church) is perhaps best known among Mesoamerican scholars for his beautiful and accurate facsimile editions of various Mexican codices, which he produced at great expense and gave to various institutions of learning.
47 Saville, 1928: 155–67, short report on the results of the Loubat expedition contains a few useful descriptions and of architecture, along with photographs and new drawings of four hieroglyphic tablets from the *subterraneos,* the buried passageway system in the lower level of the Palace.
48 Ibid. Saville's greatest contribution to Palenque studies is his extremely useful bibliographical study of research at the site (Saville, 1928).
49 In 1899, in one of the least known chapters of Palenque's history, some 24,000 acres of land immediately adjacent to "the ejido lands of the village of Palenque," including the ruins of Palenque, legally became the property of the Chiapas Rubber Plantation and Investment Company of San Francisco, California. This real estate reverted to Mexico after the revolution of 1910–17. Karena Shields, famed writer, actor, pilot, and photographer, spent part of her childhood (1904–13) at the Finca San Leandro, one of the four tracts of the Chiapas Rubber Plantation, where her father was in charge. This background imbued her with a deep interest in the area and its people. In the mid-1940s, Shields purchased the 200–acre parcel of land that included her childhood home. Until her death in 1972, she found time to photograph ruins and monuments in the Palenque area, to write two popular books based on her childhood and a paper on the Tzeltal Maya of Chiapas (Berlin, 1955: 205 and see Shields, 1959 and 1959a).
50 *Revista de Revistas,* México, 20 February 1921 and see Molina Montes, 1979: 3.
51 The Campeche edition of Stephens covered his travels in Yucatán in 1841 and 1842. It was issued by subscription in some 30 separate parts in 1849 and 1850 as *Viaje a Yucatán.* The text was translated by Justo Sierra O'Reilly, and the work was published without Catherwood's illustrations.
52 The Smithsonian Institution in Washington, D.C.'s repatriation of the carving came about largely through the efforts of archaeologist Zelia Nuttall and New York Senator Elihu Root (see Blom, 1982: 73).
53 In 1864, linguistic scholar Leon de Rosny photographed the Codex Peresianus, or Paris Codex, a fragment of a Maya book in the Bibliothèque

imperiale. In 1871, Brasseur de Bourbourg published the Codex Troano, a fragment in possession of the Tro family in Madrid. Shortly afterward, a second fragment, owned by the descendents of Cortés came to light. In 1882, Rosny united the two parts to form the Codex Tro-Cortesianus Codex, or Madrid Codex.
54 Förstemann's most important papers on Maya chronology and the hieroglyphs involved appeared in English translation in Bowditch, ed., 1904.
55 Gunckel, 1897, summarizes the work of various scholars of the late 19th century on the fundamental matter of the reading order of Maya hieroglyphic texts on the monuments and in the codices.
56 Goodman, 1905.
57 Rickards, 1910.

CHAPTER FOUR *Archaeology Comes to Palenque*
1 From the guest book of the Hotel Lacroix, Palenque, 28 August 1955 (Hardy, 1985: 29): "He tenido la suerte de realizar un sueño de arqueólogo: trabajar en Palenque y realizar aqui un descubrimiento importante. Un lazo eterno me une por lo tanto a este sitio marvilloso…" [translation by the authors].
2 Bernal, 1980: 160ff. Ezequiel Chávez signed for Mexico. Later directors were Boas, Tozzer, Engerrand, and Gamio.
3 Seler, 1915 and 1976.
4 Comas, 1950 and Bernal, 1980.
5 A decade later, Beyer founded the important journal *El México Antiguo,* the first of which contained the work of Beyer himself, Nicolás León, Enrique Juan Palacios, and other luminaries of the time.
6 Bernal, 1980.
7 Leifer, et al. n.d. and 2002.
8 Bernal, 1980: 142ff.
9 The archaeological publications, notably the series of Memoirs of the Peabody Museum of Archaeology and Ethnology, Harvard University that appeared between 1896 and 1932, as well as the publications of the Carnegie Institution of Washington from 1920 to 1937 together represented the beginning of a kind of "Golden Age" in the publication of the archaeology of the Maya area.
10 Leifer, et al., 2002: 140. English version courtesy of Jesper Nielsen, 2005.
11 Blom, 1982.
12 Noguera Auza, 1985: 13–64.
13 Blom and La Farge, 1926, 1: 194–95.
14 Fernández, 1985c: plates 1 and 2.
15 INAH's first director was Alfonso Caso, Herman Beyer's old student who had gained widespread fame for his discovery of Tomb 7 at Monte Albán, Oaxaca.
16 Berlin, 1942.

17 Fernández, 1985f-h.

18 Molina Montes, 1979: 6 and García Moll, 1985: 85.

19 Ruz Lhuillier, 1973: 32.

20 Ruz Lhuillier, 1952d.

21 Robertson, 1983–93, 3: 54.

22 Ruz Lhuillier, 1952d: fig. 1; and see Seler, 1915: 113–22.

23 Ruz Lhuillier, 1952e.

24 Rands and Rands, 1961 and RLR, Personal communication, 2005, on Rands and the choice of Palenque

25 Ruz Lhuillier, 1973: 32.

26 Ruz Lhuillier, 1952e and 1973: 67–75, fig. 259.

27 Ruz Lhuillier, 1973: 75.

28 Ruz Lhuillier, 1973, raises the possibility that Antonio del Río may have disturbed this floor in 1787.

29 Juan Chablé, personal communication, 1958.

30 Ruz Lhuillier, 1952 and 1952a.

31 Berlin, 1959.

32 Proskouriakoff, 1960, 1961.

33 Knorozov, 1952 and Kelley, 1962.

34 Ruz Lhuillier, 1956.

35 Incensario stands as totem poles (Sáenz, 1956).

36 Ruz Lhuillier, 1962.

37 Acosta, 1968, 1973, and 1976.

38 Acosta, 1973.

39 Hammond, ed., 1974 and Bernal, 1980.

40 Ethnology studies.

41 Willey in Hammond, 1974.

42 Keleman, 1943 and Kubler, 1962, etc. The use of the term "primitive" in referring to Native American art and the art of Africa and Oceania as well persists to this day in titles of works on the subject and in the names of museum collections or curatorships.

43 Coe, 1973.

44 Robertson in Robertson, Macri, and McHargue, eds, 1996.

45 Ibid.

46 Ibid.

47 Robertson, 1983–93.

48 González Cruz and Bernal Romero, 2000.

49 G. Stuart in Fagan, ed., 2007. Perhaps the complete Tablet of the Cross has been on exhibit ever since, first at the old Museo Nacional near Mexico City's Zócalo, and after 1963, at the Museo Nacional de Antropología in Chapultepec Park.

50 González Cruz and Bernal Romero, 2003.

51 Barnhart, 2001.

CHAPTER FIVE *The Early Lords*

1 See Schele, 1992: 86.

2 These dates come from a single passage recorded in blocks P4–Q9 in the main text of the Tablet of the Cross, but their anchor in the Long Count system has long been problematic. The passage straddles two sections of the narrative – one set in mythical time and another placed in Early Classic history – leading to confusion about where the "floating" Calendar Round stations should lie. Floyd Lounsbury, Linda Schele, and Peter Mathews (see Schele, 1992: 86) believed the dates would be best placed in historical times, just before those firmly associated with the next king.

3 The first identification of Toktahn was by Stuart and Houston, 1994: 31. The Toktahn emblem glyph appears prominently on the tablet of Temple XVI (also known as "The K'an Tok Panel") and always in connection with early rulers.

4 The Dumbarton Oaks vessel may not be a contemporary artifact. Although it is Early Classic in style, there are subtle indications that it may date from slightly later than the 5th century. This may account for the use of the standard Baakal royal title, which came to be used soon afterward.

5 The Temple XVII tablet was discovered in 1993 by Arnoldo González Cruz. In 2002 he discovered more fragments of the same panel in the course of other excavations at Temple XXI, some distance away within the Group of the Cross. Indications are that the Temple XVII tablet suffered intentional damage in antiquity. At some point, possibly in Terminal Classic times if not later, these battered glyph fragments were transported and used as construction material by squatters residing in the ruins of Temple XXI.

6 This comes from the use of the same verb glyph to record the ritual "setting" or "establishment" of a K'awiil effigy in a station of the 819–day cycle, as recorded on the Palace Tablet.

7 For a discussion of the architectural sequence of the North Group, see Tovalín and Manrique, 1996. As these authors note, the lack of distinctive ceramics in association with the building phases made absolute dating nearly impossible. No hieroglyphic dates survive in the North Group.

8 The suggestion that the tomb was re-entered in the Late Classic is presented here for the first time, based on the later style of the paintings found within the tomb, and on analysis of the archaeological stratigraphy as published in the original report (Ruz Lhuillier, 1962). In an earlier discussion of the Temple XVIII-A tomb, Schele, 1986, suggested that the tomb chamber was sealed from the inside by a woman buried alive as a sacrifice. This is surely not the case. Ruz's detailed description of the tomb reveals that the handprints in the plaster wall were made by an ancient tomb worker who exited through the hole and began sealing it from the outside.

9 See Braswell, 2004, for a recent discussion of the issues and debates surrounding the complex and varied

evidence Teotihuacan's involvement with the Maya area. At Tikal, historical evidence suggests a direct and disruptive political presence by highland individuals, Stuart, 2000. The later "founder" of the Copán dynasty also shows similar connections to the highlands (see Fash, 1991 and Stuart, 2004).

10 His extended name is *Yitk'aba'il Umam Ahkal Mo' Nahb*, most likely meaning "The (He who is) the Namesake of his Grandfather, Ahkal Mo' Nahb." Scribes seemed careful to distinguish between these two early kings, but on the Pakal sarcophagus lid he is named simply "Ahkal Mo' Nahb." We therefore follow the traditional method of designating him as the second of two rulers with the same name, hence "Ahkal Mo' Nahb II."

11 See Grube, 1996. Some details of the history have changed since Grube's analysis of events.

12 The Santa Elena panel is one of three found in a ball court; it now resides with its companions in the local museum in Balancan, Tabasco, after being removed from the site in 1986 by archaeologists Rebecca Perales and Mugarte, 1990.

13 Written on the east panel of the Temple of the Inscriptions, in blocks O8–P9 and Q4–R6.

CHAPTER SIX *King of Kings*

1 Janab Pakal is the name of the curious ancestor, with the honorific *K'inich* title being the only difference between the two names. He is known only from the mention of his name and his portrait on Pakal's sarcophagus. He may have been the father of Pakal's mother, Ix Sak K'uk'.

2 The inauguration date is recorded prominently in several inscriptions, including the inscribed texts of House E in the Palace, The Palace Tablet, as well as in the Temple of the Inscriptions.

3 "Stone seating" is at once an expression of ritual and of time-keeping. Each k'atun period of the Maya calendar consisted of 20 vague years of 360 days, sometimes called *tuun* ("stone"). Evidently the progression of years through a K'atun was in some way marked by the accumulations of individual ritual stones, with the initial period called the "seating" of a stone. The word K'atun derives from *k'altuun*, "twenty stones" (see Stuart, 1996).

4 The Sak Tz'i' ("White Dog") place was first deciphered by one of the authors (D. Stuart, 1987), but its precise identification remains elusive. Based on the distribution of references to the place, it is reasonable to assume that Sak Tz'i' probably lies in Mexico to the west of the Usumacinta River and southeast of Palenque (see Anaya Hernández, Guenter, and Zender, 2003). Recent investigations at the major ruins of Plan de Ayutla have raised hopes of finally identifying the "true" Sak Tz'i',

but as yet no firm evidence has come to light (see Tovalín and Villareal, 2003).

5 The first archaeological description of Tortuguero was by Frans Blom and Oliver La Farge, who paid a visit to the site in 1923 during the expedition leading to their famous publication *Tribes and Temples* (Blom and La Farge, 1926). The most complete description and investigation is that of Hernández Pons, 1984. The ruins once occupied a promontory on the hill given the same name, overlooking the plains of Tabasco near the town of Macuspana. Most of the monuments of the site are now housed in the Museo Carlos Pellicer in Villahermosa, Tabasco.

6 The debate about the use and function of Maya palaces is ongoing, and given the variety of architectural forms dubbed "palaces," it may be difficult to resolve. In the case of Palenque, there seems to be a general consensus that its principal galleries were not residential spaces. Although excavations by Ruz off the southwest corner of the Palace did uncover a substantial midden containing ceramics, artifacts, and organic material typically associated with domestic space (Ruz, 1962 and Liendo Stuardo, 2003), we find it more likely that the royal residence was elsewhere, perhaps in the Otolum Group. The middens from the palace may have been associated with functionaries who lived in the auxiliary buildings of the Palace, or even with very late "squatter" occupants.

7 It is possible that House B was a member of the "five houses," if not House A–D. The lack of any dedication text in House B, a well-preserved but small building, leads us to provisionally assign an early House A–D phase to Pakal's reign. This would still agree with the view of Tovalín and Bravo, 2001, that an earlier House A–D phase may have dated to the reign of K'inich Kan Bahlam or somewhat earlier.

8 Several photographs were published by Berlin, 1955. Other unpublished images were kindly provided to us by Lauren Essex, daughter of Karena Shields. One tablet from Miraflores, sawn away from one larger fragment documented by Berlin, is now in the collections of The Virginia Museum of Fine Arts, Richmond.

CHAPTER SEVEN *The House of Resurrection*

1 For compelling discussions of present-day Maya ancestral veneration, see Vogt, 1976, and also Carlsen and Prechtel, 1991. McAnany, 1995, offers a useful overview of Classic Maya ancestor worship in general.

2 Ruz Lhuillier, 1973, gives the complete account and original analysis of the discovery.

3 Schele and Mathews, 1998, provide a vivid overview of the Inscriptions panels and the tomb. Schele was the first to remark on the similarity to the later K'atun histories from colonial Yucatán.

4 According to the most recent analysis by Schele and Mathews, 1998: 100, there are two dedication dates to consider for the Temple of the Inscriptions: 9.12.16.12.6 (688) and 9.12.18.2.17 (690).

5 See Berlin, 1970, for a detailed discussion of Galindo's letter.

6 From Ruz Lhuillier, 1952, one of the first publications on the tomb discovery in English.

7 The *el* reading for the *k'in* bowl element was first proposed by Stephen Houston (personal communication, 1992).

8 See Taube, 2003, for a thorough overview of serpent and centipede iconography in Maya art. The interpretation of the centipede maw of the sarcophagus as a place of emergence differs from Taube's, however.

9 Freidel, Schele, and Parker, 1993: 393–403.

10 An eastern tree made of jade is depicted on page 49 of the central Mexican *Borgia Codex*. In the codex the cosmic trees of the four world quarters are depicted emerging from the skeletal earth, with birds atop each. The eastern tree is decorated with jade *chalchihuitl* jewels, with the others having their own distinctive features. The idea of the eastern tree as a resplendent tree of wealth and lordly status clearly had wider distribution outside of Palenque and the Maya area.

11 See Schele and Mathews, 1998: 23–125, for a description of these elaborate patterns in the ancestral portraits of the sarcophagus.

12 Martin's interpretations of the sarcophagus and maize god imagery are part of his broader study of cacao symbolism, Martin, 2006.

13 The inscription on the sarcophagus was first studied by Berlin, 1959, when he made the historically important identification of personal names. Lounsbury later offered a more in-depth treatment of the horizontal text, positing that the repetitious event glyph signified "death."

14 The beliefs surrounding Maya concepts of death and regeneration are ably discussed by Carlsen and Prechtel, 1991 and in Carlsen, 1997: 47–67.

15 See Robertson, 1983–93 and especially Schele and Mathews, 1998: 128–30, for a more in-depth discussion of the wall figures of the tomb.

16 The earliest assessment of Pakal's skeleton was by Dávalos Hurtado and Romano, 1954. The debate over Pakal's age stemmed from the publication of the dynastic reconstructions of Mathews and Schele, 1974, which led Ruz, 1977, to counter with his own advocacy of the results of the bone analysis. Some have sided with Ruz in this debate, Marcus, 1992, believing that "science" trumps written history, but Urcid, 1993, gives cogent reasons for casting doubt on the techniques used to age an adult skeleton past middle age. The most thorough and up-to-date discussion about Pakal's

skeleton can be found in Tiesler and Cucina, 2006.

17 Several articles devoted to the analysis of Pakal's skeleton are collected in a recent book edited by Tiesler and Cucina, 2006.

18 The tomb of the "Red Queen" is described in Gonzáles Cruz, 2000 (and see Fagan, 2007, pp. 94–97).

19 Based on the preliminary findings of physical anthropologist Vera Tiesler of the Universidad Autónoma de Yucatán.

20 For a discussion of the Temple XII tomb see López Jiménez, 2001.

CHAPTER EIGHT *Gods and Rulers*

1 The throne found in front of the Oval Palace Tablet, largely destroyed in del Río's time, was clearly a late addition, possibly from the reign of K'inich K'an Joy Chitam. Its inscription records the accessions of K'inich Kan Bahlam and K'inich K'an Joy Chitam, Schele and Mathews, 1979, so it presumably replaced another earlier throne that had stood in the same place. Could one of the two early thrones now found in the nearby *subterraneos* of the Palace have been the original?

2 The Toniná war is recorded in the panel of Temple XVII and, as Mathews has shown, it was also once on the sanctuary panel of Tablet of the Sun, visible only in Armendáriz's drawing of 1787.

3 See Martin's 2003 analysis of the complex history recorded on Morál-Reforma, Stela 4.

4 Berlin's 1963 original identification of the gods was soon followed by Kelley's 1965 seminal analysis of the mythological context of the Palenque Triad.

5 The meaning and symbolism of GI remains obscure, but have been analyzed most recently by D. Stuart, 2005. Based on an argument first put forward by Lounsbury, 1985, it has long been thought that GI and GIII of the Palenque Triad corresponded to the famous Hero Twins of *Popol Vuh* mythology, Hunahpu and Xbalanque. This association is no longer compelling, as Coe, 1991, makes clear in his essay detailing the proper identification of the Hero Twins in Classic Maya art.

6 The name of Unen K'awiil was clarified only recently through a revealing spelling first pointed out by Marc Zender, written on an inscribed shell excavated by Ricardo Armijo Torres at Comalcalco (cited in Martin, 2002).

7 These triadic sets are still poorly understood. Another three gods are cited collectively as being "ordered" at the onset of the current creation era (13.0.0.0.0 4 Ajaw 8 Kumk'u).

8 The rites of god-dressing are widespread culturally, and are also firmly rooted in Spanish folk Catholicism. The modern Maya practice in highland Chiapas, with clear pre-hispanic associations, is vividly described by Vogt, 1976.

9 Arnoldo González's excavations in the basal platform of Temple of the Sun revealed the remains of earlier phases (cited in Cuevas, 2000). Although not confirmed with the other temples of the Cross Group, there is no reason to believe that the three temples visible today were built on virgin soil – earlier versions of all three probably existed in the same area.

10 This is not to dismiss all connections between Classic Maya art and the *Popol Vuh*, but it is fair to say that interpretations of Classic Maya religious iconography based on the *Popol Vuh* have been overemphasized over the last few decades (Coe, 1973 and Tedlock, 1985). While strands of individual stories that we read in the *Popol Vuh* have deep and obvious reflections in the ancient art, they are few.

11 The decoration of the temples is documented in Volume IV of Robertson's great work on Palenque architecture and sculpture (1983–93).

12 The identification of these sacred points on the landscape of ancient Palenque was first proposed by Stuart and Houston, 1994.

13 See Baudez, 1996, for a similar analysis of the three temples and their complementary symbolic programs.

14 Some of these cache offerings were found by del Río, and are now housed in the Museo de América in Madrid. Later scientific investigations revealed similar caches in the Temples of the Cross, the Foliated Cross, and the Sun.

15 In their highly influential book on Classic Maya religion, Freidel, Schele, and Parker, 1993: 71, posit that the "Six Sky" glyph, which they read as *Wakah Chan*, "Raised-up Sky," is the name of the Milky Way and/or the ecliptic plane. We offer a different interpretation, preferring to see it as the proper name of the Temple of the Cross and its shrine. Furthermore, *Wakah Chan* now seems an erroneous reading of the glyph, which to us still eludes a full understanding. "Six Sky" was clearly a mythical location of some sort, cited as the place of GI's "descent from the sky" and reproduced in architectural form as the highest and main temple of the complex.

16 There has been some debate over the identification of the smaller figure in the tablets of the Group of the Cross. Originally Schele, 1976, proposed that the smaller person was the deceased Pakal, shown passing authority to his son, the newly crowned king K'inich Kan Bahlam. This view is repeated in later writings as well, Schele and Freidel, 1990: 242. However, Bassie-Sweet, 1991: 200–210, made the far more convincing case that the short figure is the young K'inich Kan Bahlam at six years of age. Lounsbury (personal communication,

1988) had also reached a similar conclusion independently (see also Bassie-Sweet, 1991: 260).

17 An accessible but now outdated overview of the tablet's inscription is presented by Schele and Freidel, 1990: 246–47. Other key discussions of the Tablet of the Cross and its decipherment are by Berlin, 1965; Lounsbury, 1976, 1980, 1985; and D. Stuart, 2005, 2006.

18 Mathews, personal communication, 2002.

19 The best-known examples of this pattern are from central Mexico, where local ethnic groups were said to emerge from the "Seven Caves" (Chicomoztoc) or, in the case of the Mexica-Aztec, from the watery realm of Aztlán.

20 The creator maize god's earlier identification as a female character is reflected in the informal names sometimes used, such as "Lady Methuselah," Lounsbury, 1976, and "Lady Beastie," Schele and Freidel, 1990. The revisionist treatment of these models appears in D. Stuart, 2005: 158–85.

21 As Erik Velásquez García, 2002, has shown, there is a clear parallel is to the Aztec myth recounting how Quetzalcoatl and Tezcatlipoca formed the earth by killing the great alligator, Cipactli.

22 This "creation" event on 13.0.0.0.0 4 Ajaw 8 Kumk'u can be more accurately described as a cosmic renewal, the birth of the age in which humanity exists. The vast structure of the Maya calendar and its associated mythology shows that the religious narratives sometimes pre-dated this by millions of years. See Freidel, Schele, and Parker, 1993: 59–75, for a fuller exploration of Maya concepts of "deep time."

23 The inscriptions of the Cross Group refer to these events as both "births" and as "arrivals" at the place called Matwiil.

24 This is mentioned in the text of the south face of the platform from Temple XIX, D. Stuart, 2005.

25 The antiquated style of K'inich Kan Bahlam's costume was first noticed by Schele, 1976.

26 The proper name of House A–D, the northern gallery of the Palace, was the "headband binding house," indicating that it was a place of official investiture. House E of the Palace was the royal seat of the court, and, as we will discuss in Chapter 9, we believe the far more accessible House A–D may have been a more public space for rites associated with accession and the display of newly crowned officials.

CHAPTER NINE *A City Fades Away*

1 The exact pace of Palenque's abandonment is impossible to know based on current evidence, but the settlement surveys of Stuardo Liendo, 2003, do agree with a major depopulation after the Balunté ceramic phase, around 750–800.

2 The main contribution to the historical understanding of Tiwol Chan Mat is through the insightful study of Ringle, 1996. In his paper Ringle referred to Tiwol Chan Mat as "Lord T231."

3 See Blom and LaFarge, 1926.

4 The description of the Temple XVIII tomb can be found in Ruz, 1956.

5 In their original outline of the Late Classic dynasty, Mathews and Schele, 1974, saw Chak Sutz' as a king who reigned between K'inich K'an Joy Chitam (their "Lord Hok'") and K'inich Ahkal Mo' Nahb (their "Lord Chaacal"). Later identification of the *Sajal* title led to his demotion to a more junior, yet still important, role in the royal court, see Stuart, 1991 and Schele, 1991.

6 See Rands and Rands, 1961.

7 The original setting and excavation of the Tablet of the Slaves is described in Ruz, 1952e. The central figure on the Tablet of the Slaves was long thought to be Chak Sutz', but Wald, 1997, makes the firm case for it being the king. See Zender, 2002, for the identification of the toponym *K'ina'* with a site in the Piedras Negras region. The same conflict accounts for the display of a war captive on Palenque's Tablet of the Orator, who is identified as a *Sajal* (a title for a regional governor) of K'inich Yo'nal Ahk, king of Piedras Negras.

8 The fragment's discovery is briefly described by González Cruz and Bernal Romero, 2000, who call it the "Tablero del Bulto." In an earlier study (D. Stuart, 1998) one of the authors suggested that the panel's scene was more directly associated with Palenque's long-term subjugation to Toniná. While this remains a possibility, other interpretations ought to be entertained as well.

9 The excavations of Temples XIX and XXI have yet to be fully published, but accessible overviews are to be found in Miller and Martin, 2004 and González Cruz and Bernal Romero, 2000. The inscriptions are fully analyzed in D. Stuart, 2005.

10 Janab Pakal is mentioned on the so-called K'an Tok Panel from Structure XVI, where his accession date to his junior office is given as 14 November 718 (9.14.7.0.15 6 Men 13 K'ank'in), just three years before the king's crowning (see González Cruz and Bernal Romero, 2000).

11 This avian creature is commonly known as the Principal Bird Deity (Bardawil, 1976). Its connection to the god Itzamnaaj is so intimate that in one source the bird is simply named "The Itzamnaaj Bird."

12 Such numerological connections between important dates in Maya myth and history require much further study, but the basic structures were first described by Lounsbury, 1976, in connection with other dates at Palenque.

13 The attribution of the Tower to his reign is highly speculative, and indicated only by the two panels known as the Tablets of the Scribe and Orator, set into the Tower's base.

14 The incense burner stand, first mentioned in Chapter 5, might depict the dynastic founder, K'uk' Bahlam, but the *k'in* "sun" sign of the headdress would suggest the later king who always bears the *K'inich* honorific. Significantly, if we consider this to be his ancestral portrait, it would indicate that stone sculpture was being produced and elite courts were occupied well after K'inich K'uk' Bahlam's death; he was probably not the last king of Palenque.

15 James Porter, 1994, suggests that the Tablet of the 96 Glyphs was the seat of a small throne made with the so-called Tablet of Creation (the supposed throne's back) and two similarly carved intaglio supports. This arrangement seems unlikely to us, but many have noted that the Tablet of Creation, excavated nearby, is clearly very much like the 96 Glyphs in style, and it is reasonable that it could have somehow formed part of a larger composition.

16 Structure XVI lies directly behind the Temple of the Cross, and seems to have been a residential and/or administrative center, perhaps associated with the Cross Group. The priests named on the tablet may have held an important religious office associated with the Triad deities. For a description of the tablet and of the excavations, see González and Bernal Romero, 2000.

17 The initial discovery and description of the vessel is described by Ruz, 1952e: 39–42. Group III was Ruz's name for the square-shaped complex of rooms to the north of Group B.

18 See Schele, 1992: 103. Importantly, there is no Palenque emblem glyph in the vessel's inscription, and we should be cautious about seeing "Six Death" as a true Palenque king: he may have ruled elsewhere.

19 The mention of Baakal comes from an inscribed clay brick, which was a preferred medium for much of Comalcalco's art and inscriptions (the Nahuatl name *Comalcalco* in fact means "Place of the Brick Houses"). These have been poorly documented and studied, unfortunately, although several have been published by Álvarez Aguilar, et. al., 1988 and by Armijo Torres, 2003. The legible inscriptions on some bricks are analyzed by Romero Rivera, 1992.

20 Webster, 2002, provides an excellent summary of the evidence and debates surrounding the Maya collapse question.

21 See Liendo Stuardo, 2000 and 2003, for a sophisticated settlement analysis of the Palenque region and its changes over time.

22 Liendo Stuardo, 2000, 2002.

EPILOGUE

1 Marken, ed., 2007.

Further Reading

Acosta, Jorge R., 1968. *Exploraciones en Palenque, 1967.* Informes del Departamento de Monumentos Prehispánicos, no. 14. Instituto Nacional de Antropología e Historia, Mexico.

———, 1973. "Exploraciones y restauraciones en Palenque (1968–1970)," in *Anales del Instituto Nacional de Antropología e Historia, 1970-71.* Época 7a., Tomo III, no. 51 de la colección, pp. 21–70. Secretaria de Educación Pública, Mexico.

———, 1976. "Exploraciones en Palenque durante 1972," in *Anales del Instituto Nacional de Antropología e Historia, 1974–75.* Época 7a., Tomo V, no. 53 de la colección, pp. 5–62. Secretaria de Educación Pública, Mexico.

Alcina Franch, José, ed., 1969. *Guillermo Dupaix: Expediciones acerca de los antiguos monumentos de la Nueva España, 1805–1808.* Colección Chimalistac de libros y documentos acerca de la Nueva España, 27. Two volumes. Ediciones José Porrua Turanzas, Madrid.

Álvarez Aguilar, Luis F., Maria Guadalupe Landa Landa, José Luis Romero Rivera, 1988. *Los ladrillos de Comalcalco.* Gobierno del Estado de Tabasco, Villahermosa.

Anaya Hernández, Armando, Stanley Guenter, and Marc Zender, 2003. "Sak Tz'i', a Classic Maya Center: A Locational Model Based on GIS and Epigraphy," in *Latin American Antiquity,* 14 (2), pp. 179–92.

Anonymous, 1845. "And we shall sleep and heed it not." Poem in five verses in *The Adams Sentinel,* vol. 29, no. 35, p. 1, col. 1, top. Gettysburg, Pennsylvania (May 26).

———, 1845a. "Fragmentos sobre las ruinas de la Antigua ciudad de Palenque…" in *Registro Yucateco, periódico literario redactado poruna sociedad de amigos,* I, pp. 318–22. Castillo y Compañía, Mérida de Yucatán.

Aramoni Calderón, Dolores, 1991. "Los indios constructors de Palenque en un documento del siglo XVIII," in *Estudios de Cultura Maya,* vol. 18, pp. 417–38. Universidad Nacional Autónoma de México, Mexico.

Armijo Torres, Ricardo, 2003. "Comalcalco: La Antigua ciudad maya de ladrillos," in *Arqueología Mexicana,* vol. 11, no. 61, pp. 30–37.

Baily, J. (trans.), 1823. *A Statistical and Commercial History of the Kingdom of Guatemala, in Spanish America…by Don Domingo Juarros, a native of New Guatemala.* Printed for John Hearne, London.

Ballesteros-Gaibrois, Manuel, [1939]. *Descripción del terreno y población Antigua nuevemente descubierta en las immediaciones del Pueblo de Palenque, jurisdicción de la Provincia de Ciudad Real de Chiapa, una de las del reyno de Goatemala en la América Septentrional.* Silvio Aguirre, Madrid.

———, 1960. "Nuevas Noticias sobre Palenque en un manuscrito del siglo XVIII. Introducción de Alberto Ruz Lhuillier," in *Cuadernos del Instituto de Historia, Serie Anthrpología,* No. 11. Universidad Nacional Autónoma de México, Mexico.

———, 1993. *Estampas de Palenque.* Estudio y edición de [ ]. Colección Tabula Americae. Patrimonio Nacional, Quinto Centenario, 1492–1992. Testamonio Compañia Editorial [also see Colección de Muñoz, Madrid, 1993; and Olmos Pieri, 1993].

Bardawil, Lawrence, 1976. "The Principal Bird Deity in Maya Art: An Iconographic Study of Form and Meaning," in *The Art, Iconography and Dynastic History of Palenque, Part III: Proceedings of the Segunda Mesa Redonda de Palenque,* ed. Merle Greene Robertson, pp. 195–209. Robert Louis Stevenson School, Pebble Beach, California.

Barnhart, Edwin Lawrence, 2001. *The Palenque Mapping Project: Settlements and Urbanism at an Ancient Maya City.* Dissertation presented to the Faculty of the Graduate School of the University of Texas at Austin.

Bassie-Sweet, Karen, 1991. *Through the Mouth of the Dark Cave: Commemorative Sculpture of the Late Classic Maya.* University of Oklahoma Press, Norman.

Baudez, Claude François, 1965. "The Inscription of the Temple of the Cross at Palenque," in *American Antiquity,* 30, pp. 330–42.

———, 1993. *Jean-Frédéric Waldeck, pientre: le premier explorateur des ruines mayas.* Editions Hazan, Farigliano, Italy.

———, 1996. "The Cross Group at Palenque," in *Eighth Palenque Round Table, 1993,* ed. Martha Macri and Jan McHargue, pp. 121–28. Pre-Columbian Art Research Institute, San Francisco.

———, 2002. "Análisis epigráfico del tablero de K'an Tok, Palenque, Chiapas," in *La organización social entre los mayas prehispánicos, colonials, y modernos* (Vera Tiesler Blos, Rafael Cobos, and Merle Greene Robertson, coordinators). *Memoria de la Tercera Mesa Redonda de Palenque,* 1, pp. 401–24. CONACULTA-

INAH and Universidad Autónoma de Yucatán, Mérida.

Baudez, Claude, and Sydney Picasso, 1992. *Lost Cities of the Maya*. Harry N. Abrams, Inc., New York.

Berlin, Heinrich, 1942. "Un templo olvidado en Palenque," in *Revista Mexicana de Estudios Antropológicos*, vol. 6, nos 1–2, pp. 62–90. Sociedad Mexicana de Antrpología, Mexico.

———, 1955. "News from the Maya World," in *Ethnos*, vol. 20, pp. 201–209. Stockholm.

———, 1959. "Glifos Nominales en el Sarcófago de Palenque: un ensayo," in *Humanidades*, vol. 2, no. 10, pp. 2–8. La Facultad de Humanidades de la Universidad de San Carlos de Guatemala.

———, 1963. "The Palenque Triad," in *Journal de la Société des Américanistes*, vol. 52, pp. 91–99. Musée de l'Homme, Paris.

———, 1965. "The Inscription of the Temple of the Cross, Palenque," in *American Antiquity*, vol. 30, pp. 330–42.

———, 1970. "Miscelánea Palencana," in *Journal de la Société des Américanistes*, vol. 59, pp. 107–28. Musée de l'Homme, Paris.

Bernal, Ignacio, 1980. *A History of Mexican Archaeology: The Vanished Civilizations of Middle America*. Thames & Hudson, London and New York.

Bernal Romero, Guillermo, 2002. "Análisis epigráfico del tablero de K'an Tok, Palenque, Chiapas" in *La organización social entre los mayas prehispánicos, colonials, y modernos*, Vera Tiesler Blos, Rafael Cobos, and Merle Greene Robertson, coordinators. *Memoria d la Tercera Mesa Redonda de Palenque*, 1, pp. 401–24. CONACULTA-INAH and Universidad Autónoma de Yucatán, Mérida.

———, Martha Cuevas García, and Arnoldo González Cruz, n.d. *Palenque, Chiapas, México: Guía Esencial*. CONACULTA-INAH, Mexico.

Blom, Frans, 1982. *La ruinas de Palenque, Xupá y Finca Encanto*. Presentación de Roberto García Moll. Instituto Nacional de Antropología e Historia [third edition, 1991], Mexico.

———, and Oliver LaFarge, 1926. *Tribes and Temples: A Record of the Expedition to Central America Conducted by the Tulane University of Louisiana in 1925*. Two volumes. The Tulane University of Louisiana, New Orleans.

Bonaccorsi-Hild, Doris, 2001. *Teobert Maler: Soldat Abenteurer, Gelehrter auf den Spuren der Maya*. Ibera Verlag, Vienna.

Bowditch, Charles P., ed., 1904. *Mexican and Central American Antiquities, Calendar Systems, and History*. Smithsonian Institution, Bureau of American Ethnology, Bulletin 28. Government Printing Office, Washington, D.C.

Brasseur de Bourbourg, M. l'Abbe, [1866]. *Recherches sur les ruines de Palenqué et sur les origins de la civilization du Mexique*. Arthus Bertrand [see Waldeck and Brassseur de Bourbourg 1866, below], Paris.

Braswell, Geoffrey E., ed., 2004. *Teotihuacan and the Maya: Reinterpreting Early Classic Interaction*. University of Texas Press, Austin.

Brunhouse, Robert L., 1973. *In Search of the Maya: The First Archaeologists*. University of New Mexico Press, Albuquerque.

———, 1975. *Pursuit of the Ancient Maya*. University of New Mexico Press, Albuquerque.

Cabello Carro, Paz, 1989. *Coleccionismo americano indígena en la España del siglo XVIII*. Ediciones de Cultura Hispánica, Madrid.

———, 1992. *Política investigadora de la época de Carlos III en el area maya: descubrimiento de Palenque y primeras excavaciones de carácter científico*. Ediciones de la Torre, Madrid.

Carlsen, Robert S., 1997. *The War for the Heart and Soul of a Highland Maya Town*. University of Texas Press, Austin.

———, and Martin Prechtel, 1991. "The Flowering of the Dead: An Interpretation of Highland Maya Culture," in *Man*, 26, pp. 23–42.

Carmack, Robert M., 1973. *Quichean Civilization: The Ethnohistoric, Ethnographic, and Archaeological Sources*. University of California Press, Berkeley, Los Angeles, London.

Castañeda Paganini, Ricardo, 1946. *Las Ruinas de Palenque: Su descubrimiento y primeras exploraciones en el siglo XVIII*. Guatemala.

Catherwood, Frederick, 1844. *Views of Ancient Monuments in Central America. Chiapas, and Yucatan*, London.

Charnay, Désiré, 1885. *Les anciennes villes du nouveau monde, voyages d'explorations au Mexique et dans l'Amérique Centrale, 1857–1882*. Librairie Hachette, Paris.

———, and M. Viollet-le-Duc, 1863. *Cités et ruines Américaines: Mitla, Palenqué, Izamal, Chichen Itza, Uxmal*. A. Morel, Paris.

Cline, Howard F., 1947. "The Apocryphal Career of J. F. Waldeck, Pioneer Americanist," in *Acta Americana*, vol. 5, no. 4, pp. 278–300. University of Michigan, Ann Arbor, Michigan.

Coe, Michael D., 1973. *The Maya Scribe and His World*. The Grolier Club, New York.

———, 1989. "The Hero Twins: Myth and Image," in *The Maya Vase Book*, vol. 1, pp. 161–83. Kerr Associates, New York.

———, 1992. *Breaking the Maya Code* (2nd edn, 1999). Thames & Hudson, London and New York.

Colección de Muñoz, 1993. *Descripción del terreno y poblacion Antigua, nuevamente descubierta, en las inmediaciones del pueblo de Palenque*. Academia de la Historia, Signatura A/118 dentro de esta colección; Signatura 9/4853 general de la Academia, Folio 186 al 209. Testamonio Compañia Editorial, Madrid [companion to Ballesteros-Gaibrois 1993 (see above)].

Comas, Juan, 1950. "Bosquejo histórico de la Antropología en México," in *Revista Mexicana de Estudios Históricos*, vol. 11, pp. 97–192.

Cuevas García, Martha, 2000. "Los incensarios del Grupo de las Cruces, Palenque," in *Arqueología Mexicana*, vol. 8, no. 45, pp. 54–61. Editorial Raíces, Mexico.

Davis, A., 1842. *Antiquities of Central America, and the Discovery of New-England by the Northmen, Five Hundred Years Before Columbus*. Ninth Edition, Dutton and Wentworth's Print, Boston.

Davis, Keith F., 1981. *Désiré Charnay, Expeditionary Photographer*. University of New Mexico Press, Albuquerque.

Del Río, Antonio, and Paul Felix Cabrera, 1822. *Description of the Ruins of an Ancient City, Discovered near Palenque, in the Kingdom of Guatemala, in Spanish America; translated from the original manuscript report of Captain Don Antonio del Rio: followed by Teatro Critico Americano; or, a Critical Investigation and Research into the History of the Americas, by Doctor Paul Felix Cabrera, of the City of New Guatemala*. Henry Berthoud, London.

Dupaix, Guillermo, *see* Alcina Franch, 1969; Baradére, 1834; Kingsborough, vols IV and VI, 1830; and Villaseñor Espinosa, 1978.

Evans, R. Tripp, 2004. *Romancing the Maya: Mexican Antiquity in the American Imagination, 1820–1915*. University of Texas Press, Austin.

Fagan, Brian, ed., 2007. *Discovery! Unearthing the New Treasures of Archaeology*. Thames & Hudson, London and New York.

Fash, William L., 1991. *Scribes, Warriors, and Kings: The City of Copán and the Ancient Maya* (2nd edn, 1993). Thames & Hudson, London and New York.

Fernández, Miguel Angel, 1985. "Informe de los trabajos realizados en la zona arqueológica de Palenque, Chiapas, durante las temporadas de 1934–1945," in *Palenque, 1926-1945*, compiled by Roberto García Moll, pp. 87–247. Instituto Nacional de Antropología e Historia, Mexico.

Ferrer, Juan Antonio, 1993. "La ruta de los viajeros," in *Arqueología Mexicana*, vol. 1, no. 2 (June–July), pp. 83–85. CONACULTA-INAH, Mexico.

Forresta, Merry A., and John Wood, 1995. *Secrets of the Dark Chamber: The Art of the American Daguerrotype*. Smithsonian Institution Press, Washington, D.C.

Förstemann, Ernst, 1897. "Die Kreuzinschrift von Palenque," in *Globus*, vol. 72, no. 3 (17 July). Friedrich Vieweg and Sohn, Braunschweig [see Bowditch, ed., above. pp. 547–55 for English translation].

Franco, María Teresa, 2000. "Presentación," in *La Guerra entre los antiguos mayas*, ed. Silvia Trejo, Memoria de la Primera Mesa Redonda de Palenque. Instituto Nacional de Antropología e Historia y Consejo Nacional para la Cultura y los Artes, Mexico.

Freidel, David, Linda Schele, and Joyce Parker, 1993. *Maya Cosmos: Three Thousand Years on the Shaman's Path*. W. Morrow, New York.

García Moll, Roberto, ed., 1982. *Las ruinas de Palenque, Xupá, y Finca Encanto por Franz Blom*. Instituto Nacional de Antropología e Historia [and see Blom, 1991, above], Mexico.

———, 1985. *Palenque, 1926–1945*. Instituto Nacional de Antropología e Historia (another edition, 1991), Mexico.

———, 2003. "Algo sobre papeles viejos de Palenque," in *Arqueología 30* (2nd edn), pp. 27–36. Instituto Nacional de Antropología e Historia, Mexico.

García Saíz, Maria Concepción, 1994. "Antonio del Río y Guillermo Dupaix: el reconocimiento de una deuda histórica," in *Anales 2, Museo de América*, pp. 99–119. Ministerio de Cultura, Madrid.

Gendrop, Paul, 1974. "Consideraciones Sobre la Arquitectura de Palenque," in *Primera mesa Redonda de Palenque, Part II*, ed. Merle Greene Robertson, pp. 81–87. Robert Louis Stevenson School, Pre-Columbian Art Research, Pebble Beach, California.

González Cruz, Arnoldo, 2000. The Red Queen. www.mesoweb.com/palenque/features/redqueen/01.html

———, 2004. "Las máscaras de la reina roja de Palenque, Chiapas: símbolos de poder," in *Arqueología Mexicana* (special edition), no. 16, pp. 23–25. Editorial Raíces, Mexico.

———, and Guillermo Bernal Romero, 2000. "Grupo XVI de Palenque: Conjunto arquitectónico de la nobleza provincial" in *Arqueología Mexicana*, vol. 8, no. 45, pp. 20–27. Editorial Raíces, Mexico.

———, 2003. "El Trono del Templo XXI de Palenque, Chiapas: El reinado de K'inich Ahkal Mo' Nahb III," in *Arqueología Mexicana*, vol. 11, no. 62, pp. 70–75. Editorial Raíces, Mexico.

Goodman, Joseph T., 1905. "Maya Dates," in *American Anthropologist*, n.s., vol. 7, no. 4, pp. 642–47. Lancaster, Pennsylvania.

Graham, Ian, 1963. "Juan Galindo, Enthusiast," in *Estudios de Cultura Maya*, vol. 3, pp. 11–36. Universidad Nacional Autónoma de México, Mexico.

————, 2002. *Alfred Maudslay and the Maya: a Biography*. University of Oklahoma Press, Norman.

Graham, John, n. d. *Reading the Past: Olmec Archaeology and the Curious Case of Tres Zapotes Stela C*. Paper prepared for Mesa Redonda Olmeca, 2005, expanded April 2005.

Griffin, Gillett G., 1974. "Early Visitors to Palenque," in *Primera Mesa Redonda de Palenque, December 14–22, 1973*. Part 1, ed. Merle Greene Robertson, pp. 9–34. Robert Louis Stephenson School, Pebble Beach, California.

Grube, Nikolai, 1996. "Palenque in the Maya World," in *Eighth Palenque Round Table, 1993*, ed. Martha Macri and Jan McHargue, pp. 1–14. Pre-Columbian Art Research Institute, San Francisco.

Gunckel, Lewis W., 1897. "The Directions in Which the Maya Inscriptions Should Be Read," in *American Anthropologist*, vol. 10, no. 5, pp. 146–62. Judd and Detweiler, Washington, D.C.

————, 1897a. "The Numeral Signs in the Palenque Tablets," in *American Antiquarian and Oriental Journal*, 19, pp. 1–10.

Hammond, Norman, ed., 1974. *Mesoamerican Archaeology: New Approaches*. University of Texas Press, Austin.

Hardy, Arnulfo, 1985. *Palenque pasado y presente*. Gobierno del Estado de Chiapas, Tuxtla Gutiérrez.

Hermann, Andreas, 1992. *Auf den Spuren der Maya: Eine Fotodokumentation von Teobert Maler (1842–1917)*. Herausgegeben von Rainer Springhorn. Akademische Druck- u. Verlagsanstalt, Graz, Austria.

Hernández Pons, Elsa C., 1984. *Investigaciones arqueológicas en el valle del Río Tulija, Tabasco-Chiapas*. Universidad Nacional Autonomia de México, Mexico.

Holden, Edward S., 1881. "Studies in Central American Picture-Writing," in *First Annual Report of the Bureau of American Ethnology, 1879–1880*, pp. 205–45. Government Printing Office, Washington, D.C.

————, 1881a. "The Hieroglyphs of Central America," in *The Century [Magazine]: a Popular Quarterly*, vol. 23, no. 2, pp. 228–41. The Century Company, New York.

Holmes, William H., 1897. *Archaeological Studies among the Ancient Cities of Mexico. Part II, Monuments of Chiapas, Oaxaca, and the Valley of Mexico*. Anthropological Series, vol. 1, no. 1. The Field Museum, Chicago.

Humboldt, Al[exander] de, 1810. *Vues des cordillères, et monuments des peuples indigènes de l'Amérique*. Chez F. Schoell, Paris.

Juarros, Domingo, 1808–18. *See Baily, 1823*.

Keleman, Pal, 1943. *Medieval American Art*. Two volumes. MacMillan, New York.

Kelley, David H., 1962. "Fonetismo en la escritura maya," in *Estudios de Cultura Maya*, vol. 2, pp. 277–317. Universidad Nacional Autónoma de México, Mexico.

————, 1965. "The Birth of the Gods at Palenque," in *Estudios de Cultura Maya*, vol. 5., pp. 93–134.

Kingsborough, Lord, 1829–48. *Antiquities of Mexico…* Nine volumes, London.

Kirchhoff, Paul, 1943. "Mesoamérica," in *Acta Americana*, vol. 1, pp. 92–107. University of Michigan, Ann Arbor, Michigan.

Kluckholn, Clyde, 1935. "A Note on the Sources of Drawings in the Del Rio Volume on Palenque," in *Maya Research*, ed. Frans Blom, vol. 2, no. 3, July. The Alma Egan Hyatt Foundation, New York.

Knorozov, Yuri V., 1952. "Drevnyaya Pis'mennost' Tsentralnoy Ameriki [The Ancient Script of Central America]," in *Sovietskaya Etnografiya*, vol. 3, pp. 100–18.

Lacroix González, Domingo, 1976. *Gotas de recuerdo*. Fondo de Cultura Tabasqueña, Villahermosa, Tabasco.

Larrainzar, Manuel, 1875–78. *Estudios sobre la historia de América, sus ruinas y antigüedades*. Five volumes, Cárlos Ramiro, Mexico.

Leifer, Tore, Jesper Nielsen, and Toke Sellner Reunert, n.d. "Restless Blood: Frans Blom, Adventurer and Maya Archaeologist." Sample chapters translated by Anne-Marie Overbye and Tore Leifer. Courtesy of the authors from 2002 *Det urolige blod: Biografi om Frans Blom*. Høst and Søn, København.

Liendo Stuardo, Rodrigo, 2000. "Reyes y Campesinos: La población rural de Palenque," in *Arqueología Mexicana*, vol. 8, no. 45, pp. 34–37. Editorial Raíces, Mexico.

————, 2001. "Palenque y su area de sustentación: Patrón de Asentamiento y organización política en un centro Maya del Clásico," in *Mexicon*, vol. 23, no. 2, Verlag Anton Saurwein, Markt Schwaben, Germany.

————, 2002. "Organización social y producción agrícola en Palenque," in *La organización social entre los mayas prehispánicos, colonials, y modernos*, Vera Tiesler Blos, Rafael Cobos, and Merle Greene Robertson, coordinators. Memoria de la Tercera Mesa Redonda de Palenque, 1, pp. 305–27. CONACULTA-INAH and Universidad Autónoma de Yucatán, Mérida.

————, 2003. *The Organization of Agricultural Production at a Maya Center. Settlement Patterns in the Palenque Region, Chiapas, Mexico*. Serie Arqueología de México. University of Pittsburgh Latin American Archaeological Publications/INAH.

López Bravo, Roberto, 1994. "Exploraciones Arqueologicas en el Grupo C de Palenque," in *Cuarto*

Foro de Arqueologia de Chiapas. Instituto Chiapaneco de Cultura.

———, 1995. *El Grupo B, Palenque, Chiapas. Una Unidad Habitacional Maya del Clasico Tardio.* BA thesis, ENAH, Mexico.

López Jiménez, Fanny, 2001. "El descrubimiento del la tumba 1 del Templo de la Calavera y su contexto arquitectónico en Palenque, Chiapas," in *Pueblos y Fronteras*, 1, pp. 115–29. UNAM, Mexico.

Lounsbury, Floyd G., 1974. "The Inscription of the Sarcophagus Lid at Palenque," in *Primera Mesa Redonda de Palenque, Part II*, ed. Merle Greene Robertson, pp. 5–20. Robert Louis Stevenson School, Pebble Beach, California.

———, 1976. "A Rationale for the Initial Date of the Temple of the Cross at Palenque," in *The Art, Iconography, and Dynastic History of Palenque, Part III: Proceedings of the Segunda Mesa Redonda de Palenque,* ed. Merle Greene Robertson, pp. 211–24. Robert Louis Stevenson School, Peeble Beach, California.

———, 1980. "Some Problems in the Interpretation of the Mythological Portion of the Hieroglyphic Text of the Temple of the Cross at Palenque," in *Third Palenque Round Table, 1978*, Part 2, ed. Merle Greene Robertson, pp. 99–115. Palenque. Round Table Series, vol. 5. University of Texas Press, Austin.

———, 1985. "The Identities of the Mythological Figures in the 'Cross Group' of Inscriptions at Palenque," in *Fourth Round Table of Palenque, 1980*, Merle Greene Robertson, general editor, and Elizabeth Benson, volume editor, pp. 45–58, vol. 6. Pre-Columbian Art Research Institute, San Francisco.

Mace, O. Henry, 1990. *Collector's Guide to Early Photographs.* Wallace-Homestead Book Company, Radnor, Pennsylvania.

MacKay, Charles, 1852. *Memoirs of Extraordinary Popular Delusions and the Madness of Crowds.* Two volumes, Office of the National Illustrated Library, London. [First edition published London, 1841.]

Marcus, Joyce, 1992. *Mesoamerican Writing Systems: Propaganda, Myth, and History in Four Ancient Civilizations.* Princeton University Press, Princeton.

Marken, Damien B., ed., 2007. *Palenque: Recent Investigations at the Classic Maya Center.* AltaMira Press, Lanham, Maryland.

Martin, Simon, 2002. "The Baby Jaguar: An Exploration of its Identity and Origins in Maya Art and Writing," in *La organización social entre los mayas prehispánicos, colonials, y modernos*, Vera Tiesler Blos, Rafael Cobos, and Merle Greene Robertson, coordinators. *Memoria de la Tercera Mesa Redonda de Palenque*, 1, pp. 305–27. CONACULTA-INAH and Universidad Autónoma de Yucatán, Mérida.

———, 2003. "Moral-Reforma y la contienda por el oriente de Tabasco," in *Arqueología Mexicana*, vol. 11, no. 61, pp. 44–47.

———, 2006. "Cacao in Ancient Maya Religion: First Fruit of the Maize Tree and Other Tales of the Underworld," in *Chocolate in Mesoamerica: A Cultural History of Cacao*, ed. Cameron McNeil. University of Florida Press, Gainesville.

———, and Nikolai Grube, 2000. *Chronicle of the Maya Kings and Queens: Deciphering the Dynasties of the Ancient Maya* (2nd edn, 2008). Thames & Hudson, London and New York.

Mathews, Peter, and Merle Greene Robertson, 1985. "Notes on the Olvidado, Palenque, Chiapas, Mexico" in *Fifth Palenque Round Table, 1983*, ed. Virginia M. Fields, pp. 7–17. Pre-Columbian Art Research Institute, San Francisco.

———, and Linda Schele, 1974. "Lords of Palenque: The Glyphic Evidence," in *Primera Mesa Redonda de Palenque, Part I*, ed. Merle Greene Robertson. Robert Louis Stevenson School, Pebble Beach, California.

Maudslay, Alfred P., 1889–1902. "Archaeology," Appendix to *Biologia Centrali-Americana*, eds Osbert Salvin and F. Ducane Godman. Five volumes (one of text, four of plates). R. H. Porter and Dulau, London [Parts 1–4 of Volume IV are devoted to Palenque; these appeared, respectively, in April 1896, September 1896, October 1897, and January 1899].

Maudslay, Ann Cary, and Alfred Percival Maudslay, 1899. *A Glimpse at Guatemala, and Some Notes on the Ancient Monuments of Central America.* John Murray, London.

McAnany, Patricia A., 1995. *Living with the Ancestors: Kinship and Kingship in Ancient Maya Society.* University of Texas Press, Austin.

Miller, Mary, and Simon Martin, 2004. *Courtly Art of the Ancient Maya.* Thames & Hudson, London and New York.

Millon, Rene, 1974. "Study of Urbanism at Teotihuacan," in *Mesoamerican Archaeology: New Approaches*, ed. Norman Hammond, pp. 335–62. University of Texas Press, Austin.

Molina Montes, Augusto, 1979. "Palenque: The Archaeological City Today," in *Tercera Mesa Redonda de Palenque, June 11–18, 1978*, vol. 4, ed. Merle Greene Robertson and Donnan Call Jeffers, pp. 1–8. Pre-Columbian Art Research Center, Monterey, California.

Morales M., Moises, 1974. "El País de Pacal," in *Primera Mesa Redonda de Palenque, Part II*, ed. Merle Greene Robertson, pp. 125–43. Robert Louis Stevenson School, Pebble Beach, California.

Morelet, Arthur, 1857. *Voyage dans l'Amerique centrale, l'ile de Cuba et Yucatan.* Two volumes. Gide and Baudry, Paris.

————, 1871. *Travels in Central America including accounts of some Regions Unexplored Since the Conquest*. From the French edition of the Chevalier Arthur Morelet by Mrs. M. F. Squier. Introduction and notes by E. Geo. Squier. Leypoldt, Holt, and Williams, New York.

Navarrete, Carlos, 2000. *Palenque, 1784: el inicio de la aventura arqueológica maya*. Universidad Nacional Autónoma de México, Mexico.

Noguera Auza, Eduardo, 1985. "La ciudad arqueológica de Palenque, Chiapas," in *Palenque 1826–1945*, compiled by Roberto García Moll, pp. 13–64. Instituto Nacional de Antropología e Historia, Mexico.

Olmos Pieri, Carlos, ed., 1993. *Estampas de Palenque*. Facsimile to accompany Ballesteros-Gaibrois, 1993.

Paillés H., María del Carmen, and Rosalba Calleja Nieto, 1993, *Primeras expediciones a las ruinas de Palenque*. INAH, Mexico.

Palacios, Enrique Juan, 1935. "Mas gemas del arte Maya en Palenque," in *Anales del Museo Nacional de Arqueológia, Historia, y Etnología*, series 5, vol. 2 [no. 25 of the collection], pp. 193–224. Museo Nacional, Mexico.

————, 1936. "Inscripción Recientemente Descubierta en Palenque," in *Maya Research*, ed. Frans Blom, vol. 3, no. 1, pp. 3–17. Department of Middle American Research, The Tulane University of Louisiana, New Orleans.

Pendergast, David M., ed., 1967. *Palenque: The Walker-Caddy Expedition to the Ancient Maya City, 1839–1840*. University of Oklahoma Press, Norman.

Perales, Rebecca, and Jacobo Mugarte, 1990. "Investigaciones Arqueológicas en Santa Elena, Balancán, Tabasco," in *Tierra y Agua: La Antropología en Tabasco*, 1, pp. 63–64.

Porter, James, 1994. "Palace Intaglios: A Composite Stairway Throne at Palenque," in *In Seventh Palenque Round Table, 1989*, ed. Virginia M. Fields, pp. 11–18. Pre-Columbian Art Research Institute, San Francisco.

Priest, Josiah, 1833. *American Antiquities and Discoveries in the West*. Packard, Hoffman, and White, Albany.

————, 1841. *American Antiquities and Discoveries in the West* (fifth edition). J. Munsell, Albany.

Proskouriakoff, Tatiana, 1960. "Historical Implications of a Pattern of Dates from Piedras Negras, Guatemala," in *American Antiquity*, vol. 25, pp. 454–71. Salt Lake City.

————, 1961. "The Lords of the Maya Realm," in *Expedition*, vol. 4, no. 1, pp 14–21. The University Museum, Philadelphia.

Rafinesque, C[onstantine] S[amuel], 1832. *The Atlantic Journal, or Friend of Knowledge*. Philadelphia.

————, 1836. *A Life of Travels and Researches in North Americas and South Europe... F. Turner*, Philadelphia.

Rands, Robert L., 1957. "The Ceramic Position of Palenque, Chiapas," in *American Antiquity*, vol. 23, no. 2, pp. 140–50.

————, 1974. "A Chronological Framework for Palenque," in *Primera Mesa Redonda de Palenque*, Part 1, ed. Merle Greene Robertson, vol. 1, pp. 35–39. Robert Louis Stevenson School, Pebble Beach, California.

————, and Barbara C. Rands, 1959. "The Incensario Complex of Palenque, Chiapas," in *American Antiquity*, vol. 25, no. 2, pp. 225–36.

————, 1961. "Excavations in a Cemetery at Palenque," in *Estudios de Cultura Maya*, vol. 1, pp. 87–106. Universidad Nacional Autónoma de México, Mexico.

Rau, Charles, 1879. "The Palenque Tablet in the United States National Museum, Washingon, D.C.," in *Smithsonian Contributions to Knowledge*, vol. 22, article V, November. The Smithsonian Institution, Washington, D.C.

Real Academia Española, 1984. *Diccionario de la lengua Castellana, en que se explica el verdadero sentido de las voces, su naturaleza y calidad*. Facsimile of the 1737 edition in three volumes. Editoral Gredos, Madrid.

Rickards, Constantine George, 1910. *The Ruins of Mexico*. Volume I. H. E. Shrimpton, London.

Riese, Frauke J., 1993. *Antonio del Río: Beschreibung einer alten Stadt, die in Guatimala (Neuspanien), unfern Palenque entdeckt worden ist*. Dietrich Reimer Verlag, Berlin.

Ringle, William M., 1996. "Birds of a Feather: The Fallen Stucco Inscription of Temple XVIII, Palenque, Chiapas," in *Eighth Palenque Round Table, 1993*, ed. Martha Macri and Jan McHargue, pp. 45–62. Pre-Columbian Art Research Institute, San Francisco.

————, and Thomas C. Smith-Stark, 1996. *A Concordance to the Inscriptions of Palenque, Chiapas, Mexico*. Middle American Research Institute, Tulane University, Publication 62. New Orleans.

Robertson, Merle Greene, 1983–93. *The Sculpture of Palenque*. Four Volumes (I: The Temple of the Inscriptions [1983]. II: The Early Buildings of the Palace and the Wall Paintings [1985]; III: The Late Buildings of the Palace [1985]; IV: The Cross Group, the North Group, the Olvidado, and Other Pieces [1991]). Princeton University Press, Princeton, New Jersey.

————, ed., 1974. *Primera Mesa Redonda de Palenque, Parts I and II*. Two volumes. Robert Louis Stevenson School, Pebble Beach, California.

Robertson, Merle Greene, Martha Macri, and Jan McHargue, eds, 1996. *Eighth Palenque Round Table, 1993*. Pre-Columbian Art Research Institute, San Francisco.

Romero Rivera, José Luis, 1992. "Tres tablillas de barro con inscripciones glíficas de Comalcalco, Tabasco," in *Comalcalco*, Elizabeth Mejía Pérez Campos, compiler, and Lorena Mirambell Silva, coordinator, pp. 255–69. INAH, Mexico.

Ruz Lhuillier, Alberto, 1952. "Importante découverte à Palenque dans la pyramide du 'Temple des Inscriptions,'" in *Journal de la Société des Américanistes*, vol. XLI, pp. 383–86. Musée de l'Homme, Paris.

——, 1952a. "Exploraciones en Palenque," in *Proceedings of the Thirtieth International Congress of Americanists, Held at Cambridge, 18–23 August 1952*, pp. 5–22. The Royal Anthropological Institute, London.

——, 1952b. "Importante découverte à Palenque dans la pyramide du 'Temple des Inscriptions,'" in *Journal de la Société des Américanistes*, vol. XLI, pp. 383–86. Musée de l'Homme, Paris.

——, 1952c. "Exploraciones en Palenque," in *Proceedings of the Thirtieth International Congress of Americanists, Held at Cambridge, 18–23 August 1952*, pp. 5–22. The Royal Anthropological Institute, London.

——, 1952d. "Exploraciones arqueológicas en Palenque: 1949," in *Anales del Instituto Nacional de Antropología e Historia, 1952*. Series 6a, vol. IV, no. 32, pp. 49–60. Instituto Nacional de Antropología e Historia, Secretaria de Educación Pública, Mexico.

——, 1952e. "Exploraciones arqueológicas en Palenque: 1950 and 1951," in *Anales del Instituto Nacional de Antropología e Historia, 1951*. Series 6a, vol. V, no. 33, pp. 25–45 and 47–66. Instituto Nacional de Antropología e Historia, Secretaria de Educación Pública, Mexico.

——, 1954. "Exploraciones en Palenque: 1952," in *Anales del Instituto Nacional de Antropología e Historia, 1952*. Series 6a, vol. VI, no. 34, pp. 79–112. Instituto nacional de Antropología e Historia, Secretaria de Educación Pública, Mexico.

——, 1956. "Exploraciones arqueológicas en Palenque: 1953, 1954, 1955, & 1956," in *Anales del Instituto Nacional de Antropología e Historia*, vol. X, no. 39, pp. 69–116, 117–84, 185–240, and 241–99. Instituto Nacional de Antropología e Historia, Secretaría de Educación Pública, Mexico.

——, 1962. "Exploraciones arqueológicas en Palenque: 1957 and 1958," in *Anales del Instituto Nacional de Antropología e Historia*, vol. XIV, no. 43, pp. 35–90 and 91–112. Instituto Nacional de Antropología e Historia, Secretaría de Educación Pública, Mexico.

——, 1973. *El Templo de las Inscripciones, Palenque*. Colección Científica, Arqueología, 7. Instituto Nacional de Antropología e Historia, Mexico.

Sáenz, César A., 1956. *Exploraciones en la pirámide de la Cruz Foliada*. Informes de la Dirección de Monumentos Prehispánicos, no. 5. Instituto Nacional de Anthropología e Historia, Mexico.

Saville, Marshall H., 1928. Biliographic Notes on Palenque, Chiapas. *Indian Notes and Monographs*, vol. 6, no. 5. Museum of the American Indian, Heye Foundation, New York.

Schele, Linda, 1976. "Accession Iconography of Chan Bahlum in the Group of the Cross," in *The Art, Iconography and Dynastic History of Palenque*, Part III, ed. Merle Greene Robertson, pp. 9–34. Robert Louis Stevenson School, Pebble Beach, California.

——, 1986. "Architectural Development and Political History at Palenque," in *City States of the Maya: Art and Architecture*, ed. Elizabeth. P. Benson, pp. 110–38. Rocky Mountain Institute for Pre-Columbian Studies, Denver.

——, 1991. "A New Look at the Dynastic History of Palenque," in *Supplement to the Handbook of Middle American Indians*, vol. 5, *Epigraphy*, ed. Victoria R. Bricker, pp. 82–109. University of Texas Press, Austin.

——, 1992. Notebook for the 16th Maya Hieroglyphic Workshop at Texas, March 14–15, University of Texas Department of Art and Art History, Austin.

——, and David Freidel, 1990. *A Forest of Kings: The Untold Story of the Ancient Maya*. William Morrow, New York.

——, and Peter Mathews, 1979. *The Bodega of Palenque, Chiapas, Mexico*. Dumbarton Oaks, Washington, D.C.

——, 1998. *The Code of Kings: The Language of Seven Sacred Maya Tombs and Temples*. Scribner, New York.

——, and Mary Ellen Miller, 1992. *The Blood of Kings: Dynasty and Ritual in Maya Art*. Kimbell Art Museum, Fort Worth Texas.

Seler, Eduard, 1915. *Beobachtungen und Studien in den Ruinen von Palenque*. Abhandlungen der königlich preussischen Akademie de Wissenschaften jahrgang 1915, philosophisch-historische klasse, no. 5, Berlin.

——, 1976. *Observations and Studies in the Ruins of Palenque*, trans. Gisela Morgner; eds Thomas Bartman and George Kubler. Robert Louis Stephenson School, Pebble Beach, California.

Shields, Karena, 1959. *The Changing Wind*. Thomas Y. Crowell Company, New York.

————, 1959a. "Influence of Agrarian Colonization on the Indigenous Tzeltal Community at Octen, Chiapas," in *Kroeber Anthropological Society Papers*, vol. 21, pp. 25–30. Department of Anthropology, University of California, Berkeley.

Stephens, John L., 1841. *Incidents of Travel in Central America, Chiapas, and Yucatan*. Two volumes. Harper and Brothers, New York.

————, 1843. *Incidents of Travel in Yucatan*. Two volumes. Harper and Brothers, New York.

————, 1970. *Incidents of Travel in Egypt, Arabia Petrea, and the Holy Land*, ed., and with an introduction by, Victor Wolfgang von Hagen. University of Oklahoma Press, Norman.

————, 2006. *The Palenque Mythology. Sourcebook for the XXX Maya Meetings*. Department of Art and Art History, University of Texas at Austin.

Stuart, David, 1993. "Historical Inscriptions and the Maya Collapse," in *Lowland Maya Civilization in the Eighth Century A.D.*, eds Jeremy A. Sabloff and John S. Henderson, pp. 321–54. Dumbarton Oaks, Washington, D.C.

————, 1995. *A Study of Maya Inscriptions*. Ph.D. Dissertation, Vanderbilt University, Nashville, Tennessee.

————, 1996. "Kings of Stone: A Consideration of Stelae in Classic Maya Ritual and Representation," in *RES: Anthropology and Aesthetics*, nos 29 and 30, pp. 148–71.

————, 1997. "Kinship Terms in Maya Inscriptions," in *The Language of Maya Hieroglyphs*, eds M. Macri and A. Ford, pp. 1–11. Pre-Columbian Art Research Institute, San Francisco.

————, 1998a. "'The Fire Enters His House': Architecture and Ritual in Classic Maya Texts," in *Function and Meaning in Classic Maya Architecture*, ed. S. D. Houston, pp. 373–425. Dumbarton Oaks, Washington, D.C.

————, 1998b. "Testimonios sobre la guerra durante el Clásico Maya," in *Arqueología Mexicana*, no. 32, pp. 6–13. Editora Raices, Mexico.

————, 1998c. The Deciferment of T128. Unpublished manuscript in possession of the author.

————, 2000a. "The 'Arrival of Strangers': Teotihuacan and Tollan in Classic Maya History," in *Mesoamerica's Classic Heritage: From Teotihuacan to the Aztecs*.

————, 2000b. "Ritual and History in the Stucco Inscription from Temple XIX at Palenque," in *The PARI Journal*, vol. 4, no. 1, pp. 1–4. Pre-Columbian Art Research Institute, San Francisco.

————, 2000c. "Las nuevas inscripciones del Templo XIX," in *Arqueología Mexicana*, no. 45, pp. 28–33. Editora Raíces, Mexico.

————, 2002. The Maya Hieroglyph for "Blood." Unpublished manuscript in possession of the author.

————, 2003a. On the Paired Variants of TZ'AK. *Mesoweb*: www.mesoweb.com/stuart/notes/tzak.pdf.

————, 2003b. A Cosmological Throne at Palenque. *Mesoweb*: www.mesoweb.com/stuart/notes/throne.pdf.

————, 2003c. "Long Live the King: The Premature Demise of K'inich K'an Joy Chitam," in *The PARI Journal*, vol. 4, no. 1, pp. 1–4.

————, 2004. "The Beginnings of the Copán Dynasty: A Review of the Hieroglyphic and Historical Evidence," in *Understanding Early Classic Copan*, eds E. Bell, M. Canuto, and R. J. Sharer, pp. 215–48. The University Museum, University of Pennsylvania, Philadelphia.

————, 2005. *The Inscriptions from Temple XIX at Palenque: A Commentary*. The Pre-Columbian Art Research Institute, San Francisco.

————, and Ian Graham, 2003. *Corpus of Maya Hieroglyphic Inscriptions: Piedras Negras*. Peabody Museum of Archaeology and Ethnology, Harvard University, Cambridge, Massachusetts.

————, and Stephen Houston, 1994. "Classic Maya Place Names," in *Studies in Pre-Columbian Art and Archaeology*, 33. Dumbarton Oaks, Washington, D.C.

Stuart, Gene S., and George Stuart, 1993. *Lost Kingdoms of the Maya*. National Geographic Society, Washington, D.C.

Stuart, George E., 1989. *The Beginning of Maya Hieroglyphic Study: Contributions of Constantine S. Rafinesque and James H. McCulloh, Jr*. Research Reports on Ancient Maya Writing, No. 29. Center for Maya Research, Washington, D.C.

————, 1992. "Quest for Decipherment: A Historical and Bi[bli]ographical Survey of Maya Hieroglyphic Investigation," in *New Theories on the Ancient Maya*, eds Elin C. Danien and Robert J. Sharer, pp. 1–63. The University Museum, University of Pennsylvania, Philadelphia.

Taube, Karl, 2003. "Maws of Heaven and Hell: The Symbolism of the Centipede and Serpent in Classic Maya Religion" in *Antropología de la eternidad: la muerte en la cultura Maya*, eds Andres Ciudad Ruiz, Mario Humberto Ruz Sosa and M. Josefa Iglesias Ponce de León, pp. 405–42. Sociedad Española de Estudios Mayas, Madrid.

Tedlock, Dennis, 1985. *Popol Vuh: The Definitive Edition of the Mayan Book of the Dawn of Life and the Glories of the Gods and Kings*. Simon and Schuster, New York.

Thompson, Edward H., 1895. "Ancient Tombs of Palenque," in *Proceedings of the American Antiquarian Society*, vol. X, no. 2, pp. 418–21. Worcester, Massachusetts.

Tiesler Blos, Vera, and Andrea Cucina, 2006. *Janaab' Pakal of Palenque: Reconstructing the Life and Death of a Maya Ruler*. University of Arizona Press, Tucson.

Tovalín, Ahumada, Alejandro, and Gabriela Ceja Manrique, 1996. "Desarollo arquetectónico del Grupo Norte de Palenque," in *Eighth Palenque Round Table, 1993*, ed. Martha Macri and Jan McHargue, pp. 93–102. Pre-Columbian Art Research Institute, San Francisco.

——, and Roberto López Bravo, 2001. "Excavaciones en el norte del Palacio, Palenque," in Pueblos y Fronteras, 1, pp. 131–46. UNAM, Mexico.

——, and Victor M. Ortiz Villareal, 2003. "Plan de Ayutla, Ocosingo, Chiapas: sitio arqueologico considerado para restauración," in *Arqueologia Mexicana*, vol. 10, no. 60, pp. 8–10.

Urcid, Javier, 1993. "Bones and Epigraphy: The Accurate Versus the Fictitious?," in *Texas,* note 42. Center of the History and Art of Ancient American Culture of the Art Department of the University of Texas at Austin.

Van Stone, Mark Lindsey, 2005. *Aj-Ts'ib, Aj-Uxul, Itz'aat, & Aj-K'uhu'n: Classic Maya Schools of Carvers and Calligraphers in Palenque After the Reign of Kan-Bahlam.* Dissertation presented to the Faculty of the Graduate School, University of Texas at Austin.

["Velasquez, Pedro"], 1850. *Memoir of an Eventful Expedition to Central America; resulting in the Discovery of the Idolatrous City of Iximaya, in an Unexplored Region; and in Possession of Two Aztec Children.... Described by John L. Stevens, Esq.... Translated from the Spanish of Pedro Velasquez of San Salvador.* J. W. Bell, New York.

——, 1853. *The History of the Aztec Lilliputians: Illustrated Memoir of an Eventful Expedition in Central America....* R. S. Francis, London.

——, n.d. *Mémoire illustre d'une expedition remarquable dans l'Amerique Centrale, d'ou est résultée la découverte de la ville idolatre d'Iximaya, situé dans une region inexplorée et la possession de deux merveilleux Aztecs, Maximo (le jeune homme) et Bartola (la jeune fille)…décrite par John L. Stephens, Esq....traduit de l'Espagnol de Pedro Velazquez, de San Salvador.* n. p.

Velásquez García, Erik, 2002. "Una nueva interpretación del Monstruo Cósmico maya," in *Arte y Ciencia: XXIV Colóquio Internacional de Historia del Arte,* ed. P. Kreuger, pp. 419–57. UNAM, Mexico.

Villaseñor Espinosa, Roberto, ed., 1978. *Atlas de las antigüidades Mexicanas balladas en el curso de los tres viajes de la real expedición de antigüidades de la Nueva España emprendidos en 1805, 1806, y 1807.* San Angel Ediciones, S. A., Mexico.

Vogt, Evon Z., 1969. *Zinacantan: A Maya Community in the Highlands of Chiapas.* The Belknap Press of Harvard University Press, Cambridge, Massachusetts.

——, 1976. *Tortillas for the Gods.* The Belknap Press of Harvard University Press, Cambridge, Massachussetts.

von Hagen, Victor Wolfgang, 1947. *Maya Explorer: John Lloyd Stephens and the Lost Cities of Central America.* University of Oklahoma Press, Norman, Oklahoma.

——, 1973. *Search for the Maya: The Story of Stephens and Catherwood.* Saxon House, Westmead, Farnborough, Hants.

——, ed., 1970. *See* Stephens 1970.

Wald, Robert, 1997. "Politics of Art and History at Palenque: Interplay of Text and Iconography on the Tablet of the Slaves," in *Texas Notes on Precolumbian Art, Writing, and Culture,* no. 80. Department of Art and Art History, University of Texas at Austin.

Waldeck, Frédéric de, 1838. *Voyage pittoresque et archéologique dans la province d'Yucatan (Amérique Centrale), pendent les années 1834 et 1836.* Belizard Dufour et Co., Paris.

——, 1997. *Viaje pintoresco y arqueológico a la provincia de Yucatán,* trans. Teresa Foucaud de Romero and Ayelen Romero Foucaud. Grupo CONDUMEX, Mexico.

——, and Brasseur de Bourbourg, 1866. *Monuments anciens du Mexique: Palenqué et autres ruines de l'ancienne civilization de Mexique. Collection de Vues, Bas-Reliefs, Moreaux d'Architecture, Coupes, Vases, Terres cuites, Cartes et Plans.* Arthus Bertrand, Paris.

Warden, D[avid]. B., 1827. *Recherches sur les Antiquités de L'Amérique Septentrionale.* Extract from the 2nd volume of *Les Memoires de l'Académie des Sciences de l'Institut Royal.* Everat, Paris.

Wauchope, Robert, 1962. *Lost Tribes and Sunken Continents: Myth and Method in the Study of the American Indian.* The University of Chicago Press, Chicago.

Webster, David L., 2002. *The Fall of the Ancient Maya: Solving the Mystery of the Maya Collapse.* Thames & Hudson, London and New York.

Willey, Gordon R., T. Patrick Culbert, and Richard E. W. Adams, eds, 1967. "Maya Lowland Ceramics: a Report from the 1965 Guatemala City Conference," in *American Antiquity,* vol. 32, no. 3, pp. 289–315. University of Utah printing services, for the Society for American Archaeology, Salt Lake City.

Williams, Stephen, 1991. *Fantastic Archaeology: The Wild Side of North American Prehistory.* University of Pennsylvania Press, Philadelphia.

Zender, Marc, 2002. "The Toponyms of Piedras Negras, El Cayo and La Mar," in *Heart of Creation: The Mesoamerican World and the Legacy of Linda Schele,* ed. Andrea Stone, pp. 166–84. The University of Alabama Press, Tuscaloosa.

Acknowledgments

This book would not exist without the work of eight generations of people who participated in the discovery, exploration, and investigation of Palenque. Many are cited in terms of their works, in the list of references. Here we thank the many colleagues whose scholarship and friendship made this book possible.

For the stirring of our initial inspiration some years ago, we thank Merle Greene Robertson, the late Bob Robertson, and the late Linda Schele. For his profound insights as well as his peerless scholarship and dogged persistence, we are grateful to Robert Rands, who took the trouble to visit Boundary End farm for two days in the summer of 2005 and talk of his work at and memories of Palenque. To Gillett Griffin we owe more than he will ever know for his decades of profound scholarship and acute judgment in dealing with the art and architecture of Palenque. And we are in debt to Michael Coe and his late wife Sophie for their help in our better understanding of the ancient Maya.

To the reverend George Stuart IV of the Washington Diocese, we are grateful for his pursuit and discoveries among the obscure accounts of Palenque in U.S. newspapers of the late 19th century.

Our gratitude for both help and hospitality over the years goes to many local Palencanos, particularly Moises ("Moi") Morales, his son Alfonso Morales, and Julie Miller, as well as other members of the Morales family – Moi's brothers Carlos and Mario, and nephew David, creator of the gigantic head of Pakal that rises from the ground at the fork in the road by the Palenque cemetery. We are especially grateful to Moi for keeping us gringos on the right track in our consideration of Palenque and the Maya who still live in the region; and to Arnulfo Hardy for his excellent work on the history of the town and the ruins.

To our late colleagues in archaeology, anthropology, linguistics, ethnology, ethnohistory, history, art history, iconography, linguistics, and epigraphy we owe debts beyond measure. Aside from those colleagues recognized above, we would like to mention Jorge Acosta, Ignacio Bernal, Gertrude Duby Blom, Paul Gendrop, Giles Healy, Kathryn Josserand, George Kubler, Augusto Molina Montes, John Montgomery, Barbara Rands, Edwin Shook, Evon Z. Vogt, Robert Wauchope, and Gordon R. Willey.

Our special thanks go to our many colleagues and friends still engaged in the quest to understand the ancient Maya and the history of research in their area, among them, Armando Anaya, Joann Andrews, Barbara Arroyo, Anthony Aveni, Ed Barnhart, Karen Bassie-Sweet, Claude Baudez, Guillermo Bernal Romero, Martha Cuevas García, Hector Escobedo, Federico Fahsen, Barbara Fash, William L. Fash, Arnoldo González Cruz, Ian Graham, Stanley Guenter, Julia Guernsey, Norman Hammond, Stephen Houston, Rodrigo Liendo Stuardo, Roberto López Bravo, Simon Martin, Peter Mathews, Alonzo Mendez, Mary Miller, Jorge Pérez de Lara, Christopher Powell, William Saturno, Joel Skidmore, Kirk Straight, Karl Taube, Vera Tiesler, Erik Velásquez García, and Marc Zender.

Our heartfelt gratitude is also due to Roberto García Moll, who has served us all well by publishing archival records of early archaeological research at Palenque. Without Roberto's work, our own effort would have been far more difficult.

To our colleague Laura Filloy we owe our gratitude, not only for her and her colleagues' role in the new reconstruction of the magnificent funerary mask of K'inich Janab Pakal, but also for sharing her work with us. And Leonardo López Luján of the Templo Mayor Museum in Mexico City provided us with crucial help, both in locating rare published sources, and in correcting and adjusting bibliographic details.

A special note of thanks is also due to the Lak'ech study group of Pleasant Valley State Penitentiary, Coalinga, California, especially Uguku Usdi (Cherokee), for the group's inspiring work in the pursuit of productive knowledge of Maya astronomy, calendrics, and epigraphy.

Several students at Harvard University and at the University of Texas aided directly or indirectly in the production of this book: Michael Carrasco, Nick Carter, Elaine Day Schele, Amanda Garbee, Thomas Garrison, Lucia Henderson, and Ann Seiferle-Valencia.

For other help, ranging from matters of bibliography to sources of illustrations, we thank Andre Barbeau, Arthur Dunkelman, Kenneth Garrett, Merle Greene Robertson, Stephen Houston, Jay I. Kislak, Autumn Mather, David Schele, and the following institutions: Bibliothèque Nationale, Paris; the library of the Center for Maya Research, Barnardsville, N.C.; the archives and library of the Instituto Nacional de Antropología e Historia, Mexico City; Library of Congress, Washington, D.C.; National Geographic Society, Washington, D.C.; and the Newberry Library, Chicago.

Finally, we thank Colin Ridler, Ilona de Nemethy Sanigar, Rowena Alsey, and Jane Cutter of Thames & Hudson for their extensive help in the preparation, design, and production of this book.

Sources of Illustrations

Index

GAYLORD RG